Forgotten Broadway: Dramatizing Women's Limited Choices in Selected Plays by Rachel Crothers

Forgotten Broadway: Dramatizing Women's Limited Choices in Selected Plays by Rachel Crothers

He and She
A Little Journey
Mary the Third
Let Us Be Gay

RACHEL CROTHERS
Edited by
KARIN MARESH

methuen | drama
LONDON · NEW YORK · OXFORD · NEW DELHI · SYDNEY

METHUEN DRAMA
Bloomsbury Publishing Plc, 50 Bedford Square, London, WC1B 3DP, UK
Bloomsbury Publishing Inc, 1359 Broadway, New York, NY 10018, USA
Bloomsbury Publishing Ireland, 29 Earlsfort Terrace, Dublin 2, D02 AY28, Ireland

BLOOMSBURY, METHUEN DRAMA and the Methuen Drama logo are trademarks of
Bloomsbury Publishing Plc

First published in United States of America 2026

Copyright © Karin Maresh, 2026
He and She © Rachel Crothers, 1920
A Little Journey © Rachel Crothers, 1918
Mary the Third © Rachel Crothers, 1923
Let Us Be Gay © Rachel Crothers, 1929

The authors have asserted their right under the Copyright, Designs and Patents Act, 1988,
to be identified as author of this work.

For legal purposes the Acknowledgements on p. vi constitute an extension of this copyright page.

Cover design by Jade Barnett
Cover images: Rachel Crothers © TBC, Art deco frame © Roisa / Adobe Stock

All rights reserved. No part of this publication may be: i) reproduced or transmitted in any form, electronic or mechanical, including photocopying, recording or by means of any information storage or retrieval system without prior permission in writing from the publishers; or ii) used or reproduced in any way for the training, development or operation of artificial intelligence (AI) technologies, including generative AI technologies. The rights holders expressly reserve this publication from the text and data mining exception as per Article 4(3) of the Digital Single Market Directive (EU) 2019/790.

Bloomsbury Publishing Plc does not have any control over, or responsibility for, any third-party websites referred to or in this book. All internet addresses given in this book were correct at the time of going to press. The author and publisher regret any inconvenience caused if addresses have changed or sites have ceased to exist, but can accept no responsibility for any such changes.

No rights in incidental music or songs contained in the work are hereby granted and performance rights for any performance/presentation whatsoever must be obtained from the respective copyright owners.

All rights whatsoever in this play are strictly reserved and application for performance etc. should be made before rehearsals to Permissions Department, Bloomsbury Publishing Plc, 50 Bedford Square, London, WC1B 3DP, UK. *Let Us Be Gay* remains in copyright in the UK and is available for licence through Concord Theatricals. No performance may be given unless a licence has been obtained.

A catalogue record for this book is available from the British Library.

A catalog record for this book is available from the Library of Congress.

ISBN: HB: 978-1-3503-9871-9
PB: 978-1-3503-9870-2
ePDF: 978-1-3503-9873-3
eBook: 978-1-3503-9872-6

Series: Methuen Drama Play Collections

Typeset by RefineCatch Limited, Bungay, Suffolk
Printed and bound in the United States of America

For product safety related questions contact productsafety@bloomsbury.com.

To find out more about our authors and books visit www.bloomsbury.com
and sign up for our newsletters.

Contents

Acknowledgements vi
List of Contributors vii
Preface by Jonathan Banks viii

Introduction by Karin Maresh 1

The Plays
He and She (1911–1920) 7
A Little Journey (1918), courtesy of Mint Theatre Company 71
Mary the Third (1923) 135
Let Us Be Gay (1929) 201

Appendices 273
Select productions 274
Plays by Rachel Crothers 277

Select Bibliography 279

Acknowledgements

Thank you to Dom O'Hanlon and Bloomsbury Publishing and to the Mint Theater Company's Jonathan Bank for his company's edited script of *A Little Journey* for use in this collection, as well as his insightful preface. There are *many* librarians and archivists who have helped me through this process, too, including Annemarie Van Roessel and Nailah Holmes at the Billy Rose Theatre division, part of the New York Public Library for the Performing Arts; Rachel Bolden and the W&J Milner Library; April Anderson-Zorn at Illinois State University Library for helping me gain access to the online library system there; and Julie Neville at the Dr. Jo Ann Rayfield Archives at the Illinois State University for her assistance in helping me access the Crothers's papers housed there.

Thank you also to the administration and my colleagues at Washington & Jefferson College for their support, and to my mentor and advisor at Illinois State during my master's program, Dr. Elizabeth Reitz Mullenix, who first introduced me to the work of Rachel Crothers.

And, finally, thank you to my own cheering section, my family, who support all my adventures.

– Karin Maresh

List of Contributors

Editor

Karin Maresh, Ph.D. is a Professor of Theatre and Chair of the Communication Arts department at Washington & Jefferson College in Washington, PA. She earned her degrees from Viterbo College (B.A.), Illinois State University (M.A.), and The Ohio State University (Ph.D.), and some of her publications include "Un/Natural Motherhood in Marina Carr's *The Mai, Portia Couglan,* and *By the Bog of Cats. . . .*" (*Theatre History Studies* 2016) and an entry on Irish women directors in *International Women Stage Directors* (2013). She is also the current Vice-President for Alpha Psi Omega, the national honorary theatre society.

Preface Author

Jonathan Bank has been the Producing Artistic Director of Mint Theater Company since 1995, where he has unearthed and produced dozens of lost or neglected plays, many of which he has also directed. Under Bank's leadership Mint has earned an international reputation as the source for high-quality revivals of forgotten works and has become, in the words of *The New York Times*' Jason Zinoman, "the leading New York entrepreneur" of the neglected play business. Terry Teachout of the *Wall Street Journal* described Jonathan Bank as "one of a handful of theater artists in America whose name is an absolute guarantee of quality."

Rachel Crothers

Rachel Crothers (1870–1958) grew up in Normal-Bloomington, Illinois, in a family made up predominantly of medical doctors and pharmacists. She, however, devoted her life to the theatre, first as an actor with the Stanhope-Wheatcroft School of Acting, and subsequently achieving her greatest successes as a playwright and director. More than twenty-five of her plays graced Broadway stages, many directed by her, including *The Three of Us* (1906), *A Man's World* (1910), *Ourselves* (1913), and *When Ladies Meet* (1932).

Preface

I've made a career out of reviving plays and playwrights that have been forgotten, but I don't have any special understanding of how or why they fell out of favor in the first place. I do know that once that has happened, it's nearly impossible to undo. Mint Theater Company has produced two plays by Rachel Crothers and both times enthusiastic and influential critics have urged others to follow in our footsteps, but sadly very little has happened. I hope publication of these four plays will help to change that.

The first of our two productions was in 2006, *Susan and God*, which first caught my eye because I knew that was a great title. No doubt Crothers knew it too. Crothers directed most of her plays and produced many of them as well. She knew the commercial value of a provocative title. Possibly her keen eye for commerce negatively impacted on her posthumous reputation. That's a theory put forward by Terry Teachout in his review of our 2011 production of *A Little Journey,* Crothers' play from 1918 (Teachout was drama critic for *The Wall Street Journal* from 2003 to the time of his too-soon death in 2022.):

> How could so distinguished a female artist have vanished into the memory hole? You'd think that literary-minded feminists would have been her most outspoken champions. But Ms. Crothers, like Lillian Hellman, was a commercial playwright who specialized in "well-made" plays, a genre that became unfashionable after Tennessee Williams and Arthur Miller trashed the theatrical rulebook, and the fact that she'd been so popular in her lifetime worked against her posthumously. Not until the Mint exhumed "Susan and God" did it occur to anyone that her body of work deserved a second look (*Wall Street Journal* 17 Jun 2011).

Our production of *Susan and God* did inspire a few others around the country, all well-received. Teachout described it as a "play whose subject matter is so modern in flavor that it could have been written last week" (*Wall Street Journal*, 30 Jun 2006). *The New York Times* joined in, crediting "Ms. Crothers, whose ear for breezy dialogue, jaundiced but sympathetic eye and sharp perception of the conflicts between family and career lend the play a very contemporary tone and relevance" ("Susan and God," 27 Jun 2006). *Backstage* said the play was "so timely and engaging that it should be revived yearly at theatres needing great parts for women" (Orel 51).

Mint produced *A Little Journey* five years later, in 2011. Crothers wrote Journey nearly 20 years before *Susan and God,* and it's a "big" play, to borrow a phrase from the author—and I don't mean the size of the cast, or the technical requirements, I mean the size of the feelings that drive the play.

As soon as I was done reading the play, I knew I wanted to do it. I trusted we would figure out how to solve the problems that it presented, including some issues that were baked into the text. *Journey* primarily takes place on a four-day journey on Pullman car heading west from New York and we knew that the Black porter's dialogue would require some alteration. For example, there's no reason to stick fast to Crothers attempt to spell out dialect, an actor and director can decide how best to accurately represent appropriate speech. "Dis" became "this" and "dat" became "that" in the script handed out to the cast.

Even the stage directions contained some inflammatory language—there's simply no reason to describe an exit as "shuffling" nor was it tolerable to allow our Porter to be called "Sambo". The text printed here resolves these issues while understanding that there is an unresolved undercurrent of racism alive throughout the play.

A Little Journey was embraced by both audiences and critics. David Rooney of *The New York Times* wrote: "Unseen in a professional production in New York since its Broadway premiere, this 1918 play is a beguiling rarity and a bracing plunge into the three-act theatrical pleasures of another age, replete with sparkling dialogue and soaring sentiments" (10 Jun 2011).

Teachout continued to highlight Crothers' ability to create character through dialogue and envelop her audience:

> One of the nicest things about Ms. Crothers's plays is that they're high-minded without being the least bit stuffy. The point of "A Little Journey," for instance, is that the only alternative to existential despair is to seize each day and live it to the fullest. "Can't everyday life have in it anything you *want* to put into it?" Jim asks midway through the second act. But Ms. Crothers knew that the most effective way to preach a sermon is to embed it in a fast-moving plot and adorn it with snappy dialogue. Accordingly, "A Little Journey" sounds for most of its length not like a sobersided morality play but a sparkling comedy of manners: "Six thousand a year with a real man would be—well—I'd take a chance on it. In fact I'd grab it." "It wouldn't pay for one-third of your clothes." "Oh, slush—what do clothes mean after you've *got* a man?" Imagine a cross between "Our Town" and "The Women" and you'll get an idea of how "A Little Journey" plays (*Wall Street Journal* 17 Jun 2011).

– Jonathan Bank,
Artistic Director, Mint Theater Company

Introduction

On 25 April 1939, playwright and theatre artist Rachel Crothers (1870–1958)[1] received the 1938 achievement award from Chi Omega, a women's fraternal organization that created the national award for American women as a counterpart to the Pulitzer and Nobel prizes that almost always went to men. Eleanor Roosevelt herself took part in the selection process for this award during the first decade of its existence, and the award ceremony often took place at the White House with President Roosevelt, Eleanor Roosevelt, and many other distinguished guests in attendance. Crothers had, by 1939, garnered widespread acclaim with theatre and cinema critics and patrons. Over a span of almost four decades, about twenty-seven of Crothers's plays appeared on Broadway – many of them directed by her – some on tours, others in London and Paris, and at least half of her plays made their way onto the silver screen. Neither the duration of Crothers's career nor her abundant output is notable on its own for the early 20th century American stage, but, unlike a jack-of-all-trades like "Yankee doodle dandy" George M. Cohan, Crothers is rarely discussed outside of the occasional graduate course on women in American theatre. Judith E. Barlow includes Crothers's *A Man's World* in *Plays by American Women, 1900-1930* (1985), and Katie N. Johnson (2015) includes *Ourselves* in her volume on progressive era "prostitute" plays, but scant discussion of Crothers's work can be found outside of scholarly articles, master's theses, and doctoral dissertations. Publication and productions of her plays are even less common. How did one of the United States' top theatre artists of the early 20th century fade so quickly from our collective consciousness? Certainly, gender is in part responsible for this erasure; even during her own lifetime, Crothers couldn't escape being labeled as one of the greatest "female" playwrights of the American theatre. Feminist theatre scholars have worked tirelessly to recover the work and stories of the Susan Glaspells, Zora Neale Hearstons, and Sophie Treadwells – and thank goodness for their efforts! – but these writers' avant-garde plays are easier to praise for their creativity and forward-thinking. What to do with a playwright/director like Crothers who intentionally created mainstream, commercial fare rather than experimental works; who wrote for conservative, middle-class, white audiences on Broadway rather than a mixed audience in a little theatre looking for intellectual stimulation; and whose female characters are more likely to remain within, rather than breaking free from, the constraints of their patriarchal roles? Crothers's work does not fit neatly into the existing boundary-pushing narratives we so often gravitate to in theatre history, but a place for her can and should be made.

According to an unpublished and partial autobiography, Crothers found the theatre not through her family but playing with paper dolls in her Bloomington, IL home, dolls

---

[1] Most sources during and after Crothers's death in 1958 list her birthdate as 12 Dec. 1878, yet several documents suggest this date is inaccurate. An 1880 federal census, collected in June, lists Rachel Crothers as 9 years old, a 1940 census lists her age as 70, and a 1922 U.S. passport application that Crothers, presumably, filled out, lists her birthdate as 12 Dec. 1870. There are also very well written letters in her hand to her childhood friend, Grace, dated 1882. These documents all support the fact that Crothers was born in 1870 and *not* 1878.

that she cut from magazines and "fashion sheets," "building houses for them out of books – speaking their dialogue – living their lives – finishing one set of lives before I began another" ("The Box in the Attic," p. 11, NYPL, t-mss 2016-002). The youngest of six children, most of whom were older or had died young, Crothers turned to her playful imagination for companionship as her childhood was marred with loneliness and some financial instability; her physician father lost money in various speculations, leading her mother to pursue a career in medicine to support the family and pay off her husband's debts.[2] Her parents and their community viewed the theatre, in fact, as disreputable and unseemly, certainly not a career they would have wished for any of their children, thus most of Crothers early theatrical experiences in Illinois revolved around recitation events at school and church. She did, however, begin writing short plays, possibly as early as age 12, and by the 1890s she trained in Boston with H.M. Pitt at the New England School of Dramatic Instruction, and later in New York at the Stanhope-Wheatcroft school of acting. She subsequently joined the Felix Morris and the E.H. Sothern companies and toured as an actor for several months. Finding a little success in New York City with some of her one-act plays in 1899 at the Stanhope-Wheatcroft school where she had become a teacher, solidified her intention to pursue a career as a playwright. The Bloomington, IL paper, *The Pantagraph*, kept tabs on her, regularly reporting about their famous progeny's activities writing and directing for Broadway, such as in a 1932 article titled "One of the Wonder Workers of the Town," which lauded Crothers as "the everlasting, ever-surviving, ever-recurring, ever-writing" (*The Pantagraph* 18 Dec. 1932).

Finding copies of Crothers's plays today, even with access to a research library, is not an easy task since almost all are out-of-print and several were never published and are only available in archives. Of the few plays that have been reprinted, the best known is the 1909 *A Man's World* which examines the sexual double standard, detailing a "protest by a woman on behalf of women against the world's way of having one law for man and another for women in matters of morals," according to one archival clipping (ISU archives). It also depicts a world in which the female characters, even those like Frank Ware, the central character, seem to be independent and "have it all" still have limited life choices. Aspects of this and other Crothers's plays can appear dated and "quaint" to us today with their sometimes stereotypical characters, as well as melodramatic and occasional use of racist language common in mainstream plays of the period, but, as *New York Times* critic, Claudia La Rocco, noted regarding a 2013 Metropolitan Playhouse production of *A Man's World*, "some of the broader outlines of the standards . . . imposed on women . . . [in the plays] . . . remain exhaustingly familiar" (24 Sept. 2013). It is not surprising, then, that several colleges have produced *A Man's World* in recent decades, and productions of lesser-known Crothers's plays such as *He and She* (1920), *A Little Journey* (1918), and *Susan and God* (1937) have been mounted on both educational and professional stages. NYC's Mint Theater Company, an organization committed to staging forgotten plays from the past, staged *A Little Journey* in 2011 and *Susan and God* in 2006, successfully so according to the *Wall Street Journal*. Terry Teachout, the *WSJ*

---

[2] Her mother became the first woman doctor in Illinois. Her sister Lulu later became one of the first woman pharmacists in Bloomington.

theatre critic, deemed both plays pieces "that never should have been forgotten in the first place" (30 June 2006). The last time a Crothers play appeared on a major NYC stage occurred in 1980 when the Brooklyn Academy of Music produced *He and She*, a play about two sculptors whose marriage is tested when both compete for a major cash award. Jean Ashton, writing for *The New York Times* about this production, appropriately labeled Crothers as "The Neil Simon of her day," filling houses and turning "out a popular play almost every season" in the '20s and '30s (25 May 1980, D3). Ashton also notes that avant-garde and socially conscious writers of the era scorned Crothers, and, though she referred to herself as an ardent feminist, "the thematic concerns of her work and the direction of her career alike exemplify a female consciousness that was at once provocative and traditional" (25 May 1980, D3).

The sole biography of Crothers,[3] written by Lois C. Gottlieb in 1979, follows the narrative of many second-wave feminist texts that devote space to arguing for or against Crothers's credibility as a feminist author. For example, Gottlieb states that part of the goal of her book is to investigate "the nature of the feminism expressed in Crothers's plays" (xiv), and Anna Andes's essay, "Feminism, Sentimentality, and Realism in Rachel Crothers's Working-Women Plays," "calls for a reevaluation of Crothers's feminist voice" (123), noting that other feminist critiques of the plays either condemn them or judge them as ambiguous. Crothers's female characters are indeed more likely to follow, or endeavor to follow, the traditional paths of marriage AND motherhood, especially the women in her plays of the 1920s and 1930s. Many of them are either married and mothers, or they pine for love and its traditional outcomes that do quite often playout prior to the play's ending. Even Kitty Brown, who finds great freedom and joy after divorcing her philandering husband in *Let Us Be Gay* (1929), takes him back in the final moments of the play, admitting that she still loves him. Yet, these may only be temporary solutions that provide the veneer of happiness, according to authors Colette and James Lindroth. Kitty, they note, "is as much in retreat from loneliness and frustration as she is in love with" her husband, "and the philandering which caused her to leave him is still a part of his character" (11). The reconciliation in *Susan and God*, as well as the suggested reconciliation in *Mary the Third*, are similar in that "the problems which drove them apart . . . have not magically disappeared" (11). Crothers's women are complex. They are not radical protestors, stridently marching for votes or advocating for birth control, but nor are they Cinderellas waiting for their princes, or the secondary characters to the male hero's story. Even when Women are the central figures in all of Crothers's plays (save one – *The Heart of Paddy Whack*, written for a particular actor, Chauncey Olcott) and no matter the plot, the conflict arises due to the woman (or women) making choices that butt up against societal expectations.

What is particularly wonderful about Crothers's writing is her depiction of women who want different things in life – whether that be a family, a career, or both – while revealing that no path will be easy or necessarily lead to a fairytale ending. Some, like Frank Ware in *A Man's World*, Mary Howard in *When Ladies Meet* (1932), and Pennelope Penn in *39 East* (1919) have no intention of ending their professional careers

---

[3] As of August 2025, a second biography of Crothers has been published by author John Bassett, *Rachel Crothers: Broadway Innovator, Feminist Pioneer* (Bloomsbury Academic).

even when confronted with love. Others, like Ann Herford in *He and She* (1911–1920) and Susan in *Susan and God* (1937), sacrifice their own aspirations for the sake of their husband and child; audiences at the time read these moments as the women returning to their expected roles, but I read these as moments of defeat, of begrudging acquiescence to the patriarchal society that lacks support for working mothers. Susan Trexel (originally played by Gertrude Lawrence) is noteworthy as well for her relative disinterest in her teenage daughter, a child she hasn't seen for months at the start of the play and whom she is in no rush to visit. She has spent too many years living as a nominal single parent because her alcoholic husband "neglected" their child, and now she wants freedom. Crothers's women desire to be equal to men, to have the freedom to build an identity and financial stability that are their own while also, *sometimes*, having those coexist with marriage and motherhood. The message conveyed in many of these plays is that being a "career woman" while also being a wife and mother is not easy and *may* be impossible due to limited choices. It is notable that Crothers own life mirrors in some respects the experiences of her characters. She never married, though she did live with a female companion in her later years who "kept the house allowing . . . [Crothers] . . . the freedom to work" (Stevens-Garmon). In a 1923 interview, Crothers remarked that "'The superior man will not have the superior woman – not on the superior woman's terms" (Gottleib 120), making it clear her belief that patriarchal norms impede men from accepting the woman who is equal in career or educational status.

One of the defining factors of Crothers's plays that is not usually discussed is that they represent "early twentieth-century *white* America" (Andes 126; emphasis mine), meaning the "complex coupling of "' women' and 'work'" (Andes 126) in these plays *only* represents white women, mostly the middle or upper classes. *39 East* is an exception for its inclusion of three Black servants (2 women and 1 man), but, unsurprisingly, none are developed or involved in the wider discussion of women and work. At the start of the play, as the servants ready breakfast at the boarding house, they jovially "yessah" and "grin" at the tenants coming down for the meal. The 1916 *Old Lady 31*, a play with *no* characters of color, includes the n-word, and one character in 1918's *A Little Journey* routinely remarks how untrustworthy the train porters are, even referring to their dishonesty being in their blood. References such as these do tend to be minimal and are no more present than in other popular plays of the era, but *some* editing, as has been done for this edition, is clearly necessary to make the plays palatable for today's audiences.

On Feb. 14, 1912, the *Boston Evening Transcript* published Rachel Crothers's speech given to the Drama League at the Plymouth Theatre. By then she had several successes – *The Three of Us* (1906) and *A Man's World* (1909) – and flops under her belt – *Myself-Bettina* (1908) and *Young Wisdom* (1914) – which provided her with an astute (or at least interesting) perspective on the state of American theatre and drama at the time. She asserts in the speech that "the greatest masterpiece is one which is called great by the largest number of different kinds of people, and the test and secret of the great play is that with all its fineness and beauty, it has the power to reach and touch and convince all kinds of people" (21). Meanwhile, she refers to the German and Swedish plays of the time, those that do not share the universal appeal of commercial Broadway drama, as being "secondary masterpieces," "fine play[s] which need . . . [a] special audience and which can and will make money if . . . [they] can get . . .[an] audience"

(21). In this essay and later publications and interviews, Crothers makes clear her preference for clarity and directness in plays, that it is not the playwright's job to lead the audience through a cerebral exercise, wondering what she means (Gottlieb 149). Even when writing "problem plays" in her early career, interrogating issues such as the "new woman" and "career girls" as well as young, destitute women turning to sex-work, Crothers never strayed from her primary intention to please mainstream audiences with her apolitical comedies.

French artist, Antonin Artaud, argued for doing away with plays of the past (leaving them to the graduate students), but it is possible to find things in those plays to relate to and connect to our world now. Rachel Crothers's work provides varied perspectives on the American woman's experience (albeit white woman) in a way that is not dissimilar to playwright Wendy Wasserstein's depictions—think of *The Heidi Chronicles*—demonstrating that no specific path, whether traditional or unconventional, in life will lead all women to contentment. In a country that continues to debate and control the choices women can make regarding their own futures, Crothers's plays remain relevant.

The Plays

Of the four plays included in this collection, only one, *Let Us Be Gay*, remains covered by copyright in the UK, thus why this book isn't yet available there. Minor edits have been made to *A Little Journey* and *Mary the Third* in order to omit racist language, and some grammatical edits have been made to *He and She*, *A Little Journey*, and *Mary the Third*. Other than these changes, the plays are true to Crothers's original texts.

He and She

Tom Herford, *a sculpter*
Ann Herford, *his wife*
Daisy Herford, *his sister*
Millicent, *his daughter*
Dr. Remington, *his father-in-law*
Keith McKenzie, *his assistant*
Ruth Creel, *his wife's friend*
Ellen, *a maid*

Act One

Scene: The Herford Studio.

The room is in the basement floor of a large old-fashioned house in lower New York—and shows that it has been made over and adapted to the needs of a sculptor.

At right center back are double doors opening into the workroom. At right of these doors is a recess showing it has been cut in. The ceiling of the half of the room which is towards the audience is much higher than the other part—showing that the room which is on the floor above has been used to give height to this part of the studio.

The break made in the ceiling is supported by an interesting old carved column—very evidently brought from Italy—and in the overhanging part of the wall is set a very beautiful old Italian frieze in bas relief—a few faded colors showing.

At lower left is a large studio window.

At lower right side a single door leading into hall. At upper left corner, a cupboard is built in, in harmony with the construction of the room, and showing, when opened, drawers and compartments for holding sculptors' tools, etc.

Before the window, at right center, is a scaffold built to hold a section of a frieze. At its base is a revolving table, holding modeling clay, tools, etc. In front of the scaffold is a short pair of steps. At centre, is a long table holding rolls of sketches, a desk set—a book or two, pencils, compasses, several pieces of modeling.

There are a number of chairs about and a piece of rich brocade in vivid coloring thrown over the back of one.

The room is simple, dignified, beautiful, full of taste and strength. Soft afternoon sunshine streams in from the wide window. **Keith McKenzie** *and* **Tom Herford** *are lifting one section of a bas relief frieze about 3 by 5—and placing it on the scaffolding.*

McKenzie *is about 35, tall, good-looking, in a pleasing, common-place way; also wearing a sculptor's working clothes—but of a practical and not artistic sort.*

Tom Hereford *is 40, a fine specimen of the vigorous American-artist type. Virile, fresh, alive and generous in nature and viewpoint. He wears the stamp of confidence and success.*

Tom (*as they lift the frieze*)   Come on! There she is! Put her over—no, this way, about half a foot. That's right. There! Let's have a look. (**Tom** *goes down to hanging switch and turns on the light. As he does so, he says:*) Wait! (*The lights are turned up.*) (*Turning to* **Keith**.) What do you think?

Keith   It's a great thing, Governor! Going to be a walk-away for you. You'll win it as sure as guns. I *know* it. I bet you land the $100,000.00 as sure as you're standing there, governor.

Tom Oh, I don't know. The biggest fellows in the country are going in for this competition.

Keith Well—you're *one* of the biggest. *I* think you're *the* biggest—and you've turned out the best thing you've ever done in your life. (*Going to stand above table.*)

Tom That's damned nice of you, McKenzie. It does look pretty good out here. Doesn't it? (*He goes up on the steps—to touch the frieze.*)

Keith (*after a pause*) Governor.

Tom (*working at his frieze*) Um?

Keith I want to ask you something. Not from curiosity—but because—I'd like to know for my own sake. You needn't answer of course—if you don't want to.

Tom Go on. Fire away.

Keith Have you ever been sorry that Mrs. Herford is a sculptor—instead of just your wife?

Tom Not for a minute.

Keith I've been thinking a lot about it all lately.

Tom About you and Ruth, you mean?

Keith Yes. She'll marry me in the fall if I let her keep on working.

Tom And?

Keith Well—I—Hang it all! I don't *want* her to. I can take care of her now. At first it was different—when I was grubbing along—but since I've been with you, you've put me on my feet. I'll never be *great*—I know that all right—but I can take care of her.

Tom (*working at frieze*) But she *wants* to keep on, doesn't she?

Keith Yes, but —

Tom Good Heavens, boy—you're not bitten with that bug I hope. "I want my girl by my own fireside to live for me alone."

Keith Oh —

Tom Why Ruth Creel's a howling success—the way she's climbed up in that magazine—why in the name of Christopher, do you want her to stop?

Keith (*at right end of table, figuring mechanically on some papers on- table*) How can she keep on at that and keep house too?

Tom Well they *do*, you know—somehow.

Keith Oh, Mrs. Herford's different. She's working right here with you—and her time is her own. But Ruth's tied down to office hours and it's slavery—that's what it is.

Tom *She* doesn't think so. Does she?

Keith I want a home. I want children.

Tom Of course. But that doesn't mean she'll have to give up her profession forever.

Keath Oh, I'm strong for women doing anything they want to do—in *general*—But when it's the girl you love and want to marry, it's different.

Tom It ought not to be.

Keith When you come down to brass tacks —

Ann (*coming quickly in from the workroom, and stopping as she sees the frieze*) Oh Tom!

Ann Herford *is 38. Intensely feminine and a strong vibrating personality which radiates warmth and vitality. She wears a long linen working smock—a soft rich red in color. Her sleeves are rolled up and her general appearance shows that she is at work and has stopped only to look at* **Tom***'s frieze.*

Keith Looks great out here—doesn't it, Mrs. Herford?

Ann Um.

Keith Aren't you—more sure now than ever it will win?

Ann Um.—(*Starting to speak and checking herself.*)

Tom What?

Ann Nothing. Your horses *are* marvelous, Tom. I wish we could see it all together—now. Don't you? The rest of the twenty sections—so we could see how much we—how much we—*feel* the running.

Tom Don't you feel it in this piece?

Ann Of course.

Keith I do—tremendously. I think it's wonderful. (*He goes into workroom.*)

Tom Ann—what were you going to say a minute ago about the frieze?

Ann A—I don't know.

Tom Don't hedge. Several times lately you've started to say something and haven't got it out. What is it? Any suggestions?

Ann How do you feel about it yourself, boy? Are you satisfied?

Tom Does that mean you aren't?

Ann I asked you.

Tom Well—it's the best that's in me. Why? What's the matter? You don't like it after all.

Ann Like it? It's a strong—noble—beautiful thing.

Tom *But—*

Ann Dearest—is it—just exactly what your first conception of it was? Has it turned out just as you first felt it?

Tom Why yes—not absolutely in detail of course. It's improved a lot I think—in the working—but in the main, yes—it's *just* the same. Why do you say that?

Ann You know of course, but —

Tom Say it—Say it. What have you got in your mind?

Ann I don't know that I can—but in the beginning it had a feeling of swiftness, of rushing—swirling—as if your soul were let loose in it, Tom—too big, too free to be held in and confined. But, somehow, now that it's finished —

Tom Go on.

Ann That wild thing has gone out of it. It's crystalized into something magnificent but a little conventional.

Tom Good heavens, Ann, you can't call that *conventional*?

Ann Well—orthodox then. It's noble of course—but that inexplainable thing which made it great—is *gone*—for me. Perhaps it's just me—my imagination—because I care so much.

Tom It is imagination. It's much stronger than when I began.

Ann Is it?

Tom Of course. You're trying to put something fantastic into it which never was there at all. That's not *me*. What I've done I've got through a certain strong solid boldness. That's why I think this stands a good chance. It's the very best thing I've ever done, Ann, by all—

Kieth (*opening the workroom door*)   Governor—will you show Guido and me about something please—Just a minute? (*There is a slight pause.*) (**Tom** *looks at the frieze.*)

Tom I don't see what you mean at all, dear girl. Thanks a lot—but I think you're wrong this time. (*He goes into workroom.* **Ann** *looks again at the frieze as* **Ruth Creel** *comes in from hall.*)

Ann (*going quickly to* **Ruth**)   Oh, Ruth—bless you! (*She kisses her warmly.*)

Ruth I came straight from the office and I'm dirty as a pig. (**Ann** *points to* **Tom***'s frieze.*) Is that it? (**Ann** *nods.*) Well?

Ann Oh, Ruth—I'm sick in the bottom of my soul. I hope—I hope—I'm wrong. I *must* be wrong. Tom knows better than I do; but—I can't help it. I tell myself I'm a fool—and the more I try to persuade myself the more it comes back. Ruth, it isn't the same. It isn't. What ever it was that lifted it above good work and made it a thing of inspiration—is gone. It's gone—*gone*.

Ruth Have you—told Tom how you feel?

Ann Just this minute. He says I'm wrong absolutely—that it's the best thing he's ever done.

Ruth I hope to God you are wrong but I bet you're not. You *know*. Did you—have you told him the other thing?

Ann Not yet. But I've finished it.

Ruth Absolutely?

Ann I worked down here last night till three o'clock this morning.

Ruth Well—how is it?

Ann Oh, I don't dare think. It can't be as good as it seems to me.

Ruth *Of course* it can. Why shouldn't it be? Aren't you going to offer it to him right away—before it's too late?

Ann How *can* I? It frightens me to pieces to even think of it—but, oh,—my dear, my dear—it's alive and fresh and *new*. It is. It is. If he only would take it—my idea—and put his wonderful work—his wonderful execution into it.

Ruth Perhaps he'll be *fired* with it—jump at it.

Ann I'm afraid, he won't—and I'm afraid of *this* for him. It would nearly kill him to lose. He's counting on winning. Keith and everybody are so dead sure of him.

Ruth Show him yours for goodness—

Ann Be careful. He'll be back in a minute.

Ruth I'll skip upstairs and make myself presentable.

Ann Go in my room, dear. (**Ruth** *goes out through hall.* **Tom** *and* **Keith** *come back from workroom.* **Ann** *goes to* **Tom**—*they stand a moment—looking at the frieze.* **Ann** *slaps* **Tom** *on the back, without speaking, and goes on into workroom.*)

Keith (*after a pause*)   I agree with you in general, governor. But when it comes down to the girl you love and want to marry, it's different.

Tom Why is it?

Keith The world has got to have homes to live in and who's going to make 'em if the women don't do it?

Tom (*smiling at* **Keith** *tolerantly*)   Oh, come—come.

Keith Do you mean to say you wouldn't rather your sister Daisy was married and keeping her own house instead of working here as your secretary?

Tom But she *isn't* married—and she won't live with Ann and me unless it's a business proposition. I respect her *tremendously* for it—tremendously.

Keith Well, Daisy's a big, plucky, independent thing anyway—but Ruth's a little delicate fragile —

Tom With a mind bigger than most of the *men* you know.

Keith Oh, mind be damned. I want a wife.

Daisy (*coming in from the hall*) Oh—Tom—it's out here. How corking!

Daisy Herford *is 28—strong, wholesome, handsome, with the charm of health and freshness. She wears a severe serge gown and carries a pencil and stenographer's pad.*

Tom Well—sis, how do you like it?

Daisy I adore it. I hope you haven't any doubts now about winning.

Tom I've plenty of 'em—but somehow today it looks as if it stood a pretty good chance.

Daisy Chance! I never was so sure of anything in my life.

Keith Daisy—maybe you know just *what* ought to be *where* with *this stuff*.

Daisy I've been itching to get at it. Let's put all the tools on that side.

Keith I *have* started.

Daisy And throw the trash in here. (*Pushing the box with her foot.*)

Keith Can you help me now?

Daisy Yes. Tom, do you want me to write to the Ward people about that marble again?

Tom Yes I do. Shake them up. Tell 'em if it isn't here by the first of the month I won't take it.

Daisy (*making a note in her notebook*) Um—um.

Millicent Herford *rushes in from hall at left.* **Millicent** *is 16—pretty—eager—full of vitality and will—half child, half woman. She is charmingly dressed in an afternoon frock and picture hat and is at the moment happy and exhilarated.*

Millicent Father, where's mother?

Tom In the work room. But you can't go in. (*As* **Millicent** *starts to workroom.*)

Millicent Why not?

Tom She's finishing something and said not to let *any* one stop her.

Millicent Oh *dear*! I think I *might*. It's awfully important. Couldn't I just poke my head in the door a minute?

Tom Not for a second.

Millicent Sakes, I wish Mother wouldn't work in my Christmas vacation. It's an awful bore. Don't you think she might stop the little while I'm at home, Aunt Daisy?

Daisy None of my business. Don't ask me.

Keith   If you ask *me*—yes I think she might.

Tom   That's nonsense. Your mother's doing about everything that *can* be done to make your vacation a success, isn't she?

Millicent   Yes, of course.

Tom   Then I don't see that there's any reason why she shouldn't be allowed a little time for herself.

Millicent   But I want her *now*. Aren't my new pumps stemmy. Aunt Daisy?

Daisy   Aren't they what?

Millicent   Stemmy. Wake up, Aunt Daisy. Oh, the luncheon was gorgeous. All the girls were there and the matinee was heavenly.

Keith   What play?

Millicent   "The Flame of Love." You needn't laugh, father. It's the best play in town. The leading man is a peach. Honestly, he's the best-looking thing I ever saw in my life. We were all crazy about him. Belle Stevens took off her violets and threw them right *at* him. She makes me tired, though. I don't think seventeen is so terribly much older than sixteen, do you. Aunt Daisy?

Daisy (*still at the cupboard*)   It depends on whether you're sixteen or seventeen—how much older it is.

Millicent   I don't care—I wouldn't wear a ring as big as hers if I had one. Oh, Aunt Daisy, may I borrow your earrings? (*Going to* **Daisy**.)

Daisy   Help yourself.

Millicent   Thanks, you're a duck. I could combostulate you for that. How much longer do you think mother will be, daddie?

Tom   Couldn't say.

Millicent   Well, tell her I *have* to see her the minute she comes out. Don't forget. (*She hurries off through hall.*)

Tom   She's grown up overnight somehow. I can't get used to it.

Keith   And she went away to school a few months ago just a girl. Amazing, isn't it?

Daisy   Not a bit. What do you expect? She's free now—cut loose. Boarding school does that pretty quickly.

Tom   I suppose so—and I suppose it's good for her. (*Looking at the frieze he goes into the workroom.*)

Keith   The Governor's darned cheerful about the frieze today.

Daisy   I should think he *would* be. It's great. (**Keith** *and* **Daisy** *go on clearing out cupboard.*)

Keith   I'd give a good deal to know what Mrs. Herford actually thinks of it.

Daisy Why she *loves* it.

Keith She looks at it with such a sort of a—I don't know. I can't help wondering if she *is* so dead certain of it as the rest of us are.

Daisy I hope she doesn't discourage Tom. After all *he* likes it and he knows more about it than anybody else. Ann's criticism is wonderful, of course, but still Tom is the artist.

Keith You're just as jealous for your brother as you can be, aren't you, Daisy? All right for the missus to be clever, but you want Tom to be supreme in everything, don't you?

Daisy He is. (*Leaning over the box.*)

Keith You're a brick. Daisy, have you ever been in love in your life?

Daisy What do you mean? (*Lifting her head—startled and embarrassed.*)

Keith I've been thinking an awful lot lately about this business of married women working. What do *you* think of it—now honestly?

Daisy What difference does it make—what I think?

Keith Of course, there's no reason on earth why you shouldn't be in it. You don't care a hang for men—and —

Daisy You mean men don't care a hang for me.

Keith No I don't. I don't mean that at all. But you're so independent men are sort of afraid of you.

Daisy Oh, don't apologize. You mean I'm a plain, practical girl meant to take care of myself.

Keith Well—that's what you *want* to be, isn't it?

Daisy Never mind about me. change the subject.

Keith You needn't be so touchy. I talk awfully frankly about my affairs and you never say a word about yourself.

Daisy Why should I? I'm not interesting and you're not interested.

Keith I am too. You're the best pal a fellow ever had. I don't know any other girl I could have worked with all his time—day in and day out and not either been dead sick of or sort of—you know sweet on, in a way.

Daisy You needn't rub it in.

Keith Why, Daisy, old girl, what *is* the matter? What in the dickens are you so huffy about?

Daisy Just let me and my idiosyncrasies alone, please.

Keith Heavens! Can't I say what I think?

Daisy No, you can't. I don't want to hear it. I know just what I seem like to other people—so there's no use explaining me to myself.

Keith All I meant was if you *were* in love would you give up your job and—

Daisy But I'm *not* in love, so stop thinking about it.

Keith Gosh! I thought *you* had common sense, but you're just as queer as the rest of them. What I want to know is – if a girl loves a man well enough to marry him why in hell she can't stay at home and –

Daisy What's the matter? (*As* **Keith** *cuts his finger on the tool he is holding.*) Did you cut your finger?

Keith Not much.

Daisy (*with a sudden tenderness*) Let me see.

Keith It's nothing.

Daisy It is too. Hold still. I'll tie it up for you. (*She ties his finger with her own handkerchief.*) Anything the – hold still. Anything the matter with one of your fingers would put you out of commission.

Keith Might be a good idea. I don't think Ruth believes in me much. Doesn't think I'll get much farther.

Daisy (*warmly*) I don't know why. I think you've got plenty for her to believe in. Well—speaking of angels. How are you, Ruth? (*As* **Ruth** *comes in from the hall.*)

Keith Oh—hello, dear.

Ruth Hello. What's the matter?

Keith Nothing.

Daisy Keith was waxing emphatic about *you* and over emphasized a finger. (*She turns back to cupboard.*)

Ruth I'm sorry. (*Touching* **Keith**'s *hand as he comes down to her.*)

Keith How are you?

Ruth Dead. This day's been twenty-four hours long. (*Sitting at left end of table.*)

Keith (*coming down to* **Ruth**) Has anything gone wrong?

Ruth No—but a young author from the eloquent West has been fighting me since nine o'clock this morning.

Keith What about?

Ruth He's got a perfectly magnificent story—or idea for one, rather—but it's so crudely written that it's impossible to publish it.

Daisy I suppose you can re-write it for him.

Ruth   No, he won't let me. Wants to do it all himself. Oh, he's so stubborn and so funny and so splendid. So outlandishly conceited and so adorably boyish I wanted to slap him one minute and kiss him the next.

Keith   Why didn't you do both and you'd have got what you wanted.

Ruth   I was afraid to risk it.

Keith (*nodding towards* **Tom***'s frieze*)   Doesn't that hit you in the eye?

Ruth   Awfully like Tom, isn't it? Strong and splendid.

Keith   What are you thinking —

Ruth   Oh, nothing—only I wish Ann had—I wish Ann had gone in for this competition too.

Keith   What?

Daisy   Why on earth should she?

Ruth   Why shouldn't she?

Daisy   Ruth, you're daffy about Ann. Always have been.

Keith   She does beautiful work for a woman—but ye gods—she's not in *this* class.

Ruth   And she never *will* be if she's held back and told she's limited. I think she has genius and the sooner she makes a bold dash and tries for something big the better.

Daisy   Nonsense! Tom's pushed her and believed in her always. You can't say *he's* held her back.

Ruth (*to* **Keith**)   I've heard *you* say she has genius—lots of times.

Keith   So she has—in a way. She has more imagination than the governor, but, great Peter, when it comes to execution and the real thing she isn't *in* it with him. How could she be? She's a woman.

Ruth   Don't be any more antediluvian or prehistoric than you can help, Keith. Don't *you* think Ann's more original and really innately gifted than Tom is, Daisy?

Daisy   *I do not*. She's terribly good. Of course—no doubt about that—but good Lord, Tom's *great*—a really *great* artist. (**Daisy** *starts to hall door.*)

Ruth   Why do you go, Daisy?

Daisy   Must. I have bushels of letters to get off.

Ruth   You look as fresh and rosy as if you were just beginning the day. How do you do it?

Daisy   Oh, I'm not expressing my soul in my job—merely earning by bread and butter. I suppose that's why I look so husky at twilight. (**Daisy** *goes out through hall.*)

Ruth (*looking after* **Daisy**)   Do you know—I don't believe Daisy likes me anymore.

Keith (*sitting on left end of table near* **Ruth**)   Kiss me. (**Ruth** *leans her head towards* **Keith**. *He kisses her cheek.*)

Ruth   She's so marvelously good-natured—queer she's getting snappy at me lately.

Keith   I'm awfully glad you came.

Ruth   Does it hurt? (*Touching his finger.*)

Keith   Not much.

Ruth   I wonder why she doesn't like me?

Keith   What are you talking about? I'm asked to stay to dinner, too.

Ruth   That's nice.

Keith   I can't bear to see you so tired, dear.

Ruth   I'll be all right when I have some tea.

Keith   This time next year you could be in your own home—away from those damnable office hours and the drudgery—if you only would. If you only *would*.

Ruth   It never seems to occur to you that I might be a little less tired but bored to death without my job.

Keith   If you really cared for me the way you used to—you wouldn't be bored.

Ruth   Oh let's not begin that.

Keith   But do you love me, dear. *Do* you?

Ruth   I've been telling you so for a pretty long time, haven't I.

Keith   Are you tired of it?

Ruth   There isn't any reason on earth why you should *think* I am.

Keith   Well, I do think it. I worry about it all the time. I know you're brilliant and successful—but you—after all you say you love me—and I don't see—(*He stops with a sigh.*) You're awful pretty today. Your face is like a flower.

Ruth   Oh —

Keith   Yes, it is. I love you so.

Ruth   Dear old boy! I love you.

Keith   Do you, Ruth? *Do* you?

Ruth   I've never loved anyone else. You've filled all that side of my life and you've made it beautiful. We must hang together dear—(*Putting both her hands over one of his.*) And understand and give things up for each other. But it must be fifty-fifty, dearest. I can make you happy, Keith—Oh I can. And I'll be so happy and contented with you if you'll only—(**Keith** *turns away impatiently.*) I've never had a home for a minute—in my whole life—nor a relative since I was three—of any sort or description—not a soul who belonged to me but you.

Keith I want you to have the sweetest little home in the world.

Ruth Think of having our own little dinners and all the nice people we know at our table—*ours*.

Keith Yes—but—*how can you do it if you're away all day?*

Ruth Oh Keith, dear boy, you—the whole trouble is you think housekeeping is making a home—and the two things aren't the same at all—at all, at all.

Keith Well, they can't be separated.

Ruth Oh, yes, they can. Love—love makes a home—not tables and chairs. We can *afford* more if I work, too. We can *pay* someone to do the stuff you think I ought to do. And you'll go on climbing up in your work and I'll go on in mine and we'll both grow to something and *be* somebody and have something to give each other. It will be fair—we'll be pulling together—pals and lovers like Tom and Ann. That's why they're so ideally happy.

Keith Yes, but we're different. We couldn't —

Ruth You're not fair, Keith.

Keith Great guns, Ruth—neither are you.

Ruth I am. I am perfectly. (*Their voices rise together.*)

Tom (*coming back from the workroom*)   What's the row? Hello, Ruthie Creel.

Ruth (*giving her hand to* **Tom**)   Hello, you nice Tommie Herford. I always lose my heart to you in your working clothes.

Tom You have my heart in any kind of clothes.

Ruth Keith's cross with me, Tom. You're much nicer to me than he is.

Keith You never spring any of your revolutionary speeches on Herford. You save all your really soothing remarks for me.

Ruth Tom, am I revolutionary? Aren't I just a little cooing dove?

Tom Absolutely.

Daisy (*coming in from hall*)   Dr. Remington's here. Millicent's bringing him down. But he says he wants to sit upstairs on the parlor sofa, not down in the cellar. Tom, will you sign these letters now? (**Daisy** *puts the letters on the table*—**Tom** *goes towards the table as* **Millicent** *comes in from the hall bringing* **Dr. Remington** *by the hand.*)

Dr. Remington *is 65. He is inclined to portliness and his keen humor and kindliness are combined with an understanding and wisdom which make him a very strong and a very lovable man. His manner and speech are a little deliberate. He has a twinkling readiness to tease but the weight and dignity of a successful and important physician.*

Tom Hello—hello—hello.

Remington   How are you?

Keith (*taking* **Remington***'s overcoat*)   How are you. Dr. Remington? (**Ruth** *comes to the doctor to take his hat and stick.*)

Remington   Hello, McKenzie. And here's that pretty little Ruth thing—knowing so much it makes my head ache.

Ruth   So long as it's your head and not mine I don't mind.

Millicent   Oh, thank you for the chocolates, grandfather. They're just the kind I adore. I could absolutely combostulate you—(*Giving him a violent hug.*) Five pounds, daddie.

Tom   You're a fine doctor!

Remington   Chocolate's about the best medicine I know of if you want a girl to love you. Where's your mother?

Millicent   In the cave. (*Pointing to workroom.*)

Remington   Can't she be excavated? Go and dig her out.

Millicent   They won't let me. You do it.

Remington   Hasn't anybody got the courage to do it? (**Keith** *starts towards the door with box.*)

Daisy   Not me.

Remington   Well, McKenzie, go and tell her to let the work go to thunder and come and see her dad. (**Keith** *goes into workroom.*) Is that the thing that's going to get the hundred thousand for you?

Tom   If—yes.

Remington   Well, go to it—boy. I hope you hit it. (*Sitting in the large chair at left.*)

Tom   Thanks. I'm doing my durndest. Daisy, you've got some of these dimensions wrong. Keith will have to give them to you again.

Daisy   Oh, I'm sorry.

Remington   It's a good thing you're working for your own brother, Daisy—nobody else would have you.

Daisy   You're the only person in the whole world who isn't impressed with my business ability.

Remington   Stuff! I wager you say in your prayers every night—Oh, Lord, deliver me from this job and get me a good husband.

Daisy (*laughing with the others and going to* **Remington**)   That's a very stemmy tie you're wearing. Do you get me?

Remington   Not exactly. All I know is I'd rather be stemmy than seedy.

Keith (*opening the workroom door*)   Don't you want me to carry that in for you, Mrs. Herford?

Ann (*from within*)   No, no—I'd rather do it myself.

Keith   It's too heavy for you.

Ann   No it isn't. (**Ann** *comes in carrying the figure of a woman in the nude—about a foot high. The figure is in wet clay and stands on a modeling hoard.*)

Tom   Steady there! Steady! Let me take it.

Ann   Don't touch it!

Remington   Hello there!

Ann   Hello, daddy! I couldn't come out until I finished my lady. Isn't she nice? She's ready to be cast now. Come and look at her, Tom. She isn't so bad?

Tom   She looks pretty good to me.

Remington   She looks a little chilly to me. Why don't you put a full suit of clothes on one of 'em——just for a change, Ann?

Ann   You nice, horrid, sweet, adorable, cross old thing! Why didn't you come yesterday? I don't see why I love you so when you never do anything I want you to.

Remington   If I did I wouldn't be half as irresistible. Aren't you going to stop for the day now and pay a little attention to me?

Ann   I *am*.

Millicent   Mother, when can I see you? Alone I mean.

Ann   After awhile. Have you had a nice day, dear?

Millicent   Gorgeous! But I have to see you about something.

Ann   You do? (*Holding* **Millicent**.) Look at her—dad. Hasn't she grown?

Millicent   Mother, may I stay home from school one more day?

Ann   Gracious! Is that what you want to see me about?

Millicent   That's just one thing. Can't I, mother? All the girls are staying over. Mayn't I? Please—please.

Ann   I have to think a little. Let's wait and talk it over. Daisy, aren't we going to have some tea?

Daisy   It will be ready in a minute.

Remington   Thank God! Then we'll go upstairs.

Ann   No, down here—it's much nicer. You'll have to get used to it, dad.

Millicent   Well—you be thinking—but you be thinking—*yes*—for I've just *got* to stay over. I've just got to. It would be perfectly ridiculous if I didn't. (*She goes out through hall.*)

Remington (*nodding after* **Millicent**)   Getting more like you every day, Ann.

Ann   She's *your* grandchild, you know.

Remington   I like 'em that way. I'd rather she was stubborn as a mule than have a wabbly spine.

Ann (*taking off her smock*)   But a little wabbling once in a while is rather a pleasant thing to live with. For instance, it would make me very happy indeed if you wabbled enough to admit that this is a beautiful studio and that having it in the house where we live is the most sensible thing in the world.

Remington   It would be all right if you'd stay upstairs and mind your own business. Tom, if you don't look out you'll be so mixed up you'll be upstairs keeping house and Ann will be downstairs keeping shop.

Tom   I don't know how I'd keep house—but Ann could keep shop all right.

Remington   Is that the way you feel about it, McKenzie? When you're married are you going to stay at home and polish up while Ruth goes on running the magazine?

Keith   It looks as if that's about the way it'll have to be.

Ruth (*bringing the cake down to table*)   That's a splendid suggestion, Dr. Remington. Keith thinks somebody's got to do it for a successful marriage—and *I* won't—so why not you, dear? (*Pointing at* **Keith**.) (**Keith** *looks at* **Ruth** *and turns away in hopeless disgust*.)

Remington (*winking at* **Ruth** *and lowering his voice to her*)   Keep at it. He'll come to it. (**Ann** *laughs as she cuts the cake*.)

Keith   I don't see that it's so funny.

Remington (*going to table to get a piece of cake*)   You bet it's not funny. Daisy, would you like your husband to wash the dishes if you happened to be too much occupied to do it yourself?

Daisy   I'd kill him if he did. (*Bringing the cream and sugar to large table*.)

Remington   Oh—well—with one perfectly normal woman in the room I'm much more comfortable. (*He settles himself elaborately in his chair at left*.)

Keith   I'm serious. I'd like to know if there's anything queer or preposterous in a fellow wanting a girl to give up hard, slavish work and let him take care of her when she marries him.

Ruth   When she wants to do the work. Don't leave that out.

Tom   I don't see that you, Keith, or any other fellow has got any kick coming so long as the girl makes you happy.

Keith   I'd like to hear your angle on it if you don't mind, doctor.

Ruth   Yes. Keith loves to hear his mid-Victorian ideas well supported.

Remington   Oh, I'm not so moth-eaten as I may look. In fact, I'm a damned sight more advanced than you women are. You're still yelling about your right to do anything on land or sea you want to do. We gave you that long ago.

Ann   So nice of you!

Ruth (*sitting below the table at right*)   Why talk about it all then? What else is there to it?

Remington   Put this in your pipe. The more women make good—the more they come into the vital machinery of running the world, the more they complicate their own lives and the more tragedies they lay up for themselves.

Ruth   The more they escape—you mean.

Ann (*as she pours the tea*)   There isn't a single hard thing that can happen to a woman that isn't made easier by being able to make her own living. And you know it.

Remington   Oh. It's a hopeless subject for conversation. What everybody says is true. There's the rub.

Daisy   Two?

Remington   Three. (**Keith** *gives a cup of tea to* **Remington**.)

Tom   Go on. What were you going to say?

Ann   Yes, go on, dad.

Remington (*to* **Ann**)   You hang on to yourself then till I get through. The development of women hasn't changed the laws of creation.

Ann   Oh yes it has. (**Remington** *looks at her.*) Sorry. Go on.

Remington   Sex is still the strongest force in the world. (*He looks at Ann again.*)

Ann (*smiling*)   Go on.

Remington   And no matter how far she goes she doesn't change the fundamental laws of her own —

Tom   Individuality?

Ruth   Type?

Daisy   Character?

Keith   Ego.

Ruth   Psychology.

Ann   Species.

Tom   Breed.

Daisy   Spots.

Remington   *No!*—Mechanism—mechanism. And when the sensitive—involved—complex elements of a woman's nature become entangled in the responsibility of a man's work—and the two things fight for first place in her—she's got a hell of a mess on hand.

Ann   But her psychological mechanism *has* changed.

Remington   No.

Ann   Yes.

Tom   Yes, I think it has.

Keith   It couldn't.

Ruth   But it *has*. Women who are really doing things nowadays are an absolutely different breed from the one-sided domestic animals they used to be.

Ann   But men don't realize how deeply and fiercely creative women love their work.

Remington   That's just it—Just what I'm getting at. A woman of genius puts in her work the same fierce love she puts into her child or her man. That's where her fight is—for one or the other of 'em has got to be the stronger in her. It isn't a question of her *right* to do things—nor her ability—God knows—plenty of 'em are beating men at their own jobs now. Why, I sometimes think she'll go so far that the great battle of the future will be between the sexes for supremacy. But I tell you—she has tragedies ahead of her—the tragedy of choice between the two sides of her own nature.

Ruth   Well, thank you—I'll take any and all of the hard things that go *with* my job—but none of the ones that come from being a dub and giving it up.

Remington   How about you, Daisy? Could any man on earth make you stop typewriting and live for him alone!

Daisy   Oh, I'm not in this class. Ann and Ruth both have men to depend on if they want them. I'm taking care of myself because I've *got* to—and I must say this soul tragedy of choice stuff makes me a little tired. (*She starts toward hall.*)

Remington (*stopping* **Daisy** *by taking her hand*)   If I were twenty or thirty years younger, I'd go in for you strong.

Daisy   Yes, I know—I'm just the kind that *older* men appreciate very deeply. (*She goes out.*)

Remington   Poor Daisy.

Ann   Poor Daisy. She's the happiest, most independent thing in the world. (*Straightening the things on the table—***Keith** *having taken the tea tray away.*)

Ruth   Much to be envied. No strings to *her* independence.

Keith   And so cocky and spunky—nobody can even ask her if she's ever been in love.

Remington Sure sign she has been then.

Tom But she never has.

Remington How do you know?

Tom I've been pretty close to her all my life. No blighted bud about Daisy.

Remington She's putting up a darned good bluff, I must say.

Ruth Bluff? What do you mean?

Ann Father thinks there isn't a girl alive who wouldn't rather have a beau than a job.

Remington I do. And Daisy *looks* so self-reliant she *has* to be cocky to keep up appearances. Under her skin, she's not half the man that little lady-like looking thing Ruth is.

Ruth Now, Dr. Remington, you may go upstairs.

Remington I haven't time now. I've wasted it all down here.

Ruth Oh, come and look at the living room just a minute. It's too beautiful.

Remington Has it got a carpet on it yet?

Ann Yes, absolutely finished.

Remington Because I don't mind saying my feet are like ice from this confounded brick floor.

Ruth Oh, the beautiful tiles!

Remington I'll take a little less Italian beauty and a little more American comfort in mine.

Ruth, Remington, *and* **Keith** *go through the hall.*

Tom (*stopping* **Ann** *as she starts with the others*) Ann—about this thing. Why in the name of heaven didn't you say you were disappointed in it long ago?

Ann I kept hoping each day I was mistaken; that what I missed would come back. But when I saw it out here—I'm afraid of it, Tom.

Tom Afraid of what? That I'll fail? Lose it? (**Ann** *nods.*) Nonsense! You're tired of it. There can't be such a change in it as all that. The idea's absolutely the same and I've *worked* as I never —

Ann I know. I know! And oh, the beauty—the beauty of the work! That's the pity.

Tom Pity?

Ann I mean somebody without *half* your skill as an artist may have an idea—an *idea* that's *new*.

Tom Oh bosh! Nothing can be done, anyhow. It's too late. Besides, I don't agree with you. I honestly do not, Ann. I know you're saying this because you're trying to boost me and get the best out of me; but the thing's done, you know. Don't confuse me. I must go on now. What's the use of talking about it? It's too late.

Ann No, it isn't.

Tom It is. Of course it is. You can't expect me to begin all over again and put into it a subtle intangible something I don't even feel. Damn it? It will have to fail then.

Ann (*taking hold of* **Tom** *quickly*) It can't. You've got to win, Tom. You've *got* to. It's the most important thing you've ever done. Think of where it will put you. Think of the money.

Tom I *have* thought. I've done the best that's *in* me, I tell you. It is the best, the very best I've ever —

Ann But it isn't. It isn't. It isn't as great as your last two things —

Tom Oh—

Ann Tom—listen—you don't know how hard it is to say it. I'd rather you won this than anything that could possibly happen. You know that. Don't you?

Tom Of course. But this isn't getting anywhere. It will have to go in as it stands.

Ann Wait—I—I've wanted to talk to you about something for a long time—but I wasn't sure—and now I *am*.

Tom Well—

Millicent (*coming back through hall*) Thank goodness, mother. I can't wait any longer.

Ann (*to* **Millicent**) Oh, just a minute, dear.

Tom No, that's all right. There's nothing more to be said.

Ann I appreciate what you mean—yes I do. But it doesn't get me. And all I can do is to go after it as I see it. (*He goes into workroom.* **Ann** *stands looking at the frieze.*)

Millicent (*pulling* **Ann** *toward table*) Mother—come here. Mother, *please*. Why— what I wanted to—sit down. (*Putting* **Ann** *into a chair above the long table.*) Every *one* of the girls are staying over tomorrow. It looks as if you were having such a slow time that you didn't have anything to do *but* go back to school if you don't stay. And I want—Why Fanny's going to have a party tomorrow night—just a little one, and I want to have eight of them to dinner first. (*Sitting at right end of table.*)

Ann Oh —

Millicent Only eight. You see, Fanny's brother's home, too, and—you see it's— Everybody has dinners and things you know before they go to the dance, you know, and—will you. Mother? Can't I?

Ann But dearest you've done so much since you've been home. You can't get back to school too soon. New York is dreadful. It really is! The sensible mothers can't compete with the idiotic ones who let girls do all these silly things.

Millicent Don't be foolish. Mother.

Ann And school does begin tomorrow. And they expect —

Millicent They don't expect us to be back. All the really smart girls stay over. It's only the deadly slow ones who are there on time. Please, mother—*please*. There'll only be eight of us; and Fanny's done so much for me I think it's as little as I could do to have her brother to dinner. Don't you?

Ann Is he nice?

Millicent Yes he is. He's older, you know and more fun. He got full dress clothes this Christmas—long tails, you know, and he looks perfectly—Mother, you're not listening. (**Ann**'s *eyes have gone back to the frieze again.*)

Ann Yes, I am dear—Yes I am. Full dress clothes.

Millicent Well—May I?

Ann Dearest—I may be frightfully busy tomorrow. I may have to do the most important thing I've ever done in my life and if I do it would be awfully hard to have —

Millicent Oh, now mother! Fanny's mother's had a party or something for her every single night. She took her to the Plaza to dance after the matinee today and I've never been to a hotel or any exciting place in my life. You try to keep me so young mother and, jiminy cricket, I'm sixteen.

Ann Positively ancient.

Millicent Well—sixteen's old enough for anything. Will you mother—please—*please*. (*Kissing her mother's throat.*)

Ann But what would I do if I had to do this other thing?

Millicent What other thing? Can't it wait?

Ann No it can't. That's just it. Your father may—I may be working with him all day tomorrow.

Millicent You needn't have such a terribly *elaborate* dinner,—you know, but I'm crazy to do it. In fact I just have to. I've already asked most of them and they're dying to come.

Ann You didn't. Kitten—how could you?

Millicent But Mother, it's so *important*—and I don't see how I can get out of it now. You wouldn't want me to be compromised or anything, would you?

Ann (*laughing and kissing* **Millicent**) You blessed baby—you ought to be spanked.

Millicent You're an angel, Mummie. You will—won't you? (*Putting her cheek against* **Ann**'s.)

Ann What have you got in your ears?

Millicent Earrings of course.

Ann Heavens! Take them off.

Millicent Oh, *mother*! All the girls wear them.

Ann Take them off!

Millicent But they have so much style.

Ann Style your granny! Take them off or I'll bite 'em off. (**Millicent** *squirms and giggles as Ann bites her ears.*)

Millicent Wait—wait. I will. I think you're mean to make me. You have such terribly strict ideas.

Ann Your ears are much prettier than those things. Can't you understand that nothing is so attractive as just being natural? Why cover up with stuff like that?

Millicent You *are* funny! You'll stay at home and meet everybody tomorrow night, won't you? I want them to see you. You are sweet, mummy.

Ann Do you love me a lot?

Millicent Of course. (*Kissing* **Ann**.)

Ann (*rising suddenly and going to look at the frieze*) Oh, I'm so unhappy.

Millicent Why? What's the matter? I should think you'd be tickled to death if father's going to get all that money.

Tom (*coming in from the workroom quickly*) You say—(*He stops seeing* **Millicent**.)

Millicent Aren't you coming up, now to plan it all?

Ann In a few —

Tom Go on Millicent. (**Millicent** *skips out.*) Why didn't you speak the minute you saw it go wrong—or thought you did?

Ann I was never *sure*, until today, dear.

Tom I don't agree with you at all but still it isn't exactly inspiring—knowing you think I'm going to fail.

Ann Tom—I'm sorry.

Tom It's all right—but you know I care more what you think than anybody in the world and—I—it's sort of a knockout.

Ann I had to tell you the truth—when I *was* sure. I *had* to. Tom—listen—since you've been working at this an idea has come to me. At first I thought the idea was too big for me—that I never could carry it out—and then I said I won't *let* myself be afraid—and it's grown and grown night and day. Last night I finished it—down here —

Tom The—

Ann The drawings—I want you to look at them—and if—if you like it—if you think the idea is better than yours I want you to take it—use it, instead of yours.

Tom Why Ann, you're not serious. (*She nods.*) Good heavens, child, you know—you know how tremendous this thing is as well as I do.

Ann Yes I do! But I tell you my idea is big. Oh, I knew you'd look like that when I told you. You can't believe it of course—but Tom—. It's there—something vital and *alive*—with a strange charm in it. And I offer it to you dear—if you want it.

Tom (*taking her in his arms strongly and kissing her passionately*) You generous darling! It's like you to do this. You dear—I love you for it.

Ann (*responding warmly to his love*) I want you to have it. It's more than I ever dared dream I could do.

Tom But darling—you couldn't possibly do anything for a scheme as big as this.

Ann Why do you take that for granted? Why do you say that—before you've even seen my sketches?

Tom (*after a pause*) Well—where are they?

Ann (*taking a key out of her pocket*) In the lower drawer in my cupboard.

Tom (*taking the key*) No, don't come with me.

Ann But I—

Tom I don't want you to explain anything. I want it to strike me fresh. But I'm going to hit hard—right from the shoulder. If it's good—all right. If it's bad—all right. And I expect you to take it like a man. (**Ann** nods. **Tom** *hurries into workroom as* **Ruth** *comes in from hall.*)

Ruth Have you told him?

Ann Yes—he's gone to look at my sketches now.

Ruth Ann—I've been thinking. You're a fool to give away your ideas. Make your models and send them in yourself.

Ann What?

Ruth Certainly. Why not?

Ann Oh, Ruth—I couldn't. Some day I will. Some day.

Ruth Some day! You've got the biggest idea you've ever had. Do it—send it in—yourself—on your *own feet*.

Ann Tom would think I was out of my —

Ruth *You* know it's good—don't you?

Ann Yes, I do.

Ruth It belongs to *you*—and if you don't take care of it and give it its chance, you kill something which is more important than you are. Don't forget *that*. You're not just the talented woman, you've got *downright genius*, and you ought to make everything give way to that. *Everything*. If you don't, you're weak.

Ann Wait and see what Tom says. He'll know. He's so dead right about my stuff—always.

Ruth Oh, you lucky people! Pulling together. If Keith only had a little of it towards me. Ann, what *shall* I do?

Ann (*with quick sympathy*) What, dear?

Ruth He's never, never, never going to know what a sacrifice it will be for me to stop just as I'm getting what I've slaved and struggled for all these years. And I can't bear to hurt him.

Ann Dear old Keith. He just *can't see*. And he loves you so.

Keith (*coming in from hall*) Why did you come back down here?

Ruth Just to run away from—you. No, I didn't. (*Going to him sweetly.*) You know I didn't.

Ann (*as* **Daisy** *comes in from hall*) Daisy, tell me the minute Tom comes out.

Keith (*to* **Ruth**) I'll be up in a minute. I've got to cover some stuff in there. (*Exit* **Ann** *and* **Ruth**.)

Keith You're a wonder, Daisy. You don't mind sitting up late to get your letters off, do you?

Daisy Oh, no—I'm healthy.

Keith You're a peach. I'm sorry I made you huffy. All I meant was that no man would ever think he could ask you to marry him unless he had an awfully big bank-roll to offer.

Remington *comes in from hall to get his hat and stick—just in time to hear* **Keith***'s last remark.* **Daisy** *rises—consciously.* **Keith** *goes into workroom.* **Remington** *goes to end of table.*

Daisy I suppose that speech sounded rather queer. He was talking about Ruth, of course.

Remington Don't apologize or you'll make me suspicious.

Daisy Now —

Remington It sounded very much as if he were making love to *you*.

Daisy Oh—

Remington I wish to God he would. You'd—be a much better wife for him than the other one.

Daisy You —

Remington You know you would. Why don't you go in and get him? Cut the other one out.

Daisy How *dare* you say such a thing to me?

Remington Why shouldn't I say it?

Daisy Because you have no *right* to. I haven't the slightest interest in Keith McKenzie—not the slightest.

Remington No. I can see that.

Daisy What do you mean?

Remington (*suddenly understanding*) Why my dear girl, I didn't mean anything. I'm sorry.

Daisy I don't know why in the world you said such a thing to me.

Remington Well—well—forgot it.

Daisy You don't think from anything I've ever done or said —

Remington I don't think anything—I don't know anything . . .

Daisy I don't see *why* you said it.

Ann (*coming from hall*) What's the matter?

As **Daisy** *breaks away from* **Remington** *who is holding her by the wrists.*

Daisy Let me go, please. I'm in a hurry. (**Daisy** *rushes out through hall.*)

Ann What on earth are you doing to Daisy?

Remington She's doing things to me.

Ann What?

Remington Convincing me of some of my old-fashioned ideas. (**Tom** *rushes in from the workroom with a large roll of drawings.*)

Tom Ann—they're wonderful.

Ann Oh—Tom!

Tom (*spreading the roll of sketches on the table —* **Ann** *helping him*) Beautiful! Astoundingly beautiful! Well as I know you, I didn't think you had it in you.

Ann I can't believe it. Are you going to use it?

Tom Oh, my dear girl. That's different. Now don't be hurt. Why Ann—it isn't possible. You—you're mistaken—way off. I don't know what's got into you. This is imaginative and charming and graceful—full of abandon and fantasy and even vitality—but ye gods, child, it isn't in *this* class.

Ann But you could strengthen it. It will grow. You'll see more in it. Really you will. Don't make up your mind yet.

Remington What are you talking about? What has she done?

Tom Drawings for a frieze—like this. And they're amazing, doctor. Positively amazing.

Remington You don't say.

Tom Wait—let's see what McKenzie says. McKenzie —

Ann (*pounding on the workroom door*)   Keith—Keith—come here—quickly.

Remington   Looks beautiful to me, daughter. When did you do all this? Do you mean to say you didn't know anything about it, Tom?

Tom   Not a thing. She's been—(**Keith** *comes in.*) Here McKenzie. Look at this. Here's a scheme Mrs. Herford's worked out. Begins here—See—see? Get it? What do you think?

Keith   Mrs. Herford?

Tom   Yes. Do you get it?

McKenzie   Of course.

Tom   Well? What do you say?

Keith   I say it's as beautiful as anything I ever saw.

Tom   Great! And what do you think of it for a big place like mine?

Keith   For *that*?

Tom   Yes.

Keith   Oh—I—too fanciful, isn't it? Would the crowd understand it? Needs a big clear striking thing like that. Don't you think?

Tom   Then you don't think it's as good as mine for this competition.

Keith   As yours? Heavens no!

Ann (*standing at right—facing the three men*)   Then do you know what I'm going to do?

Keith and Tom   What?

Ann   Make my models and send them in myself.

Tom, Keith and Remington   What?

Ann   Why not?

Remington   You don't mean it, daughter.

Ann   I do. I mean it with my whole soul.

Remington   Why do you want to do anything so foolish?

Ann   Because I made it. Because it's my work. You all say it's good. Why shouldn't I send it? I don't mind failure. I only want it to stand its little chance with the rest. I love it. It means more to me than I can possibly—why shouldn't I? I *want* to.

Tom   Then do it. Why not? It's your own affair. Go ahead. (*Putting out the hand of a good pal-ship to her.*)

Ann   Oh, Tom—thank you. You're splendid.

(*The curtain falls*)

Act Two

Time : *Four months later—about nine in the evening. The living room in the Herford house.*

The room is long and wide, dignified and restful in proportions. At center back a large fireplace with a severe mantel in cream marble. A wide window covers the entire left wall, and wide doors at right lead into the library. A single door at back, left of fireplace, leads into hall. The walls are hung in a soft dull silk which throws out the strong simple lines of the woodwork. A bright wood fire is burning and soft lights throw a warm glow over the gray carpet and the furniture which is distinguished and artistic but distinctly comfortable, giving the room the air of being much lived in and used.

At Curtain: *The room is empty a moment.* **Daisy** *is singing in the library at right.* **Ellen**, *a maid, middle-aged and kindly, comes from hall carrying a silver coffee service.*

Daisy (*as she comes in from library*)   Here's your coffee, girls. Come in here. Put the flowers over there, Ellen.

Ellen *moves the vase of flowers and makes room for the coffee service on table right center.* **Ruth** *comes in from the library with a book.* **Ellen** *goes to fire and pokes it, then straightens the writing things on the desk.*

Daisy   Ann, here's your coffee.

Ann (*calling from library*)   I don't want any, thank you. What time is it, Daisy?

Daisy   About nine. Why?

Ann   Oh, the postman. I'm waiting for the last mail.

Daisy   Well, don't. A watched pot you know. (*To* **Ruth**.) She's watched every mail for a week. I almost think Ann will be more disappointed than Tom himself if he doesn't get the commission. (*They take their coffee to the fire.*)

Ruth   I hope to goodness he does. Everybody's so dead sure of him.

Daisy   Almost too sure. I'm beginning to be frightened myself. The time's about up.

Ann (*hurrying in from the library*)   That's the postman—isn't it?

Ellen   No ma'am. Beggin' your pardon. It ain't—I'm listenin' too.

Ann   Are you, Ellen? Keep on and bring it up the minute it comes.

Ellen   Faith I will. I've got the habit meself lately of watchin' for the mail .

Ann   Have you?

Ellen   Every time I hear the whistle I drop whatever I'm doin' like it was hot—and run.

Ann Do you?

Ellen And just before I open the door I say—The Holy Saints be praised, I hope it's come this time—whatever it is they're lookin' for. (*She goes out through the hall.*)

Ann Oh, dear! It gets worse as the time grows shorter.

Daisy Ann, working yourself up like this won't make Tom get the commission. Stop thinking about it.

Ann But I can't, Daisy Dimple. He ought to hear tonight if he's ever going to.

Daisy Well, I'll be glad when it's all over and we know one way or the other—and can settle down to ordinary life again. It's almost given me nervous indigestion.

Ann Listen! There's the postman.

Ruth (*jumping so that her cup and saucer almost fall*) Oh, Ann, you're getting me so excited, I'll listen for the postman all the rest of my life.

Ann I know I shall. Oh, Tom must get it. He must. If he does, I'll wire Millicent. (*Taking up a picture of* **Millicent** *which stands in a frame on the table.*) I think I'll run up to school Sunday just to give her a good hug. I get so hungry for her!

Ruth Isn't it splendid the school is so really what it ought to be?

Ann Yes. So much that's sweet and right that one can't get in New York for a girl.

Daisy (*sewing on a frock which is nearly finished*) She seems pretty keen about it herself.

Ann Yes—rather. Easter vacation when I was working day and night to get my models off, she was perfectly contented to stay at school.

Ruth She's an adorable kiddie but I don't envy you your job.

Ann Why?

Ruth I think being a mother is the most gigantic, difficult, important and thankless thing in the world.

Daisy That's the most sensible remark I ever heard you give vent to, Ruth.

Ann There's something much more glorious in it than being thanked. You'll miss the most wonderful thing in the world, Ruth, if you don't have children.

Ruth I know. I know. But work has taken that all out of me. It does, you know. It would bore me stiff to take care of a baby.

Daisy That's a pleasant prospect for Keith. Do you expect *him* to do it?

Ruth (*making herself comfortable on the couch*) I'm not going to *have* children.

Ann (*going to sit at the fire*) That's perfectly fair if he knows it. No reason why you should if you don't want 'em.

Daisy Well, I think it's a *rotten* way to live.

Ruth Wait till you decide to marry somebody yourself, young lady, and see how *you* like giving up everything that interests you most.

Daisy Well, by Jove, if I ever *do* marry, I'll *marry* and do all the things that belong, to my side of the game. No halfway business for me. You might as well be a man's mistress and be done with it.

Ruth (*half serious—half joking*) That's the ideal relationship for a man and woman. Each to keep his independence in absolutely every way—and live together merely because they charm each other. But somehow we don't seem to be able to make it respectable.

Daisy I suppose that's very clever and modern.

Ruth Oh, no—it's as old as the everlasting hills. The trouble is children are apt to set in and mess things up. It's hard on *them*.

Daisy So far as I can see most everything that's modern is hard on children.

Ann (*laughing*) How's the gown getting on, Daisy?

Daisy Most finished.

Ruth That's awfully pretty.

Ann Slip it on so we can see.

Daisy Oh, I can't.

Ann (*rising and walking to* **Daisy**) Yes, you can—over that one—just to give us an idea.

Daisy I'll look a tub and it really makes me quite respectably straight up and down.

Ann You're a perfectly scrumptious size and shape. Isn't she, Ruth?

Ruth Magnificent!

Daisy Yes, Ruth, skinny women always enthuse over their fat friends.

Ruth (*rising and goes to* **Daisy**) Oh, you aren't fat, Daisy. That is, not too fat. How does this go. It's terribly complicated, isn't it?

Daisy No—perfectly simple. Wait—this goes over here.

Ann No, it doesn't, does it?

Daisy Yes, it does. Right there. Don't you see? The style of the whole gown depends on that.

Ruth You must have it on wrong side before.

Daisy Nonsense! Can't you see, Ann? It's as simple as can be.

Ann Yes, I know dear—but does this go on the shoulder—or down on your hip? (*They all talk at once for a moment on the subject of where the end of the girdle* *fastens.*) Oh, here! I see, of course! There!

Daisy   Now, does it make me look big?

Ruth   You want to look big, don't you?

Daisy   Well, I want to look life size. Don't you see how much better I am through here than I was last year, Ann? (*Touching her hip.*)

Ann   Much. The female form divine is improving all the time anyway—gradually getting back to what it was in the beginning.

Daisy   I don't expect to look like you in it, Ruth.

Ruth   Oh, don't you, dear? Then why don't you have it stick out this way as much as possible so everybody will know you *mean* to look broad? There's everything in that, you know.

Daisy   I think it would be awfully good on you—to fill out what you haven't got. Then everybody would know you didn't *mean* to look so narrow—even if you *are*.

Ann   You're both delightful. Perfect specimens of your types. When I look at Ruth I think the most alluring charm a woman can have is beautiful bones without a superfluous ounce of flesh on them. And when I look at you, Daisy, I think after all, there's nothing so stunning as a big strong girl with perfectly natural lines—so natural that we know she'd be even better looking with no clothes on at all.

Daisy   Heavens, Ann! Your sculptor's eye is a little embarrassing.

Ruth   Evidently you think my clothes help me out a good deal. But at least I'm free and comfortable, too. Can you touch the floor, Daisy?

Daisy   Of course. (*The two women bend—touching the floor with the tips of their fingers.*)

Tom, **Remington** *and* **Keith** *come in from the hall.*

Tom   What's going on?

Remington   What are you trying to do, Ruth—swim or fly?

Ann   We're just saying that the waist measure expands as we *broaden* in our ideas.

Keith   Is that the fashion now?

Ruth   Yes—broad and free.

Remington   That's *one* thing you women have to acknowledge men have more sense about than you have.

Ann, Ruth, Daisy   What?

Remington   Our figures. We've had the same shape since the Garden of Eden and you've had hundreds of absolutely different kinds.

Ann   Turn around, Daisy, I want to try something. (*She accidentally sticks a pin into* **Daisy**'s *shoulder.*)

Daisy Ouch!

Ann Oh, I'm sorry! You seem to be so close to your clothes.

Remington What are you doing to her?

Daisy She's sticking pins into me.

Ann For her own good. Isn't that pretty?

Tom What?

Ann The frock.

Tom Is that new?

Keith Which?

Daisy Do you mean to say you don't realize I have on something different from what I wore at dinner?

Ruth No use dressing for Keith. He never sees anything.

Daisy I'm going to undress now. Perhaps that will interest you more. (**Ann** *begins to unfasten the gown.*)

Remington Much more.

Ann Was *that* the postman?

Daisy No, it was *not*.

Remington The postman habit is getting on my nerves. You're all jumping and listening till you'll have St. Vitus dance if you don't stop.

Ann How can we help it?

Remington After all, a few other competitions have been lost and won—and people have lived through it. It's not the only thing in life.

Tom You'd think it was if you had $100,000 at stake. (**Ellen** *comes in from hall and takes out the coffee tray.*)

Ann Aren't we going to have some bridge? Who wants to play? I know you do, daddy.

Remington I have to get even with you for that last rubber, Tom.

Tom You can't do it.

Daisy I want to play, with you, doctor.

Remington Come on.

Ruth I'm afraid to play *against* you.

Remington (*turning at the library door*) What's that?

Others What?

Remington The postman!

Others Oh! (**Ruth** and **Daisy** *go into library R. with* **Remington**.)

Ann (*to* **Tom** *and* **Keith**) Coming?

Tom You go, Keith. I want to look at the paper a minute.

Keith Oh, my game's no good. You go.

Ann Now don't stay out here and listen and wait. If there is any mail Ellen will bring it straight up.

Tom I won't. I'll be with you—in two minutes.

Ann Anyway—tonight doesn't necessarily decide it. There may be still two or three more days. Isn't that so, Keith?

Keith Yes, I think so.

Remington, Ruth, Daisy (*calling from the library*) Come on. Come on.

Ann Coming. (*She goes in.*)

Keith That's straight. I do think so—(*A pause.* **Tom** *reads.*) Don't you?

Tom I'm trying to—but these last few days of waiting have been —

Keith Don't lose your nerve, Herford. I'm just as sure as I was the first day. If by any wild chance you *don't* get it—it will be a fluke.

Tom Oh, no. Oh, no, not by any means. The men judging this *know*. I'd trust them with anything. The fellows who lose will have no kick coming on that score.

Keith Well—I don't see how you *can* lose.

Tom A man's a fool to let himself count on an uncertainty. I don't mean that I've lost sight of the fact that I might lose—not for a second—but I confess—as the time has grown shorter I've realized I *want* it even more than I thought I did.

Keith Of course you want it. Aside from the glory—it's an *awful lot of money*—governor, an awful lot of money.

Tom *It is.* It would put us straight—clear up the house entirely and make it possible to do only the things a fellow wants to do. That's what I'm after. Then—No more competitions for me, thank you. Is that the 'phone? I'm as bad as Ann—jumping and listening. Damn it! I want to *know*—one way or the other.

Keith Of course, you do. The cursed waiting is enough to make you cut your throat.

Ellen (*opening the hall door*) The telephone for Mr. Herford.

Tom Who is it?

Ellen I couldn't just get the name, sir.

Keith Want me to go?

Tom   If you don't mind, old man. (**Ellen** *goes out.*)

Keith (*starting to the door and turning*)   It couldn't be—you wouldn't get word that way—would you?

Tom   Uh?—Oh—nonsense! No—no—nonsense! I'll go—No, I—you go—old man. That's not it—of course. (**Tom** *listens a moment—showing a tense anxiety.*)

Ruth (*coming in from the library*)   They're waiting for you, Tom. The cards are dealt. Where's Keith?

Tom   He'll be back in a minute.

Ruth   Aren't you going in?

Tom   Why don't you take my place? I don't feel a bit —

Ruth   I did offer to, but Dr. Remington said he would like to *play* bridge this evening, not *teach* it. Wouldn't it be seventh heaven to speak the truth on all occasions as unconcernedly as Dr. Remington does? Imagine the sheer bliss of letting go and spitting it all out. Have you ever counted the lies you told in just one day, Tom?

Tom   No—I've never had time. (**Tom** *starts to go into the library and turns to see if* **Ruth** *is coming.*)

Ruth   No—I'm going to wait for Keith. (**Tom** *goes in —* **Ruth** *reads for a moment.*)

Keith (*coming back from the hall*)   That was —

Ruth   What?

Keith   Millicent or her school or something. Such a bad connection; they're going to call again in a few minutes. Is that dress new, dear?

Ruth   I've had it three years.

Keith   It's awfully pretty. I wish you'd wear it all the time.

Ruth   I do.

Keith   Aren't we going in to play?

Ruth   No, I don't feel like it. Come and sit down, dear. Oh, are you going to sit way over there?

Keith   Not 'specially. (*Drawing chair near the couch —* **Keith** *sits facing* **Ruth**.)

Ruth   Comfortable?

Keith   Not very.

Ruth   Have you read this?

Keith   No. Any good.

Ruth   Yes—Good enough. (*She rises, going to the fireplace.*)

Keith   What's the matter? I thought you wanted to talk. Where are you going?

Ruth   No place.

Keith   You got the fidgets, too?

Ruth   Sort of.

Keith   Well, stop it. Herford's going to be all right. There'll be news in a day or so now.

Ruth   I wasn't thinking of that. I have something to tell you.

Keith   Then why don't you come and tell it?

Ruth   And if you aren't fine about it—it will be the greatest disappointment in my whole life.

Going to **Keith** *and putting a hand on his shoulder.*

Keith   You mean if I don't think just what you want me to about it. Go on. I s'pose I know, anyway.

Ruth   Then if you do—but you don't. It's so wonderful you couldn't guess. And you'll just *have* to see it the right way, because if you don't it would mean you're what I know you're *not*. Down in your real soul, Keith, you're generous and fair and right.

Keith   Suppose you communicate it to me first and discuss my soul afterwards.

Ruth (*sitting on couch facing* **Keith**)   Well—Oh you *will* be sweet won't you, Keithie?

Keith   I can see it's going to be something very pleasant for *me*.

Ruth   It is if you . . .

Keith   It's wonderful if I'm not a fool and a pig. Yes, I know. Go on. Go on.

Ruth   Now don't begin that way —please dear. Don't shut up your mind before I even tell you.

Keith   Suppose you *do* tell me.

Ruth   Well—last week there was a row in the office over a matter concerning the policy of the magazine and I differed with all the men in my department. At last I was sent for by the Editor in Chief. He was terribly severe at first, and I was frightened to pieces—but I stuck to my guns—and bless your soul he sent for me again today and said they had had a meeting of the directors and that they decided—oh, it's too —

Keith   What? What?

Ruth   They had decided to make me Editor of the Woman's Magazine. (*Fighting back her tears.*) Isn't it funny?

Keith   And I suppose all this introduction means you accepted—without even asking me?

Ruth   Why, of course. Oh, Keith, don't you understand what this means to me?

Keith   I understand that unless it means more to you than I do—you wouldn't hesitate a minute to chuck it.

Ruth   It's hopeless—we'll never—never see it the same way.

Keith   You've never made the slightest effort to see it *my* way.

Ruth   What you ask of me is to cut off one half of my life and throw it away. What I ask of you is only an experiment—to let me try and see if I can't make things comfortable and smooth and happy for us—and still take this big thing that has come as a result of all my years of hard work and fighting for it.

Keith   You'll never stop if you don't now. Once you get deeper in it you'll be swamped—eaten up by it.

Ruth   Don't, Keith. I can't bear it. It's too unutterably selfish.

Keith (*rising and pushing his chair away*)   All right—I'm selfish—but I'm human—and I'll bet my hat I'm just like every nine men out of ten. What in the name of heaven does loving a girl amount to if you don't want to take care of her from start to finish? A man's no good if he doesn't feel that way, I tell you. He's a pup—and ought to be shot.

Ruth (*rising*)   But what about *me*—and what I want and have to have—in order to be happy.

Keith   That's it. That is the point. You won't be happy without it. You want the excitement of it—that hustle and bustle outside.

Ruth   I want it just as you want your work—and you haven't any more right to ask me to give up mine than I have to ask you to stop *yours*.

Keith   You simply don't *love* me.

Ruth   What rot! What nonsense!

Keith   You don't love me.

Ruth   It's hopeless. You've decided then. You won't compromise—so we'll end it.

Keith   What do you mean?

Ruth (*going to the hall door*)   You've made your own choice. We'll end it now.

Keith (*following her*)   No—Ruth—I won't give you up.

Ruth   You have. You have given me up.

Keith   Ruth—wait.

Ruth   It's best, Keith. Don't hate me. You'll see it's best in a little while. We'll learn to be friends. I want you to be happy, dear boy—I do. And I couldn't make you so. We'll end it now. It's the best for us both.

Keith   Ruth —

She goes out quickly, closing the door. **Keith** *turns to the fire.*

Daisy (*knocking and opening the library door*)   Excuse me. May I come in to get my sewing? Where's Ruth?

Keith (*with his back to* **Daisy**)   Don't know.

Daisy   Well, don't bite my head off. I can always tell when you and Ruth have been discussing the *emancipation* of women.

Sitting below table and taking her dress to sew.

Keith   You *all* think you're superior beings.

Daisy   Of course.

Keith (*beginning to walk about*)   Yes, you do. You're just as bad as the rest of them—worse. The minute a woman makes enough to buy the clothes on her back, she thinks she and God Almighty are running the earth and men are just little insects crawling around. (**Daisy** *laughs.*) Oh, you can laugh. It's so—and you *know* it. Every one of you that have got the bee in your bonnet of doing something—*doing* something, are through with the men. Look at *you*. You've cut men out entirely and you think you're too smart to marry one. Now, don't you? Isn't that the reason?

Daisy (*threading her needle*)   Don't bully-rag me. Say it all to Ruth.

Keith   I tell you it's all rot—business for women. It spoils every one of you. Why aren't you in a home of your own instead of hustling for your bread and butter? It's because you're too damned conceited. You think you know more than any man you ever saw and you think you don't need one. You wait—You'll see—someday.

Going back to the fire.

Daisy   You amuse me.

Keith   There you *are*—that's about what I'm for.

Daisy   There's a button off your coat. Looks horrid.

Keith   I know. I've got it.

Putting his finger in waistcoat pocket.

Daisy   Have you got it there? (**Keith** *shows her the button.*) Come here, I'll do it.

Keith   Never mind. I'll *nail* it on.

Daisy   Come here. (**Keith** *goes slowly to her.*) You'll have to take your coat off. It's bad luck to sew anything on you.

Keith   Oh —

Daisy   Go on—take it off. (**Keith** *takes off his coat reluctantly and watches* **Daisy** *as she examines the coat.*) Good Gracious, the lining's ripped, too.

Keith   Yes.

Daisy Poor old fellow! Are these some of your stitches?

Keith (*drawing the chair from C. and sitting L. before* **Daisy**) What's the matter with 'em?

Daisy Looks like carpet thread. (*Snipping some threads.*) See, I'll just draw this together and that'll be all right.

She begins to sing an old ditty — **Keith** *gradually hums with her, keeping time with his hands and feet and relaxing into a good humor.*

Keith (*soothed for a moment*) How does it happen you're so handy with a needle? I thought you were all for business.

Daisy Well, I can sew a button on if *you can.*

Keith I tell you it changes all women—business. They make a little money themselves and want luxury and won't live without it.

Daisy Sometimes—yes. But there are lots and lots and lots of women taking care of themselves—putting up the bluff of being independent and happy who would be so glad to live in a little flat and do their own work—just to be the nicest thing in the world to some man.

Keith Wouldn't you think that Ruth would like that better than the office?

Daisy No—not the lamp light and the needle for Ruth. Keith, don't ask her to give up her work—don't you see, she's more clever, in her way than you are in yours. She'll go further, and if you make her stop, she'll hate you some day because she'll think you've kept her back. That's a hard thing to say—but it's the truth.

Keith You mean I'm a failure.

Daisy (*genuinely*) No—no—I don't mean that, Keith.

Keith I work—Gosh, how I work, but I'll never *do* anything. Why haven't I got what Mrs. Herford's got? She sent models off for this frieze that any *man* would be proud to send. Why couldn't I?

Daisy Seems kind of mixed up and unfair—doesn't it?

Keith You bet it's unfair. I work like a dog and never get anywhere. If Ruth throws me over, I'll never have the home I'm working for. That's what I want—a home. I'll never have it now.

Daisy Oh, yes you will.

Keith I'm done for.

Daisy No, you're not. There are too many women in the world—who—could—love you.

Keith I'm no good.

Daisy Some woman might think that you—your—the way you work—and your honesty and *loyalty* are the greatest things a man can have.

Keith Um!

Daisy *Some* woman might use all her cleverness and ingenuity to make the little flat beautiful—to show you what your own home—could be—to give you a better dinner than you thought you could afford.

Keith (*sitting with his head in his hands*) That kind of a woman is a thing of the past.

Daisy Oh no, they're not. They're lying around *thick*. The trouble is—a *woman* can't *ask*. Even if a man is—just at her hand—and she knows she could make him happy—she can't *tell* him—she can't open his eyes—she has to hide what might make things right for both of them. Because she's a woman.

Keith Oh—love doesn't cut much ice with a woman. Women are all *brain* nowadays.

Daisy (*with sudden warmth*) That's enough to use all the brains a woman's got—to make a home—to bring up children—and to keep a man's love.

Keith (*raising his head slowly and looking at* **Daisy**) I never expected to hear *you* say a thing like that. There's some excuse for *you* being in business.

Daisy Yes, of course. (*Rising and holding the coat.*) I'm not the marrying kind.

Keith (*getting into the coat*) Much obliged. Would *you* be willing to give up work and marry a man on a small salary—if you loved him?

Daisy You make me laugh.

Keith What's the matter, Daisy?

Daisy Nothing.

Keith I never saw tears in your eyes before. Women are funny things.

Daisy Yes, we're funny. There's only one thing on earth funnier.

Keith What?

Daisy Men.

Remington (*coming in from the library*) Did I leave my other glasses in here?

Daisy (*beginning to look for them*) I haven't seen them.

Remington I've lost one game because I didn't have 'em and I don't propose to give 'em another.

Daisy What a shame! Help look for them, Keith.

Remington I'm pretty blind—but thank God not quite as bad as you, Keith.

Keith What? There's nothing the matter with my eyes.

Remington (*looking insinuatingly at* **Daisy**) Don't you think there is, Daisy

Daisy (*trying to look unconscious*) Are you *sure* you left those glasses in here?

Remington It's as bad a case of short sightedness as I ever saw.

Daisy Oh—

The doctor holds her and turns her, pushing her toward **Keith**.

Remington Daisy, don't you see that queer blind look in his eyes?

Daisy No—I don't.

Keith What do you mean? (**Remington** *laughs*.) Do you see the joke, Daisy?

Remington It's no joke—is it Daisy?

Daisy I don't know what on earth you're talking about. I'm going to get those glasses. (*Going to hall door*.) You probably left them in your hoat in the call. I mean in your hall in the coat—I mean —

Remington That's all right, Daisy—we know what you mean. At least I do.

Daisy Oh you—(**Ellen** *comes in from hall*.) What is it, Ellen?

Ellen The telephone. Miss Herford.

Daisy For me?

Ellen They said any one of the family.

Daisy I'll go.

She goes out followed by **Ellen**.

Remington *There's* a woman who knows how to take care of a man.

Keith I'm afraid that's not her object in life. They all have something else to do.

Remington What's the matter with you?

Keith I'm done for.

Remington Ruth, you mean?

Keith She won't marry me unless she goes on working.

Remington She's right, too.

Keith What?

Remington Of course. You haven't any more right to ask that clever little woman to throw away half her life and to be the tail to your kite than you have to ask her to cut her throat. Open your eyes and look around. There are always other women.

Keith *Never*. Never in the world for me.

Remington I give you about three months.

Keith Do you think I could ever —

Remington Certainly, I do. Look at Daisy, for instance. A fine, sweet wholesome girl with no kinks and no abnormal ambition.

Keith   Daisy?

Remington   Don't blow your brains out for a couple of days. Talk it over with her. She thinks you're about the finest thing going.

Keith   *What*?

Remington   Fact! Don't try to hold on to the woman who's getting away from you but take the one who is coming your way.

Keith   You're crazy. Mad as a hatter. What are you giving me?

Remington   Just a little professional advice—*free*. She's head over heels in love with you, I tell you.

Daisy (*coming in from hall in great excitement. She has a case for glasses in her hand*)   Dr. Remington, that was long distance. They telephoned from school that Millicent has gone.

Keith   Gone?

Remington   Gone where?

Daisy   Left school suddenly tonight without saying a word to anyone.

Remington and Keith   What?

Daisy   As soon as they knew—they 'phoned the station and found she had taken the train for New York.

Remington   What train?

Daisy   The one that gets here at nine o'clock.

Keith (*looking at his watch*)   It's 9:15 now.

Daisy   Shall I tell Ann?

Remington   No—no—wait. We'll give her fifteen minutes more to get to the house. No use frightening Ann.

Keith   Do you think she *is* coming home?

Daisy   Why do you say that, Keith? What put such an idea into your head?

Keith   Why wouldn't she say so—wire or write or something?

Daisy   Oh, it's too horrible. Doctor, oughtn't we to tell them now?

Remington   No—no —

Daisy   But we're wasting time. What if she *shouldn't* come?

Keith   I think I'll dash down to the station anyway. The train might be late.

Remington   No—no. They'd ask where you'd gone. Wait fifteen minutes—I think she'll be here. I don't want to frighten —

Anne *comes in from the library.*

Anne Well, I never saw people so wildly keen about playing as you are. What's the matter with you?

Remington I've been waiting all this time—for my glasses. Come on Daisy.

Taking the glasses from **Daisy**, *he goes into library.*

Ann You look worried, Daisy.

Daisy No—I'm only —

Ellen (*coming in from hall with eight letters on a small tray*) The mail, Mrs. Herford.

Ann Oh! (*She snatches the letters, taking off the three top ones.*) It's come! Tom's letter.

Keith and Daisy What?

Ellen *goes out through hall L. C.*

Ann It is! It is—as true as I live.

Keith Great Scott!

Daisy Then he's got it. He's got it.

Ann Sh! Ask him to come here.

Daisy It's too good to be true. It's too good!

Daisy *goes into the library.*

Keith I can't tell you how glad I am, Mrs. Herford. I can't tell you.

Ann (*scarcely able to speak*) Ask him to come here.

Keith (*going into library*) Mrs. Herford wants you, Governor.

Tom (*within*) Come and play, Ann.

Ann (*throwing the other letters on the table*) Come here just a minute, Tom, please.

Tom (*coming to door*) What is it?

Ann Shut the door. It's come. (*Showing the letter.* **Tom** *opens and reads it. A look of sickening disappointment comes into his face.*) No? Oh, Tom!

Tom I was their *second* choice!

Ann Oh, Tom, don't take it like that. What difference does it make after all? You know you did a big thing. It's all luck—anyway.

Tom I'll pull up in a minute. Well, it means taking hold of something else pretty quick. Going at it again.

Ann Yes, keeping at it—that's it. What a TERRIBLE lot chance has to do with it.

Tom Oh no, that isn't it.

Ann Yes, it is, too.

Tom No—I failed. I didn't get it, that's all.

Ann You'll do something greater—next time—because of this.

Tom (*taking her hand*) You're a brick! Now, see here, don't you be cut up about this. It's not the end of everything, you know. Stop that! You're not crying, I hope?

Ann No, I'm not. Of course, I'm not! (*With passionate tenderness.*) Oh, my boy. I never loved you so much—never believed in you as I do now. This is only a little hard place that will make you all the stronger.

Tom Dear old girl! What would I do without you? I'll tell the others and get it over. (*Rising, he stops, staring at one of the letters on the table.*) Ann!

Ann Um?

Tom (*taking up a letter*) Ann—here's one for you, too.

Ann What? (*She tears open the letter.*) Tom! They've given the commission to me! Look! Read it! Is that what it says? Is it? Now aren't you glad you let me do it? You haven't lost! We've got it. Say you're glad. Say you're proud of me, dear. That's the best part of it all.

Tom Of course, I am, dear, of course I am.

Ann Oh, Tom, I wanted you to get it more than I ever wanted anything in my life, but this is SOMETHING to be thankful for. Doesn't this almost make it right?

Tom Yes, dear, yes. Don't think of me. That's over—that part of it. Tell the others now.

Ann Wait!

Tom Aren't you going to?

Ann I only want to be sure that you're just as happy that *I* won, as I would have been if YOU had.

Tom Of course, I am. You know that.

Kissing her.

Ann Tell the others, then, Tom—I can't.

Tom (*opening the library doors*) What do you think has happened?

Daisy (*rushing in*) Tom got it. Didn't you, Tom? You did. You did! Oh, I'm so glad. (*She kisses him.*)

Keith (*following* **Daisy** *in*) Well—governor—what did I tell you?

Remington (*in doorway*) Pretty fine —isn't it?

Ann You tell them, Tom.

Tom Ann got it!

Daisy What?

Tom Isn't it great?

Ann You won't believe it. But you can see the letter. Now, father, don't you think getting that is better than being nursemaid and housekeeper? Now, don't you, honestly?

Remington I do not.

Ann What?

Remington I do not.

Ann Oh, I can laugh at your theories now. You haven't a leg to stand on. Has he, Tom? Be a dear father and say you're glad.

Remington I'm not. I'd rather you'd failed a thousand times over—for your own good. What are you going to do with Millicent while you're making this thing?

Ann How can you be so hard and narrow. Father?

Remington What if you did win? You've got something far greater than making statues to do.

Tom Doctor, you're excited.

Remington Not a bit. I'm only telling the truth. This is your business you know—and it would have been far better for *both* of you if *you'd* won the thing.

Tom I don't see the argument. Ann got it because she sent in a better model than I did. I don't see that anything else has anything to do with the case.

Tom *goes out through hall.*

Ann (*turning to sit on the couch*) At least *Tom's* glad I got it.

Remington He's stung to the quick. You've humiliated him in his own eyes (*He goes to the fireplace.*)

Ann I *can't* understand why you feel this way about it, father.

Daisy Oh, its *natural* enough.

Ann (*turning to* **Daisy** *in amazement*) Aren't you glad for me—Daisy?

Daisy Yes, but—I—I'm awfully sorry for Tom.

She goes out through hall.

Ann What's the matter with them all, Keith?

Keith Oh—as Daisy says—it's natural, Mrs. Herford.

He goes out after **Daisy***.*

Remington (*coming down to* **Ann**) Daughter, I'm afraid I was a little too stiff just now. I didn't mean to be unkind.

Ann (*rising and starting to hall door*) Oh, it doesn't matter.

Remington (*stopping her*)   Yes, it does matter. I wouldn't hurt you for the world.

Ann   But you've *always* fought me, Father. You've *never* thought I had any right to work—never believed in my ability, now that I've proved I have some—Why can't you acknowledge it?

Remington   Ann, this is a dangerous moment in your life. Tom's beaten—humiliated—knocked out. You did it—he can't stand it.

Ann   What have I done? Tom has a big nature. He's not little and petty enough to be hurt because I won.

Remington   You're *blind*. He's had a blow tonight that no man on earth could stand.

Ann   Not Tom. I won't believe it.

Remington   Yes, I say. I know what I'm talking about. Ann, be careful how you move now. Use your woman's tact, your love. Make Tom know that he is the greatest thing in the world to you—that you'd even give up all this work idea—if—he wanted—you to.

Ann   *What*? Tom wouldn't let me.

Remington   Ask him. Ask him. See what he'd say.

Ann   Why, I wouldn't insult him. He'd think I thought he was —

Tom *comes in from the hall —* **Ann** *checks herself and turns away quickly to fire.*

Tom (*after a pause*)   What's the matter?

Remington   Nothing—nothing. Ann and I were just having a little argument as usual. I'll be back in a few minutes.

Looking at his watch he goes into hall.

Tom (*going slowly to* **Ann**)   I hope you're not still fighting about the—your frieze?

Ann   They're all so funny, Tom—the way they act about it. It hurts. But so long as you're glad, it doesn't matter what anyone else thinks. Say you're glad, dear. I want you to be as happy as I would be if you had won.

Tom   You know I am, dear. You know that.

Ann (*with a sigh of relief* **Ann** *sits at left of fire*)   Think how I'll have to work. I can't even go to the country in the summer.

Tom (*sitting opposite* **Ann** *at the fire*)   And what will you do with Millicent this summer?

Ann   Oh, there are lots of nice things for her to do. The money! Think what it will mean to you!

Tom   Let me tell you one thing, Ann, in the beginning. I'll never touch a penny of the money.

Ann   What?

Tom   Not a cent of it.

Ann   What are you talking about?

Tom   That's your money. Put it away for yourself.

Ann   I never heard you say anything so absolutely unreasonable before in my life.

Tom   If you think I'm unreasonable, all right. But that's understood about the money. We won't discuss it.

Ann   Well, we *will* discuss it. Why shouldn't you use my money as well as I yours?

Tom   That's about as different as day and night.

Ann   Why is it?

Tom   Because I'm taking care of *you*. It's all right if you never do another day's work in your life. You're doing it because you want to, I'm doing it because I've got to. If you were alone it would be a different thing. But I'm here, and so long as I am I'll make what keeps us going.

Ann   But I'll help you.

Tom   No, you won't.

Ann   I *will*. I'm going on just as far as I have ability to go, and if you refuse to take any money I may make—if you refuse to use it for our mutual good, you're unjust and taking an unfair advan—Oh, Tom! what are we saying? We're out of our senses—both of us. You didn't mean what you said. Did you? It would—I simply couldn't bear it if you did. You didn't—did you?

Tom   I did—of course.

Ann   Tom—after all these years of pulling together, now that I've *done* something, why do you suddenly balk?

Tom (*rising*)   Good Heavens! Do you think I'm going to use your money? Don't try to run my end of it. It's the same old story—when you come down to it, a woman can't mix up in a man's business. (*He moves away.*)

Ann   Mix up in it? Isn't it a good thing for you that I got this commission?

Tom   No. I don't know that it's a good thing from any standpoint to have it known that I failed, but my wife succeeded.

Ann   I thought you said you were glad—proud of me.

Tom   It's too—distracting—too—takes you away from more important things.

Ann   What things?

Tom   Millicent and me.

Ann   Oh, Tom don't. You know that you and Millicent come before everything on earth to me.

Tom   No.

Ann You do.

Tom We don't—now. Your ambition comes first.

Ann (*she rises, going to him*) Tom, I worship you. You know that, don't you?

Tom I'm beginning to hate this work and everything in connection with it.

Ann But you taught me—helped me—pushed me on. What's changed you?

Tom I let you do it in the first place because I thought it was right. I wanted you to do the thing you wanted to do.

Ann Well?

Tom I was a fool. I didn't see what it would lead to. It's taking you away from everything else—and there'll be no end to it. Your ambition will carry you away till the home and Millicent and I are nothing to you!

Ann Tom—look at me. Be honest. Are you sorry—*sorry* I got this commission?

Tom I'm sorry it's the most important thing in the world to you.

Ann Oh! Why do you say that to me? How can you?

Tom Haven't I just seen it? You're getting rid of Millicent now because you don't want her to interfere with your work.

Ann No!

Tom You're pushing her out of your life.

Ann No!

Tom You said just now you were going to send her away alone in the summer. I don't like that. She's got to be with you—I want you to keep her with you.

Ann But that's impossible. You know that. If I stop work now I might as well give up the frieze entirely.

Tom Then give it up.

Ann What?

Tom Give up the whole thing—forever. Why shouldn't you?

Ann Do you mean that?

Tom Yes.

Ann Tom—I love you. Don't ask this sacrifice of me to prove my love.

Tom Could you make it? Could you?

Ann Don't ask it! Don't ask it for your own sake. I want to keep on loving you. I want to believe you're what I thought you were. Don't make me think you're just like every other man.

Tom I am a man—and you're my wife and Millicent's our daughter. Unless you come back to the things a woman's always had to do—and always will—we can't go on. We can't go on.

Ann (*following him around the table*) Tom—if you're just a little hurt—just a little jealous because I won

Tom Oh

Ann That's natural—I can understand that.

Tom Oh—don't

Ann But, oh, Tom, the other—to ask me to give it all up. I could never forgive that. Take it back, Tom—take it back.

Tom Good God, Ann, can't you see? You're a woman and I'm a man. You're not free in the same way. If you won't stop because I ask it—I say you *must*.

Ann You can't say that to me. You can't.

Tom I do say it.

Ann No!

Tom I say it because I know it's *right*.

Ann It isn't.

Tom I can't make you see it.

Ann It isn't.

Tom I don't know how—but everything in me tells me it's right.

Ann Tom—listen to me.

Tom If you won't do it because I ask you—I demand it. I say you've *got* to.

Ann Tom—you can kill our love by just what you do now.

Tom Then this work *is* the biggest thing in the world to you?

Ann What is more important to us both—to our happiness than just that?

Millicent (*calling outside door L. C.*) Mother! (*A startled pause as* **Ann** *and* **Tom** *turn towards hall door.*) Mother! I'm home, where are you?

Millicent *opens the hall door and rushes into the room.*

Ann Millicent! What are you doing here?

Millicent I came home, mother.

Ann Why?

Millicent Because I had to.

Ann Are you ill, dear?

Millicent No. No.

Tom   Is anything wrong at school?

Millicent   No, but I won't go back.

Tom   But why won't you? What's the trouble?

Millicent   I won't go back.

Tom   But you can't do a thing like this. I won't allow it.

Millicent   You wouldn't let me come home when I wanted to and now I can't go back. I won't—everything's different now. I won't go back and you can't make me.

She turns and rushes out of the room and **Tom** *and* **Ann** *stare at each other as the curtain falls.*

Act Three

Time: *Half an hour later.*

Scene: *Same as Act II.* **Ruth** *is writing at the desk.* **Daisy** *opens the hall door and stops, listening back into the hall.*

Ruth (*quickly*)   What's the matter?

Daisy   Nothing. I was looking to see who went up the stairs. It's Dr. Remington.

Ruth   How's Millicent now?

Daisy   Ann's with her—getting her to bed.

Ruth   Do you know yet why she came home?

Daisy   I don't know whether Ann's got it out of her yet or not.

Ruth   What do you think? Why on earth didn't she tell them at school?

Daisy   I haven't the dimmest—but she didn't do it without some good reason. I'll bet anything on that. Millicent's a pretty level-headed youngster.

Ruth   She's a pretty self-willed one. Ann will send her right back of course.

Daisy   I don't know whether she will or not. Millicent's got some rather decided ideas of her own on that.

Ruth   But she'll *have* to go. Why shouldn't she? Ann will make her.

Daisy   Tom will have something to say about it.

Ruth   It's for Ann to decide surely.

Daisy   Not at all. I don't see why. She is Tom's child, too, you know, and this is his house and he pays the bills at school and if he doesn't want her to go back you can bet she jolly well won't go. I only hope Millicent tells the whole business whatever it is. Ann is so excited over the frieze I don't know whether she'll have the patience to handle Millicent right or not. She's not easy.

Ruth   It's awful for Ann to be upset now—of all times—when she has to begin this gigantic work.

Daisy   Oh—I wish the damned frieze were in Guinea and that Ann had nothing to do but take care of Tom and Millicent—like any other woman. I'd give *anything* if she hadn't won the competition.

Ruth   Daisy!

Daisy   Oh, I would. I have a ghastly feeling that something horrible is going to come of it—if it hasn't already come.

Ruth   What do you mean?

Daisy   I tell you it is not possible for a man and woman to love each other and live together and be happy—unless the man is—*it*.

Ruth Speaking of the dark ages! You ought to live in a harem. How any girl who makes her own bread and butter can be so old fashioned as you are—I can't see.

Daisy You've got so used to your own ideas you forget that I am the average normal woman the world is full of.

Ruth Nonsense! You're almost extinct. I'm the average normal woman the world is full of—and it's going to be fuller and fuller.

Daisy I'll bet on plenty of us—left—(*Indicating herself.*) on Judgment day.

Ruth I want to laugh when I think how mistaken we've been calling you a bachelor girl. Why you'd make the best wife of anybody I know.

Daisy I s'pose you mean that as an insult.

Ruth But you *seem* so self-reliant men are sort of afraid of you —

Remington (*coming in from hall and feeling a certain restraint in the two girls*) Am I in the wrong camp.

Ruth and **Daisy** No, no. Come in.

Remington I have to stay some place. I'm going to hang around till Millicent quiets down—and then I'll clear out.

Daisy Is she ill?

Remington Oh, no. Just a little worked up and excited.

Ruth Why do you think she came home, Dr. Remington?

Remington I don't know what to think—unless she has "*boy*" in the head.

Daisy Goodness no! Not yet!

Remington She's sixteen. You can't choke it off to save your life.

Ruth Oh, she's a baby!

Remington Don't fool yourself. She won't wait as long as you two have to sit by her own fireside with children on her knee.

Ruth Oh—

Remington That's the only thing in the game that's worth a cent—anyway. (*As* **Keith** *comes in from the hall.*) Isn't that so, Keith?

Keith What's that?

Remington I've just been telling these two that love and children are the greatest things on earth. Ruth doesn't agree with me—but Daisy —

Ruth I must go.

Daisy I must go up to Ann. (**Ruth** *goes out.*)

Remington Let *me* go. They both seem terribly anxious to get out when you come in, Keith. Or maybe I'm in the way. I'll go.

Daisy Don't be silly. I really must see if I can do anything for Ann.

Remington No, you mustn't. She's waiting for me to see Millicent. By the way, Keith—tomorrow's Sunday. I always take a run into the country in the motor on Sunday. Come along and bring either Ruth or Daisy. Take your choice. I know which one I'd take. (*He goes into the hall.*)

Daisy Isn't he a goose.

Keith Would it bore you to go, Daisy?

Daisy Nonsense! Ruth will.

Keith It would be awfully good of you. Tomorrow's going to be a hard day for me to get through. Ruth told me tonight that she—I'm afraid it's all over.

Daisy Why don't you compromise?

Keith There's nothing to compromise about. She's all wrong. Don't you think so?

Daisy Oh, don't ask me. I don't know anything about it.

Keith Wait a minute. I—won't you go tomorrow, Daisy.

Daisy Ask Ruth. It will be a good chance to make up.

Keith You're so *practical* and like such *different* things—maybe you'd think flying along through the country and lunching at some nice little out-of-the-way place was too frivolous —

Daisy Oh yes, I don't like anything but being shut up in the house all day, pounding at my typewriter and splitting my head to get the bills straight. To actually go off with a man—for a whole day—and have a little fun—like any other woman—would be too unheard of. Of course, I couldn't do anything as silly as that.

Keith Oh —

Daisy I wouldn't be amusing anyway. Dr. Remington—well, he's sixty, and you'd be thinking of Ruth and I'd sit there like a stick—the sensible, practical woman who couldn't possibly be interesting and fascinating because no man would take the trouble to find out how devilish and alluring and altogether exciting I could be if I had the chance.

She throws open the door and goes out. **Keith** *stares after her.*

Tom (*coming in from library after a moment*) I thought you'd gone, McKenzie.

Keith No, but I'm going.

Remington (*coming back from hall*) Good night, McKenzie. I'll dig you up in the morning, ten o'clock. Sharp, mind. And I'll call for Daisy first.

Keith (*at hall door*) All right. Much obliged, Doctor. (*Turning back.*) How'd you know it was Daisy?

Remington I didn't—but I do now.

Keith Good night. (*He goes out.*)

Tom Well—how is she? How is Millicent?

Remington Oh, she's not ill—but the child's nervous as a witch—all strung up. She's worried about something—got something on her mind and naturally her head aches and she has a little fever—but that won't hurt her.

Tom Got something on her mind? What?

Remington She didn't confide in me.

Tom What *could* she have on her mind?

Remington I don't think she's committed murder—but she's *got* a mind, you know—There's no reason why she shouldn't have something *on* it.

Tom Well, *I* don't know what to do with her.

Remington If you think she ought *not* to go back to school, say so. Tell Ann those are your orders.

Tom I don't give orders to Ann.

Remington The devil you don't. She'd like it. A woman—a dog and a walnut tree—the more you beat 'em, the better they be.

Tom The walnut tree business doesn't work with Ann. I made a food of myself tonight by telling her I wouldn't touch the money she gets out of this thing. She doesn't understand. I've made her think I'm jealous because she won.

Remington Well, aren't you?

Tom *No*! I tell you it's something else. Something sort of gave way under my feet when I opened her letter.

Remington I know. I know.

Tom Doctor, for the Lord's sake, don't think I'm mean. I don't want to drag her back—but she seems gone somehow—she doesn't *need* me anymore. *That's* what hurts.

Remington Of course, it hurts.

Tom Much as I've loved to have her with me—working away at my elbow—wonderful as it all was—sometimes I've wished I hadn't seen her all day—that I had her to go home to—fresh and rested—waiting for *me* and that I was running the machine alone for her. She'll never understand. I've acted like a skunk.

Remington Y-e-s—I guess you have—so have I—unjust—pig-headed. No more right to say the things I've said to her than I have to spank her—except that she's—the most precious thing in the world to me—and I'd rather see her happy—as a woman—than *the greatest artist in the world.*

Tom   That's it. I want her here—*mine*. But I s'pose that's rotten and wrong.

Remington   Yes—I s'pose it is. But you're despising yourself for something that's been in your bones—boy—since the beginning of time. Men and women will go through hell over this before it shakes down into shape. *You're* right and *she's* right and you're tearing each other like mad dogs over it because you love each other.

Tom   That's it. If another man had got it I'd take my licking without whining. What's the matter with me? Why can't I be that way to *her*?

Remington (*shaking his head with a wistful smile*)   Male and female created He them. I don't take back any of the stuff I said to her before she went into this. She's fighting you now for her rights—but she laid her genius at your feet once and she'd do it again if —

Ann (*coming in from the hall and speaking after a pause*)   Well, father—what do you say about Millicent?

Remington   My advice is that you let her stay at home for a while.

Ann   This is only a caprice—and it would be the worst thing in the world to give in to her. Unless you say as a physician—that she's too ill to —

Remington   I don't say she's too ill—physically. You must decide for yourself. I'll go up and see her again and if she isn't asleep then I'll give her a mild sleeping powder. Ann, I put her in your arms first—and the look that came into your eyes then was as near divinity as we ever get. Oh, my daughter—don't let the new restlessness and strife of the world about you blind you to the old things—the real things. (*He goes out.*)

Ann (*after a pause*)   You agree with me, don't you, that it's better for her to go back.

Tom   Do whatever you think best.

Ann   But what do you think?

Tom   It doesn't matter what I think, does it?

Millicent (*opening the door*)   Mother, aren't you coming back? (**Millicent** *wears a soft robe over her night gown. Her hair is down her back.*)

Ann   Millicent—why did you get out of bed?

Millicent   I couldn't sleep. (*Running and jumping into the middle of the couch.*)

Ann   Run back—quickly.

Millicent   In a minute. It's so quiet upstairs I couldn't sleep. I'm used to the girls.

Ann   You'll catch cold.

Millicent   Goodness, mother, I'm roasting.

Ann   *Millicent*—what *shall* I do with you.

Millicent   Is that what you and dad were talking about? What did Grandfather say? I don't care what he says. I'm not going back to school. You're on my side—aren't you, Dad?

Tom Whatever your mother thinks is right, of course.

Millicent Is it true—what Daisy told me—that you got the contract for a big frieze and not father? Is it? Is it, father? (*Looking from one to the other.*)

Ann Millicent, go to bed.

Millicent I think that's perfectly horrid, mother. Why should they give it to you? I think father ought to have it—he's the man. Don't you think people will think it's funny that you didn't get it? I should think it would make them lose confidence in you. (*A pause.* **Tom** *stalks out—closing the door.*) Is father hurt because you got it? I should think he would be.

Ann Millicent, I've had quite enough of this. Go up to bed at once.

Millicent Will you come up and sleep with me?

Ann Of course not. (*Walking about restlessly.*)

Millicent Why not?

Ann Neither one of us would sleep a wink.

Millicent That wouldn't matter. I don't want to be alone.

Ann Come now—I won't speak to you again.

Millicent What have you decided about school?

Ann I'll tell you in the morning.

Millicent I won't go up till you tell me.

Ann Millicent—you will go at once, I say.

Millicent Oh, Mother, don't be cross. Sit down and talk a minute.

Ann It's late, dear. You must —

Millicent That's nothing. We girls often talk till twelve.

Ann Till twelve? Do the teachers know it.

Millicent Oh, mother, you're lovely! Don't you suppose they *know* that they don't know everything that's going on? Come and sit down, Mummie.

Ann No! You must go to bed.

Millicent But I won't go back to school.

Ann (*going to* **Millicent**, *who is still on the couch*) You make it terribly hard for me, Millicent. You don't know what's good for you, of course. I don't expect you to—but I *do* expect you to be obedient.

Millicent But, Mother, I tell you I —

Ann Don't be so rebellious. Now come upstairs, please dear, and —

Millicent But I won't go back to school, mother, dear. I won't.

Ann   You say I treat you like a child. You *force* me to. If you don't want me to punish you—go upstairs at once and don't say another word.

Millicent   I won't go back.

Ann   Stop, I say!

Millicent   I know what I want to do. I'm sixteen.

Ann (*their voices rising together*)   You're my child. You will obey me.

Millicent   But I won't. You don't understand. I can't mother, I can't—I can't.

Ann   Why? Why can't you?

Millicent   Because I—I'm going to be married.

Ann   You silly child!

Millicent   It's the truth, Mother. I am.

Ann   Don't say a thing like that, even in fun.

Millicent   It's the truth, I tell you. I'm going to be married.

Ann   Some time you are, of course—you mean.

Millicent   No—now—soon. That's why I left. That's why I'm not going back.

Ann (*after drawing a chair to the couch and sitting before* **Millicent**)   What do you mean?

Millicent   I—he—we—we're engaged.

Ann   He—who?

Millicent   You—You don't know him.

Ann   Who?

Millicent   He's—he's perfectly wonderful.

Ann   *Who is he?*

Millicent   Now, Mother, wait. He—he isn't rich —

Ann   Well—

Millicent   He's poor—but he's perfectly wonderful—he works and he's so noble about it.

Ann   What does he do?

Millicent   He-he—Oh, mother, it's hard to explain because he's so different.

Ann   *What does he do?*

Millicent   Well—just now he—he drives the motor at school—because you see he's so proud he —

Ann   Drives the motor—a chauffeur, you mean?

Millicent   People call him that, of course—but he isn't—(**Ann** *rises*.) Mother—(**Ann** *goes to the door and locks it—going back to* **Millicent**, *who had risen*.) Now, Mother, don't look like that.

Ann   Sit down.

Millicent   *Don't* look like that. Let me tell you about it.

Ann (*sitting again*)   Yes, tell me about it.

Millicent   Oh, I—hardly know how to begin.

Ann   He drives the motor—the school motor, you say?

Millicent   Yes—to the trains, you know—and into town and to church.

Ann   Who is his father?

Millicent   Why—I—I don't know who he is. I've never met his father.

Ann   What is his name?

Millicent   His father's name? I don't know.

Ann   The *boy's* name.

Millicent   Willie Kern.

Ann   How does he happen to drive a motor?

Millicent   Well, I don't know just *how* it happened—he's so clever you know, and of course he isn't really a chauffeur at all.

Ann   What is he then?

Millicent   Oh, Mother! He just happens to run the school motor.

Ann   And what did he do before that?

Millicent   Why he—he ran *another* motor. Oh, now, Mother, you don't understand at all. (*She breaks into sobs and throws herself full length on the couch.* **Ann** *sits rigidly*.) Just because he's poor and clever and drives a motor is no reason why you should act this way. (*Sitting up*.) He's going to do something else. He's going to come to New York to get a different position. And we'll be married as soon as he gets it, and that's why I came home—to tell you. So there—you see I can't go back to school. (*She rises and starts to the door*.)

Ann   Millicent! Come here.

Millicent   That's all there is to tell. I'm going to bed now.

Ann (*rising*)   You know this is the most wild and impossible thing in the world.

Millicent   I don't. It *isn't* impossible. I'm going to marry him. I love him better than you or father or anybody in the world and I'm going to marry him.

Ann   Stop! Do you want to disgrace us? How any child of mine could speak—even speak to such a—Oh, the disappointment! Where's your pride? How *could* you? How could you? Millicent, if you'll promise me to give this up I won't say a word to your father.

Millicent   No—no—I'm going.

Ann   Don't unlock that door.

Millicent   I want to go now.

Ann   You'll never see this boy again. Never speak to him—never write to him—never hear of him. I shall send you away where he'll never know —

Millicent (*coming back to couch*)   You won't! He loves me and I love him. He understands me. All that vacation when you wouldn't let me come home and all the other girls had gone he was just as good to me as he could be. He knew how lonely I was and he—we got engaged that vacation. You wouldn't let me come home.

Ann   Millicent—you don't know what you're saying. You don't know what you're doing.

Millicent   Oh, yes, I do. Mother. It's you that don't know. You don't understand.

Ann (*kneeling before* **Millicent**)   My darling—why—didn't you tell me this when you said you wanted to come home? Why didn't you tell me then? (*Sobbing,* **Ann** *buries her face in* **Millicent**'*s lap.*)

Millicent   I would have told you—if you'd let me come home—but you wouldn't—and I was so lonely there without the girls and—we—we got engaged. You don't understand, Mother.

Ann (*lifting her face to* **Millicent**)   Oh, yes, I do, dear. Yes, I do. Tell me—all about it. When did you first know him? How did you—happen to speak to him—I mean to—to love him.

Millicent   Oh, Mother, why I—he—I just did—he's so handsome and so nice. You haven't any idea how nice he is. Mother.

Ann   Haven't I, dear? What is he like? Tell me *everything*—how did it begin?

Millicent   He—the first time I really knew he was so different you know —

Ann   Yes, dear.

Millicent   Was one Sunday morning I was ready for church before anybody else and I went out to get in the motor and ran down the steps and fell, and he jumped out and picked me up and put me in the motor, and of course I thanked him and we had to wait quite a while for the others, and I found out how different and really wonderful he was. All the girls were crazy about him. Here's his picture. (*Drawing out a locket which is on a chain around her neck.*) It's just a little snapshot which I took myself one morning—and you can't really tell from this how awfully good looking he is. (**Ann** *seizes the locket and looks closely at the picture.*) His eyes are the most wonderful—and his lashes are the longest I ever saw. You can't see his teeth and they are—well, you'd just love his teeth, Mother.

Ann   Would I, dear? Have you seen very much of him? Have you seen him any place besides in the motor, I mean? (**Millicent** *hesitates.*) Tell me, dear—everything. I shall understand.

Millicent   Well, of course. Mother—I *had* to see him someplace else after school began again and the girls were all back and I wasn't going for the mail anymore.

Ann   Of course; and where *did* you see him?

Millicent   Why, you see, it—it was awfully hard, Mummie, because I couldn't tell anybody. Nobody would have *understood*—except Fanny. She's such a dear. She's been so sympathetic through the whole thing, and she has helped me a lot. There is a fire escape out of our room and Mondays and Thursdays at nine o'clock at night—

Ann   Oh—

Millicent   What, Mother?

Ann   Nothing—go on, dear.

Millicent   At exactly nine I'd put on Fanny's long black coat and go down, and he was always there and we always went down in the arbor just a little while.

Ann   The arbor? Where was the arbor?

Millicent   Down the path of the other side of the drive—not far from the house; but of course, nobody went near it at that time of night—in cold weather and—and we'd talk a while and then I'd run back. You don't mind, do you, Mother. What else could I do?

Ann   And—he's kissed you—of course?

Millicent   Of course.

Ann   And you've kissed him?

Millicent   (*lowering her eyes*)   Why yes—Mother—we're engaged.

Ann   And what did he say to you there in the arbor?

Millicent   I can't tell you *everything* he said, Mother.

Ann   Why not, Millicent? I'm your mother. 'No one on earth is so close to you—or loves you so much—or cares so much for your happiness—and understands so well. I remember when I was engaged to your father—I wasn't much older than you—I know, dear. Tell me what he said.

Millicent   He thinks I'm pretty, Mother.

Ann   Yes, dear.

Millicent   And he thinks I'm wonderful to understand him and to know what he really is in spite of what he happens to be doing.

Ann   Yes—and how long did you usually stay there in the arbor?

Millicent   Oh, not very long, only last time it was longer. He teased so and I couldn't help it. He—he—I—

Ann   How long was it that time?

Millicent   Oh—it—it was almost two hours last time.

Ann   And what did you do all that time? Wasn't it cold?

Millicent   He made me put on his overcoat—He *just made* me.

Ann (*holding* **Millicent** *close in her arms*)   And he held you close—and kissed you—and told you how much he loved you?

Millicent   Yes, I love him so—Mother—but—I—tonight, was the last night to go again—but I—

Ann (*holding* **Millicent** *off as she searches her face*)   Yes, dear?

Millicent   I—I was—afraid to go.

Ann (*shrieking*)   Why?

Millicent   Oh, Mother—Was it wicked to be afraid? I ran away—I wanted to be with you.

Ann *snatches* **Millicent** *in her arms. Her head falls against* **Millicent** *and* **Millicent**'s *arms hold her close as she sobs. Someone tries the door and knocks.*

Tom (*in the hall*)   Ann!—Ann!

Ann   Yes?

Tom   Why is the door locked?

Ann   Millicent and I are talking. Wait just a few minutes. And Tom—tell her grandfather not to wait to see Millicent again tonight. She's all right.

Tom   Sure?

Ann   I'm sure.

Millicent (*in a whisper—after listening a moment*)   What are you going to tell father?

Ann (*sitting on the floor*)   Well—you see, dear—you're too young to be married now—much too young—and—

Millicent   Oh, now. Mother, if you're going to talk *that* way. Wait till you see him.

Ann   That's just what I want to do. I've got such a lovely plan for us—for the summer.

Millicent   But I want to be married as soon as he gets his—

Ann   I know, his position—and while he's looking and getting settled you and I will go abroad.

Millicent   You're awfully good, Mother, but if you really want to do something for me—I'd rather you'd give me that money to be married.

Ann   But Millicent, my dear child—I *have* to go. I'm so tired. I've been working awfully hard this winter. You're the only one in the world who could really be with me and take care of me. I *need* you.

Millicent   Poor Mother – I don't want to be *selfish* and if you *need* me—I'll go.

Ann (*catching* **Millicent** *in her arms*)   Thank. you, dear.

Millicent   *If* you'll promise me that I can be married when I get back.

Ann (*getting to her feet*)   If—you—*still*—want to—marry him when you come—back with me—you may. I promise.

Millicent   Mother I—I didn't know you loved me so much.

Ann   Didn't you, dear? Now go to bed. (*They start to the door together.* **Ann** *catches* **Millicent** *again, kissing her tenderly as though she were something new and precious.*)

Millicent   What's the matter. Mother?

Ann   Nothing, dear—Good night.

Millicent   Good night.

Tom (*coming into doorway as* **Millicent** *unlocks and opens the door*)   Not in bed yet?

Millicent (*throwing her arms about her father's neck*)   Oh, dad. I'm so happy. (*She goes out.*)

Ann (*sitting at the fire*)   Come, in, Tom. I want to talk to you about Millicent.

Tom (*closing the door and going to* **Ann**)   What's the matter?

Ann   She thinks she's in love.

Tom   What?

Ann   Our baby. She wants to be married.

Tom   What do you mean?

Ann   That's why she came home.

Tom   Good Heavens, Ann! Married? What has she got mixed up in? How did such a thing happen? How *could* it?

Ann   Because I didn't let her come home when she wanted to. Don't say anything, Tom. I can't bear it now.

Tom (*putting a hand on her head tenderly*)   Don't dear! Don't! It—might have—happened—anyway.

Ann   Oh, the things that *can* happen!

Tom Has she told you everything?

Ann Everything.

Tom What have you said to her? What are you going to do?

Ann I'm going to take her away—and win her—till she gives up of her own free will—I shall have to have the wisdom of all the ages. I shall have to be more fascinating than the boy. That's a pretty big undertaking, Tom. I wonder if I'll be equal to it.

Tom You mean you're going to give up your frieze and go away with her? (**Ann** *nods her head.*) You can't do it, Ann.

Ann (*rising and moving away*) Oh, yes, I can.

Tom You cannot. Don't lose your head. You're pledged to finish it and deliver it at a certain time. You can't play fast and lose with a big piece of work like that.

Ann *You'll* have to make my frieze, Tom.

Tom I will not ! I utterly and absolutely refuse to. You make Millicent behave and break this thing up and you go on with your —

Ann I can't. I can't. She's been in danger—absolute danger.

Tom How?

Ann Oh, I'll tell you. I'll tell you. She ran away to me—to me—and I was pushing her off. My little girl! She's got to be held tight in my arms and carried through.

Tom Ann, I'm not going to allow this to wipe out what you've done. I'll settle her —

Ann Tom, you can't speak of it to her—not breathe it —

Tom Of course I will.

Ann No you won't . If we cross her she'll get at him some way—somehow.

Tom I'm not going to let you sacrifice yourself for a wayward —

Ann It's my job. She is what I've given to life. If I fail her now—my whole life's a failure. Will you make my frieze, dear, will you?

Tom No. It's *yours*. You've got to have the glory of it. Ann, I haven't been fair—but you're going to have this and all that's coming to you. I'm not going to let anything take it away from you. It's too important. My God, you've not only beaten me—you've won over the biggest men in the field—with your own brain and your own hands—in a fair, fine, hard fight. You're cut up now—but if you should give this thing up—there'll be times when you'd eat your heart out to be at work on it—when the artist in you will *yell* to be let out.

Ann I know. I know. And I'll hate you because you're doing it—and I'll hate myself because I gave it up—and I'll almost—hate—her. I know. I know. You needn't tell me. Why I've seen my men and women up there—their strong limbs stretched—their hair blown back. I've seen the crowd looking up—I've heard people say—"A woman did that" and my heart has almost burst with pride—not so much that *I* had done it—but for *all* women. And then the door opened—and Millicent came in. There isn't any choice, Tom—she's part of my body—part of my soul. Will you make my frieze, dear, will you? (*Falling against him.*)

Tom (*taking her in his arms*) My darling! I'll do whatever makes it easiest for you. Don't think I don't know *all*—*all*—it means to you. My God, it's hard.

Ann (*releasing herself and going to the hall door*) Put out the light. I hope she's asleep. (*They go out into the lighted hall. After a moment*

THE CURTAIN FALLS

A Little Journey

Characters

Julie Rutherford
Jim West
Mrs. Welch
Mrs. Bay
Lily
Leo Stern
Frank
Charles
Smith
Annie
Ethel
Kittie Van Dyck
Porter
Conductor

Act One

TIME: *A few years ago—six o'clock—an afternoon in. April.*

PLACE: *Grand Central Station—New York.*

The middle of a first-class sleeping car which is bound for the Pacific Coast.

AT CURTAIN: *The only occupants are* **Mrs. Bay** *and her granddaughter* **Lily**. **Mrs. Bay** *is a little old lady, with white hair and a pink and white smiling face, wearing a quaint grey gown and bonnet. Her grand- daughter Lily is a pretty girl of eighteen becomingly but provincially dressed for travelling—and just now is opening a suitcase and searching for something as she takes out various toilet articles.*

Mrs. Bay (*with the persistent voice of a deaf person*)   I know it's there for I put it in myself. I must have it to put over my bonnet.

Lily   Why didn't you put it on top, Grandma? I can't find it.

Mrs. Bay   Put it on what?

Lily (*raising her voice a little*)   Top—on top.

Mrs. Bay   Over my bonnet—yes.

Lily (*still louder*)   Why didn't you—Oh—Here it is.

Lily *gives* **Mrs. Bay** *a grey cotton veil which* **Mrs. Bay** *carefully puts over her bonnet.*

A dapper young **Porter** *coming in from L. end of car carries a handsome travelling bag and umbrella and puts them in section at upper L.* **Mrs. Welch** *follows him into the car. She is a large woman, good-looking in a common and flamboyant way—about forty-five years old, overdressed in the extreme height of the most extreme fashion. She carries a gold purse with vanity box and a great variety of trinkets which rattle noisily as she moves. After her enter* **Charles** *and* **Frank**, *two very young college boys who carry their own luggage, find their own section and proceed to make themselves comfortable—taking out caps to put on instead of their hats, unfolding newspapers, etc.* **Frank** *is quiet and shy with an appealing charm of manner.* **Charles** *is rather sure of himself and bears all the earmarks of a good-natured American boy with plenty of this world's goods.*

Mrs. Welch (*in a loud nasal voice*)   Nine. Number nine mine is. I have the whole section.

Porter   Yes m'am.

Mrs. Welch   Which end is the ladies' dressing room?

Porter   Right there, m'am.

Mrs. Welch (*opening her purse*) Good Lord, it ought to be *here*. (*Seating herself with an air of ownership.*) Now which way do we go?

Porter (*waiting for his tip*) This way, lady.

Mrs. Welch Oh Lord! I'll sit over here then. I can't ride backwards. Just leave my bag up on the seat. I have the *whole section*. (*Giving him his tip.*)

Porter Yes m'am.

The **Porter** *turns to go as* **Jim West** *comes in from the left. He is a tall lanky fellow dressed in loosely fitting clothes and a soft hat. He carries a large shabby suitcase. He is about thirty-eight and the thin face, brown and heavily lined, has strength, humor, and great kindness. He moves with a long, slow stride—and glancing about the car, throws his suitcase into the seat on lower side at R. of the center section.*

Jim Seven. Is this about it?

Porter Yes sir—yes sir.

Jim This car go all the way through to the coast?

Porter Yes, sir. All the way through, sir.

The **Porter** *goes out, and* **Jim**, *kicking his suitcase under the seat, starts out as a slender young woman shabbily dressed, enters. She carries a baby, a heavy satchel and a package which falls as the satchel strikes the end of the seat.*

Annie (*to the pullman porter who is helping her with her luggage*) The rest is out there.

Porter I'll get it. I'll get it. (*He goes out quickly.*)

Jim (*picking up the package*) Allow me madam. What's your number?

Annie (*in a tired voice*) Eight—upper eight.

Jim (*taking her satchel*) Here you are. Upper? That's bad business with the baby. Isn't it? We'll swop. You have my lower seven here—and I'll take yours.

Annie Oh, no. I couldn't put you to that trouble, mister.

Jim Give me your berth ticket. Here's mine. No, not that one. Here it is. (*Taking the right ticket from* **Annie**.) Porter, we're making a trade. The lady will have this one.

Porter (*bringing in the rest of* **Annie**'s *luggage*) What sir?

Annie Oh no, I couldn't take it off you. I couldn't.

Jim I prefer it up top. Better air. Great accommodation to *me*.

Annie Oh my—is it? Do you hear that, baby? We don't have to climb up after all. Thank you, sir. (*The* **Porter** *deposits the large shabby suitcase and a small satchel and starts to put the covered basket in the rack.*) Oh don't put that under there. I have to have it for the baby.

Porter   You'll have to put *some* of it under to make room. You ain't got the whole section.

He follows **Jim West** *out.*

Women's voices are heard and *Kittie Van Dyke and* **Ethel** *Halstead come in from the left.* **Kittie** *is about thirty, extremely smart—artificial—chic modern. She carries a box of violets and one of chocolates.* **Ethel** *is tall and languid—slow in speech and movement—wearing rather graceful clothes, soft and flowing in effect. She carries several books, followed by the* **Porter**.

Kittie (*in high quick tones*)   Where is it? Six she said, didn't she?

Ethel (*following slowly*)   I don't know. Heavens, isn't it stuffy!

Kittie   I wanted her to have the drawing room, but she wouldn't. She simply would *not*.

Ethel   How could she? I dare say it was all she could possibly manage to pay for her ticket.

Kitie   Yes, I know. (*Stopping where the Porter is standing.*) Is this six?

Porter   Yes, miss.

Kittie   I mean I wanted to blow her to it but she wouldn't have it.

Ethel   Very sweet of you I'm sure.

Porter *coughs slightly* to *remind the young lady of a possible tip.*

Kittie   Oh! (*Looking at* **Ethel**.)

Ethel   I'm sorry I haven't a cent. He's waiting.

Kittie (*looking at the* **Porter**)   Oh yes. Didn't the man give you anything?

Porter   No, miss.

Kittie (*winking at* **Ethel**)   That's graceful of him. *Very* Alfredesque. (*She gives the* **Porter** *some money. He goes out.* **Kittie** *sits.*) As I was saying, I'm so sorry for Julie I could die. It's appalling. She's kicked out. Literally kicked out.

Ethel (*standing languidly and condescendingly in in the aisle*)   Oh that's putting it rather—

Kittie   No, it isn't. What else can you call it when her old selfish aunt refuses to let her live with her any longer, and that *pig* of an Alfred Bemis has *not* come across and asked her to marry him?

Ethel   How could he? Julie hasn't a penny and Alfred about six thousand a year I suppose.

Kittie   Six thousand a year with a real man would be—well—I'd take a chance on it. In fact I'd grab it.

Ethel It wouldn't pay for one third of your clothes. (*Finally deciding to sit opposite* **Kittie**.)

Kittie Oh slush—what do clothes mean after you've *got* a man?

Ethel How you rave dear! It's delightful—when you spend more money on clothes than any woman I know.

Kittie (*applying her lipstick skillfully*) Of course, because I've *got* it—and haven't got anything else. But I'd rather be *in love* than rich—any day.

Ethel Not Julie and Alfred.

Kittie Not *Alfred*. But let me tell you—he's broken Julie's heart.

Ethel Piffle! Julie's heart is too well regulated for that.

Kittie That's where we're all wrong about her. She's proud and game and pulling it off awfully well but she's *killed—simply killed—*and he's a *pig* and I *despise* him—and when you think what she's going to—it's *hell*. That's what it is. Nothing else. Why don't they come in? Alfred is making anaemic love to her outside,—I s'pose—keeping it up to the last. I'm going to get them in.

Kittie *starts out as* **Julie Rutherford** *comes in followed by* **Alfred**. **Julie** *is beautiful, charming and exquisite, with an air at once appealing because of her loveliness and chilling because of the slight hauteur by which she rather holds herself aloof as something more precious than common mortals.* **Alfred** *is pale, thin. perfect in manner and dress, the ruthless bachelor—comfortable on his small income, allowing himself the luxury of loving but not of marrying.*

Kittie Oh, here you are. I was just going out for you. Come and get settled. There's only a minute.

Julie (*coming to her section*) There's plenty of time.

Ethel I hate coming into the train. Porter, do tell us when it's time to get off. Why don't you open some windows?

Porter It will be cool enough when we get started, lady.

Julie Where am I? Here? (*Sitting in* **Ethel**'*s place as* **Ethel** *rises.*)

Kittie The drawing room's taken, Julie. It's absurd for you not to have it.

Julie For goodness' sake, don't fuss, Kittie.

Ethel But it's awful—being mixed up with all kinds of people for four days.

Mrs. Welch *rings her bell violently. They all turn to look at her.*

Mrs. Welch Porter, what time is it?

Porter Seventeen minutes past.

Mrs. Welch Past what?

Porter (*as he goes out at L.*) Past six.

Mrs. Welch   Oh! (*She sets her diamond wrist watch.* **Julie** *and her friends exchange amused glances.*)

Ethel   Here are some books, Julie dear. One of them will amuse you—the other is an awful bore but everybody's reading it.

Kittie   My little offering is chocolates. Mundane but most agreeable.

Ethel   Here are some smelling-salts too. You need those more than anything else in a stuffy train.

Julie   Thanks. You act as if I were going steerage.

Ethel   You might as well. A train's so much worse than a boat. You *can* get away from people a *little* on a boat.

Julie   Let me take my violets out now. (*Opening the box and taking a deep breath of the fragrance.*) Oh aren't they luscious!

Ethel   They won't last long in this air.

The **Porter** *enters again carrying two huge travelling bags which he takes into the drawing room. A very portly gentleman by the name of* **Smith** *follows the* **Porter** *in. He carries a large roll of newspapers under his arm and puffs and blows as he wipes his face and the inside of his hat with his handkerchief which has a conspicuous colored border.* **Mr. Smith** *is about fifty and his fat puffy face is ill-natured and selfish. His clothes and his manners indicate that he has a great deal of money and very little else to recommend him.*

Mr. Smith (*as he waddles through the aisle*)   This is good business—train so far from the gates a man nearly gets left. Turn on that fan in there. It's hotter'n blazes. (*He disappears into the drawing room.*)

Kittie   That pig has it instead of you.

Julie   Thank goodness he's going to be shut up in it. I hope he never comes out.

Kittie   Isn't Julie looking lovely? I adore you when you're a little pale, dearest.

Julie   Aren't you trying some new rouge, my love?

Kittie (*opening her small mirror*)   Yes. Don't you think it's good?

Ethel   It depends upon what you mean by *good*.

Alfred (*leaning over the back of* **Julie**'s *seat*)   If you want it to be as evident as possible I should say it was a great success.

Kittie   You don't suppose for one minute I want it to look *natural* I hope?

Julie   That *would* be stupid, wouldn't it? It suits you awfully Kittie dear. You look adorably disreputable. I don't know anyone who does it so well.

Ethel   Oh I don't know—I think it's much more chic to be glaringly natural—well groomed and bravely plain. After all that's the last word in distinction.

Kittie Isn't it lucky you feel that way about it dearest?

Mrs. Welch (*to the* **Porter** *as he comes out of the drawing room*) Say, Porter, aren't we going to start on time?

Porter Yes m'am. Yes m'am.

Mrs. Welch Well it don't look like it.

Leo Stern *comes in from the R. with a travelling salesman's sample case and a very large grip.*

Leo (*to the train* **Porter** *who has just come out from* **Mr. Smith***'s drawing room*) It's a wonder you wouldn't be outside to help a fellow with his stuff. Where's seven?

Porter Right there sir. I was just comin' sir.

Leo Excuse me, lady. (*Stopping at the seat where* **Annie** *is with the baby.*) Upper seven is about mine.

Annie Certainly. I don't mean to take up all the room.

Leo (*cheerfully*) All right—all right. Don't move. Just so I have a place to put my feet.

He takes off his hat and looks about the car smiling familiarly and showing a large gold tooth. His cheaply fashionable clothes smack of his trade and his small wiry body has a certain slang in its movements.

Ethel Do go to bed early Julie and get away from it all.

Julie You speak as if there were some danger of my sitting on somebody's knee before the evening's over.

Kittie I wish you would. It would do you good.

Julie Heavens! What's that?

Sniffing as **Mrs. Welch** *sprinkles toilet water about liberally and wetting her handkerchief, spreads it on the back of her seat.*

Ethel Isn't it dreadful?

They all turn to look at **Mrs. Welch** *as she waves her hands in the air to cool and dry them.*

Julie My violets might as well die right now.

Alfred It's time for us to get off.

Kittie It just kills me, Julie. I'd rather anything had happened than this.

Julie Good-bye Kittie dear. Good-bye, good-bye.

Ethel Do write soon and wire some place on the way, won't you? It's too awful to think of you—

Julie Oh don't Ethel, dear—*please.* You'd better get off now. The time's almost—

Ethel *kisses* **Julie** *whose pride is fighting her emotion.*

Kittie Go on Ethel. I'm going to bawl and I can't help it and I don't care. It's a beastly rotten sin that you're going. (*Throwing her arms about* **Julie**—*she cries.*)

Julie Don't dear, it's awfully sweet of you—but don't—*please.*

Ethel *goes out.*

Kittie Damn it! It's all wrong—you know. If I were a *man* I'd snatch you up and *make* you stay. Good-bye—you're a peach and I love you. (**Kittie** *rushes out wiping her eyes and bumping into Jim as he comes back.*) Oh Lord—can't people *see* me!

Jim *smiles and goes on to his seat.*

Alfred (*taking* **Julie**'s *hands and sitting beside her*) This can't be the end for us, dearest.

Julie It is.

Alfred No, I won't give you up. I can't. I can't.

Julie Oh don't! It's all over.

Alfred Listen dearest. It isn't. Just because we've got the beastly luck to have no money *now* doesn't mean it will always—

Julie We've been saying these things so long.

Alfred It's money—only money. Nothing on earth would make me let you go if there—if I had enough *to*—*to*—

Julie To love me?

Alfred Enough for us to marry. You—you surely don't blame *me* for this separation—do you? Oh my dear girl—you know I adore you. It's only money that—

Julie It's *all* money of course. Why do we pretend that anything else has anything to do with *us?*

Alfred You know I love you. You know that—don't you? Are you trying to tell me that if I loved you more this wouldn't have happened?

Julie You know this couldn't have happened if we cared for each other more than anything else in the world.

Alfred But I do care for you more than for anything else in the world. You must believe me.

Julie More than for anything else except your own happiness.

Alfred *You* are my happiness.

Julie Oh no, your happiness is your comfort and your convenience. I would have been a *very* inconvenient encumbrance.

Alfred Take that back. Say you didn't mean it.

Julie I thought when I first knew I had to go—I was fool enough to think you would say "Stay and share what I have." And I would have done it Alfred—and been contented to be poor—with you—*if* you had loved. *If you had loved me.*

Alfred Don't. How can you say—

Julie I don't blame you. You can't help it. Other things come first. Good-bye—do go—you must.

Alfred How can I? You're being horribly cruel to me. It isn't true. And this isn't good-bye.

Julie Oh yes it is.

Alfred Kiss me.

Julie No.

Alfred *You must.*

"All Aboard"—is heard called outside.

Julie No, I can't. Go please.

Alfred Some day I'll have you. I won't give you up.

He kisses her hands and hurries out. The vestibule doors bang. **Julie** *leans back covering her face—shaken by sobs which she is unable to control.*

Mrs. Bay I'll be glad when we get through the river. It hurts my ears so. The concussion of air you know. It's a marvelous thing though—marvelous. I didn't think when I was your age I'd be riding right under a river in a railroad train. They're doing wonderful things these days. If they just don't go too *far* with their reckless ideas.

Lily Don't talk so loud grandma.

Mrs. Bay What?

Lily Nothing.

Mrs. Bay You jabber so I can't get half you say.

Jim (*looking out the window on the side towards the audience—then rising and leaning over the seat to speak to* **Julie**) Your friends are trying to attract your attention out there.

Julie Oh, thank you. (*She turns to the window and raises her voice to speak to her friends outside.*) Yes—yes. No, I'm all right. Don't wait. Why don't you go? What? Yes.—What? Oh yes—I will. Good-bye—good-bye.

Mrs. Welch *rises to see to whom* **Julie** *is speaking.* **Lily** *and* **Mrs. Bay** *also look out—***Annie** *tries to see—rising with the baby.* **Jim** *goes on reading. The change seen through the windows at back shows that the train is starting. The bell in the drawing room rings violently.*

Leo (*to* **Annie** *in loud and friendly tones*)   We're going now. Do you like to ride? Hello Kid! (*To the baby—dangling his watch before her.*) Coo—coo! Coo—coo! Are you a boy?

Annie   She's a girl.

Leo   All look alike to me.

The **Porter** *starts toward R. end as* **Mr. Smith** *opens the door of his room.*

Smith   What are you doing? Why don't you come when I ring? Come here and turn *off* this fan.

Porter   Yes sir. Yes sir.

Smith *goes in and the* **Porter** *follows.*

Mrs. Welch (*going down the aisle to the dressing room—blandly to* **Lily**)   Rather a disagreeable old party—isn't he?

Lily (*timidly*)   Yes.

Mrs. Bay   What did the lady say?

Lily   Nothing.

Mrs. Welch   Is your grandmother deaf?

Lily   Yes, a little.

Mrs. Bay (*sweetly to* **Mrs. Welch**)   I don't hear very well—the train makes such a noise.

Mrs. Welch *nods her head violently and exits.* **Jim** *opens a newspaper and buries himself in it.* **Julie**, *wiping her tears, opens her smelling salts.*

Charles   I wonder when we can get some food?

Frank   Dinner pretty soon I s'pose.

Charles (*nudging* **Frank** *and looking at* **Julie**)   There's a peach over there. Did you see the fellow saying good-bye to her? She feels pretty rocky.

Frank   What do you know about it? I wish I didn't have to tell dad I flunked in two exams. He may not let me go back next year.

Charles   Gee—I wish I didn't have to go back. But the more I flunk the longer they'll keep on sending me. Look at Ikey and his gold tooth.

As **Leo** *rises and yawns—stretching his arms and looking about the car,* **Julie** *tries to open her bag and hurts her finger.*

Leo (*going to* **Julie**)   Allow *me* Lady.

Julie   Oh, the Porter will do it.

Leo   I'll have it open before you can tinkle for him. (*Opening the bag.*) No sooner said than done.

Julie (*frigidly*)   Thank you.

Leo   Don't mention it. (*He strolls down the aisle to the boys.*) Smoker back this way—think?

Charles   No—the other way.

Leo   Much obliged. (*Turning and going the other way.*)

Charles   The pleasure is mine. (*To* **Frank**.) I bet he sells pants!

Leo (*stumbling and falling into* **Jim's paper as he passes him**)   Excuse me. Some spill.

The passengers all show they suddenly feel the pressure in their ears as the train goes into the tunnel.

Leo (*to* **Annie**)   Open your mouth and press your ears and it won't get you.

Annie (*looking about in distress—not understanding*)   What's the matter?

Jim   Nothing. Nothing at all—sit still.

Mrs. Bay   There! There! What did I tell you? I knew it would happen. It did before—that peculiar sensation in the ears. Open your mouth dear, and it relieves it. My—my—just think where we are and what's on top of us! What would we do if it caved in?

Charles (*making a swimming motion and lowering his voice to* **Frank**)   Swim, Grandma—swim!

The **Conductor** *comes in from the left, stopping first for* **Leo**'*s ticket.*

Leo (*looking in all his pockets*)   Hold on. I got 'em, somewhere. Wouldn't that jar you! Where is the pesky thing? Oh, here you are. (*Finding his tickets.*) Right here. Upper five. How about a lower? Couldn't you fix me up? They told me they didn't have anything but uppers. But that don't go with me. How about it?

Conductor (*laconically*)   All taken.

Leo   Oh, come off. Is that straight?

Conductor   That's what I said.

Leo   Well, fix me up, old man—if somebody don't show up.

The **Conductor** *goes on to* **Annie**. **Leo** *goes out.*

Annie (*to the* **Conductor**, *as she gives him her ticket*)   Will I be able to get this milk heated for the baby?

Conductor   Speak to the porter about that.

Annie   Oh! Thank you. I don't have to change cars at all, do I?

Conductor   This is a through sleeper.

Annie Through?

Conductor You don't change at all.

Annie That's what I thought.

Conductor Tickets, madam.

Julie *rousing herself, opens her purse indifferently and then surprised, looks for her tickets.*

Julie (*having risen and turned over everything in the two seats several times*) Why, that's funny. Where *are* they?

Conductor Perhaps in your bag, Madam.

Julie (*opening her bag*) I surely didn't put them in *it*. No—not there. Why that's too queer. I had my tickets and my berth ticket and my trunk checks all in one of those little railroad envelopes, you know. They were all together.

Conductor Have you had them since you got on?

Julie Why no—not since I came *on*—*but* they were poked at the gate—and of course I put them right back in my purse, again. Or at least I *thought* I did.

Conductor You couldn't have got through the gates without them. Take another look.
Porter—help this lady look for her tickets.

The **Conductor** *goes on to the other passengers and the* **Porter** *who has just come in from the L. with paper bags for the hats, puts the bags in a seat and goes to* **Julie**.

Conductor (*to Grandma*) Tickets please.

Porter (*to* **Julie**) Lost your pocketbook, lady?

Julie No, my tickets. I haven't lost them but I can't find them. It's the queerest thing I ever—Look under the seats please.

Porter Yes m'am.

He gets down on his knees and looks under the seats while **Julie** *stands in the aisle watching him.*

Mrs. Bay Give him your tickets, Lily. Have you got both of them? This is a long trip for an old lady like me. I say this is a long trip. I made it very comfortably two months ago, going to visit with my daughter, and I guess I can do it going home. What is it? (*As* **Lily** *nudges her to be quiet.*) Are we on time? (*The* **Conductors** *nod again.*) That's good. When I came East to visit my daughter—What *is* it, Lily? Do stop stepping on my feet.

Porter (*getting up from the floor*) No, ma'm—'taint here.

Julie Take the cushions out. Maybe it's fallen under.

The **Porter** *lifts the cushions out of the two seats. The* **Conductors** *take the boys' tickets.*

Charles   Fork out, Frankie. You've got 'em.

Porter (*to* **Julie**)   No. 'Tain't here.

Julie   Why, they must be. Look down the aisle, then, under all the. seats. Maybe I dropped it as I came in. It's a little railroad envelope you know. Look well in that dark narrow place at the end. (*Pointing to the end of the car.*)

Porter   Yes m'am. Yes m'am.

He gets down to look under **Jim**'s *seat.* **Jim** *watches* **Julie** *as she mechanically goes through the same process of moving all her things again. She opens the violet box and turns it over.*

Julie   They *must* be here.

Mrs. Welch (*giving the conductor her tickets as she comes back from the dressing room*)   Lady lost her ticket?

Conductor   Yes, madam.

Mrs. Welch   Awful careless. I always carry my purse right on my arm like this. And when I go through a crowd I just hug it up to me like that. Too bad!

Charles (*to* **Frank**)   Crawl down the aisle and look for the lady's tickets, you lazy lubber you.

Frank   You go. You're fresh. (**Charles** *goes to* **Julie**.)

Charles (*with irresistible good nature to which* **Julie** *responds*)   Have you lost something?

Julie   Yes, my tickets.

Charles   Have you looked in all your books and papers?

Julie   Oh, I hadn't thought of that. (**Charles** *helps* **Julie** *turn the leaves of her books and shake out her newspapers.*) You're awfully good. It's the most mysterious thing. If they hadn't had to be poked at the gate I'd think I hadn't brought them. I don't see—They were all together—my ticket—my berth check and my trunk checks—in one of those little railroad envelopes, you know.

Frank (*going shyly to join* **Charles**)   Where did you lose it?

Julie   That's what I'm trying to find out.

Charles (*digging* **Frank** *with his elbow*)   That was a brilliant shot.

Porter (*getting to his feet again*)   No'm. No *m'am*. 'Tain't nowheres here.

Julie   Why it must be. It couldn't disappear like that.

Mrs. Welch (*going to* **Julie**)   Where did you lose it?

Julie   I'm sure I don't know.

Mrs. Welch   Have you been in the ladies' dressing room? Maybe you left it in there.

Julie No, I haven't.

Mrs. Welch I left two valuable rings in there once and never did get them. One was a ruby—the most valuable ring I ever had, set in di'monds, you know. The other I didn't care so much for. I went right back the minute I missed them and they were gone. There was never any doubt in my mind who took them. (*Lowering her voice and glancing at the* **Porter**.) It's in the blood. (*Touching Julie's arm confidentially.*) I'd have him searched.

Julie (*very coldly*) My tickets would be of no value to him.

Mrs. Welch (*not in the least suppressed*) Oh, I don't know. He could do *something* with them.

Mrs. Bay My goodness! What's the matter? Is there an accident?

Lily No, no, Grandma. A lady has lost her tickets.

Mrs. Bay My stars! You be careful and take good care of ours. She must be a very careless young lady.

Lily Be careful, Grandma.

Conductor (*going back to* **Julie**) Haven't you found it, Madam?

Julie Not yet.

Conductor I'll be back in a little while.

The **Conductor** *goes into the drawing room.*

Mrs. Welch (*looking very accusingly at the* **Porter**) Are you sure you didn't find it, Porter?

Porter No *ma'am*. 'Tain't in this car. I know *that*.

Julie (*giving the porter some money*) Thank you very much.

Porter (*bowing elaborately*) Thank you, Miss, thank you.

Mrs. Welch What are you going to do about it?

Julie I'm sure I don't know.

Annie Excuse me, Miss. (*Rising with the baby and going to* **Julie**.) Maybe it's inside of your dress. That's where I always carry my money.

Julie Oh, no, I never have enough money to hide.

Annie *goes back to her seat.*

Frank You didn't give it up just outside the car before you got on, did you?

Julie No, I don't think I did. I begin to wonder if I ever bought a ticket at all.

Charles (*pulling* **Frank**) That will do for you.

Mrs. Bay (*unable to control her curiosity longer and moving to* **Julie***'s section*) Hasn't the lady found it yet?

Mrs. Welch   No—not yet.

Mrs. Bay   What?

Mrs. Welch (*who had seated herself in* **Julie**'s *section with comfortable familiarity; shouting at* **Mrs. Bay**)   No, no.

Mrs. Bay   Was it her railroad ticket?

Mrs. Welch (*still louder*)   Yes, her railroad ticket.

Lily (*going after her grandmother*)   Grandma, come back.

Mrs. Bay (*with cheerful persistence*)   Where was she going?

Mrs. Welch   I don't know.

Lily   Grandma, come and sit down. You'll fall over.

Mrs. Bay   Let me alone, child. I like to know a little something that's going on. The lady can't find her ticket. (*To* **Julie**.) Where did you lose it?

Julie (*laughing in spite of her irritation*)   I wish I knew.

Mrs. Bay   What?

Lily   Grandma, please come here.

Mrs. Bay   People are so careless nowadays.

Mrs. Welch (*rising and still shouting to* **Mrs. Bay**)   Yes, I always carry everything right in my purse in my hand like this—tight.

Mrs. Bay   When I travel I have a good deep pocket in my petticoat—like this. See?

Lifting her dress skirt.

Lily   Grandma!

Mrs. Bay   And buttoned up tight too.

Charles (*to* **Frank**)   She'll have to put up the money I suppose.

Conductor (*coming back to* **Julie**)   Have you found it, Madam?

Julie   Not yet. I can't understand. It's so strange.

Conductor   You say you know you had it after you came on the train?

Julie   No, I didn't say that. I'm not sure of anything. I don't remember touching it—but I do know it was *poked* at the gate.

Conductor   Yes, but can't you remember—

Julie   They were all together you know—my ticket, my berth check and my trunk checks—all in one of those little railroad envelopes. They were poked—*punched*—out there.

Conductor   Yes but punching them out there won't do. I have to have a ticket or you'll have to pay your fare.

Julie Oh, but you *know* I had a ticket. The man at the gate let me in so after all what difference does it make.

Conductor Someone else may be riding on that ticket, lady.

Julie Oh no—how could anyone? I *had* it. You surely *believe* me, don't you?

Conductor If you had it, madam, when you got on the train, where is it now?

Julie That's what I don't *know*.

Conductor That's what I've *got* to know. I have to have the ticket, madam.

Jim (*rising and leaning over* **Julie**'s *seat to speak to her*) Did one of your friends have the tickets at all?

Julie Why yes, of course, Mr. Bemis had them. He was taking charge of everything,

Jim He probably didn't give them back to you.

Julie That's it. That's just exactly the way it was. (*Looking at the Conductors.*) You understand, don't you?

Conductor I have to have your ticket, madam, or you'll have to pay your fare.

Jim *goes back to his paper.*

Julie I'll wire back at the next station and get somebody to *do* something.

Conductor Producing the ticket is the only thing that will do any good.

Julie (*not able to believe that her convenience is to be interfered with by law*) I'll wire Mr. Bemis and ask if he has my ticket—and he will wire back—some place further on.
That's all that's necessary, surely.

Charles Or you could tell him to have the ticket office telegraph you it was O.K. That would be official all right, wouldn't it?

Conductor All that takes time. You can pay your fare and it will be returned to you if the ticket is found. See?

Julie Oh but I—I'm afraid I couldn't do that.

Conductor Where was the ticket to?

Julie Greenville, Montana.

Mrs. Welch Good Lord!

Jim *looks up quickly.*

Conductor The fare is—The fare is ninety-two fifty with the sleeper. You can redeem it. The money will be refunded to you at the office when you return the ticket.

Julie Oh, but—

Conductor That's the only thing I can do.

Julie (*opening her purse helplessly*) But I—I—I don't happen to have that—that amount with me. I—I can give you twenty-five dollars. That would make it all right, wouldn't it. Till I get my ticket? I'll telegraph at the—

Conductor I'm sorry, Madam, but I can't let passengers ride on my train without their fare. That's what I'm here for.

Julie But I haven't enough money with me, don't you see?

Mrs. Welch (*calling from her seat*) Give him a check?

Conductor We don't take checks. You'll have to get off at the next stop.

Jim Pardon me. To Greenville, Montana, you say you're going?

Julie Yes.

Jim I'm going within a hundred miles or so of that myself. I'll be very glad to pay for this ticket and you can fix it up when you get there.

Julie Oh, I couldn't let you do that.

Conductor Then I'm sorry, Madam, but you'll have to get off at the next stop.

The **Conductor** *goes out.*

Julie (*to* **Jim**) Thank you very, very much. You're extremely kind, but I couldn't.

Jim I thought perhaps you'd like to go on with your journey now that you've started. I suppose you can get a train back to New York tonight.

Julie I suppose so. Thank you.

Jim *goes back to his seat and* **Julie** *sits staring desperately before her, breathing quickly. The other passengers watch for a moment and then go on with their own affairs.*

Charles Damned shame for her to have to get off. She's a peacherino.

Frank The conductor couldn't help it. She ought to take that fellow's money.

Mrs. Welch (*going back to* **Julie**) I must say I'm sorry for you. What are you going to do—get off?

Julie I suppose so.

Mrs. Welch Shame—now that you've started. Live in New York?

Julie Yes.

Mrs. Welch I do too. We're old New Yorkers *now.* But I go back to see Ma once a year. I'll always do *that.* It's nothing more than my duty. But *my!* It certainly is a dose. Nothing like New York, is there? I couldn't live any place else. When you're *in* right New York's the place. Haven't I seen you somewhere before?

Julie I don't think so.

A Little Journey   89

Mrs. Welch Seems to me I have. Did you ever come to the Queen of Hearts Bridge Club?

Julie No—I never did.

Mrs. Welch I thought maybe that was it. I meet so many there. It's a swell club. You ought to join it. It's lively all right. You know what I mean—not *too* gay—but no dead ones. I tell my husband I'd rather be dead than behind the procession.

*The **Porter** comes back with his paper bags,—going to **Annie** first.*

Annie What is it?

Porter Have your hat in a bag?

Annie What?

Mrs. Welch (*glancing at **Annie***) I guess she hasn't travelled much.

Porter A bag for your hat to keep the dust off.

Annie Oh, thank you.

*The **Porter** takes **Annie**'s hat from the rack and puts it into the bag.*

Mrs. Welch All kinds of people in this world, aren't there? (*With the amused air of an experienced traveller.*)

Julie Yes, there seem to be.

Porter Have your hats in a bag, ladies?

Julie *shakes her head.*

Mrs. Welch Take mine over there. Be careful how you put it in, too.

Porter Yes m'am.

Julie How soon do we get to the next station?

Porter Almost ten minutes now, ma'am.

Julie Do you know when the first train goes back to New York?

Porter I couldn't say, Lady. I expects there'll be one along about midnight.

*He goes to put **Mrs. Welch**'s hat in a bag.*

Mrs. Welch It'll be awful waiting, won't it? You might go to a movie to kill time. That's what I'd do. *Oh*, that *fool*'s jamming my hat in like a rag. *Here!* Be careful! I paid a hundred dollars for that hat.

*She takes the hat away from the porter and puts it into the bag herself. The porter gives two bags to Lily and she and **Mrs. Bay** go through the process of putting their hats in.*

Mrs. Bay More of their modern inventions. I approve of this one. It's very sensible. Don't you think we'd better eat our supper now?

Lily (*glancing at the boys*)   Not yet.

Mrs. Bay   I think we had. I want to get to bed early and get settled for the night.

Lily (*speaking in* **Mrs. Bay**'*s ear*)   Let's wait till the other people go into the dining car.

Mrs. Bay   Why?

Lily   Oh, because.

Mrs. Bay   Nonsense! I want my supper. Open the box.

Lily   I don't want to eat with those boys right there.

Mrs. Bay   Why not?

Lily   Oh, I don't know. It *looks* so.

Mrs. Bay   That's no reason. I don't want to get a headache. Open the box.

Lily   Oh, Grandma!

Lily *takes the shoe-box and opens it reluctantly.*

Mrs. Bay   Don't get a spot on that good skirt of yours. Fried chicken's awfully greasy. (*Tucking her napkin under her chin.*) Chicken's dreadfully high in New York now—but Carrie can afford it so I thought I might just as well let her put it in. Here—we can put the egg shells in this bag the oranges are in. (*Taking two oranges out of a paper bag and dropping one—which rolls under the boys' seat opposite.*) Now look at that! Everything jiggles so.

Lily   Oh, Grandma!

Charles *and* **Frank** *both stoop to get the orange—but it rolls further under the seat and* **Frank** *goes down on his knees to get it.*

Frank (*feeling for it*)   Must have been oiled. (*He gets lower down to look under the seat.*)

Charles   Are you *eating* it?

Mrs. Bay   Dear, dear! That's too bad—to give the young man so much trouble.

Charles *looks at* **Lily** *and they both laugh.*

Frank (*rising with the orange—his sleeve pushed up and his cap on one ear*)   Here you are.

Mrs. Bay   You keep it. We have another one and that's plenty for us. They're very nice and juicy.

Frank   No, thank you.

Mrs. Bay   I wish you would.

Lily   Oh, Grandma! (*Turning shyly to* **Frank**.) Thank you very much for getting it.

Frank   Don't mention it. (*He goes back to his seat.*)

Mrs. Bay (*eating her fried chicken with great relish and cracking an egg on the arm of the seat*)   What's the matter? Take your chicken, child. It's very nice.

Lily *eats a piece of bread and butter—keeping her back to the boys.* **Julie** *again looks in her bag and her purse and shakes out the books and papers, occasionally wiping her eyes.*

Charles   Me for food. Come on Frank.

Frank   Are you blowing me to it?

Charles   I'll match you for it.

Charles *follows* **Frank** *out with his hands on* **Frank***'s shoulders, pushing him along.*

Mrs. Welch (*powdering her nose elaborately, and going down the aisle to* **Julie**)   Have you decided to get off?

Julie   It seems to have been decided for me.

Mrs. Welch   It's a shame. Well, good-bye, goodbye.

Julie *nods slightly and* **Mrs. Welch** *moves on, stopping by* **Annie**.

Mrs. Welch   My, what a little baby to travel with! I should think you'd be afraid to, aren't you?

Annie   You can when you have to.

Mrs. Welch   Why don't you put it in short clothes?

Annie   I don't just happen to have any.

Mrs. Welch   You ought to get some. Hello baby. See it look at me. Kind a' cute. Bye, bye, Cutie.

She goes out. **Annie** *rocks the baby in her arms, singing softly.*

Porter (*following the conductor in*)   All right, Lady.

He takes **Julie***'s bag out.*

Conductor   This is the station. We're pulling in now.

Julie   Yes, I know. The Porter has my bag.

Conductor   I'm extremely sorry, Madam—but it's the only thing I can do.

Lily (*to her grandmother*)   Oh, I think that's awful! She's going.

Julie *rises and goes slowly to the door—***Jim** *watches her. She turns suddenly and goes back to him.*

Julie   I—I think I *will* let you, if you—if you'll be so good.

Jim   You'll go on?

Julie   I can't get off. I *can't*. If you'll be good enough to lend me the money, I shall be very much—

Jim Of course.

Porter (*coming back*) This way out, Lady.

Jim She's not getting off. Tell the conductor to come here.

Porter Them was his orders, sir. The lady is to get off.

Jim Tell him to come here.

Porter We only stops a minute. You'll have to hurry, Lady.

Jim You do as I tell you, will you? Tell that conductor to come here.

Porter Yes sir, yes sir.

He hurries out.

Julie (*calling*) Don't put my bag off. Oh, it's too dreadful. How can I thank you? You're very very kind to do this.

The train stops. There is the sound of newsboys calling outside.

Jim Not at all. I just happened to have the money with me. Why shouldn't it be used? That's what it's for.

Conductor (*hurrying in*) Madam, I told you you'd have to—

Jim Hold on. This lady has decided to let me lend her the money. How much did you say the fare is?

Conductor Ninety-two dollars and fifty cents.

Jim (*counting the bills*) Twenty, forty, sixty, ninety-two and a half. There you are.

Conductor Here's your receipt.

Giving the slip of paper to **Julie**—*he goes out.*

Julie You see it's—very important that I go on. I mean I—I simply had to. It's a—the circumstances are—I *have* to go on. I can't go back, and I don't know what I should have done, if you hadn't been so good. I never can thank you enough.

Jim We all get caught in a snag once in a while. Somebody usually helps us out.

Julie If you'll give me your name and address, please. And this is mine. (*Taking a card from her purse.*) Or at least it was. That was my New York address. I'll write the other.

Jim I haven't got a card.

Julie Just put it on one of mine, then, please. (*As he gives the card back to her.*) Thank you. My brother will send the—the amount as—a—just as soon as possible—of course –and he will be extremely indebted to you for your kindness. (*Reading what he has written on the card.*) "Jim West, High Forks, Montana." Is that all that's necessary? Will a letter reach you with just that?

Jim   Oh yes, that'll me. I have a sort of a—well, I don't know just what you would call it. A kind of a camp up in the mountains there.

Julie   Isn't there a town—at all?

Jim   No—fifty miles from a town.

Julie   But will a letter—

Jim   Oh yes, they throw the mail bag off to us.

Julie   And it's only a camp?

Jim   We *call* it a camp. We've got about forty log houses and a store and a kind of a shed where the trains stop long enough for things to get off. And a good many things do get off—from pretty much all parts of the country. It's, you might say, as cosmopolitan a mixture of human beings as you can find put together anywhere. (*Slowly sitting opposite* **Julie**.)

Julie   How strange! What sort of a place is it?

Jim   A place where a man can come when he's down and out and stay till he gets on his feet again, if he's willing to fall in with the law.

Julie   The law? (*A little interested in spite of herself.*)

Jim   The law is work. Work and get your living out of the earth.

Julie   How extraordinary!

Jim   Oh, no—it's ordinary enough. You don't happen to have stumbled on to it. We're all so busy digging in our own potato patches we don't see much of the other fellow's.

Julie   And that's where we ought to stay—in our own.

Jim   (*trying to put her at ease, his kindness covering his shyness. He speaks with a whimsical smile and a wistful hesitancy*)   Don't you think it's—good—for us to be jerked out of them once in a while?

Julie   No—I don't think that. Will you take this as security, please, for the—for the money? (*Taking a brooch from her dress.*)

Jim   What?

Julie   There might be some delay. I mean my brother might not—There might be some slight delay in getting it back to you.

Jim   Of course.

Julie   And I want you to take this as a sort of security.

Jim   What do you mean?

Julie   Just that. It insures you against any possible loss—in case anything should go wrong.

Jim I am insured.

Julie What?

Jim I've got all the security I want.

Julie You haven't *any*. You must take-

Jim You said you'd send the money as soon as you could—didn't you?

Julie Yes, but that's nothing after all. You don't know who I am or what might happen and this makes it safe.

Jim (*taking the pin and looking at it*) The pin is worth a good deal more than the price of the ticket—isn't it?

Julie Of course.

Jim And how do you know I'd give this up—once I got it?

Julie Because—you *would*.

Jim How do you know?

Julie Just because—I *know*.

Jim Then you must give me credit for as much good judgment as you evidently think you have yourself. It's my gamble. I'll wait. If I lose the money it's my own fault. (*Laying the pin on her book.*)

Julie Please take it.

Jim No thank you. I want to see how good a guess I've made. I haven't been fooled many times. It would take all the fun out of it to have any sort of security.

Julie I'm afraid I don't see any fun in this situation.

Jim Oh I—didn't exactly mean *that*.

Julie Just what—did—you mean then?

Jim Well—to see a pesky little ninety-two fifty help a—somebody like you out of a—a—hole—was—I mean it was the biggest chance of doing something agreeable that I've had in a long long time.

Julie You're very good to put it that way. The "pesky little ninety-two fifty"—may not be very large to you—but it means a very great deal to me. It saved me from something hideous and humiliating, and I appreciate it more than I can possibly tell you.

Jim Then I'm lucky. Ever been West?

Julie No.

Jim You'll like it—if you don't go with your mind made up *not* to. But I'm afraid that's what you *have* done.

Julie No, I haven't, but I don't belong there.

Jim We belong *every*where—don't we?

Julie Oh no, we don't. We all have our own places and can't be pulled up by the roots and live.

Jim Don't you think we're all on one root and can live *any* place if we will?

Julie No, I don't.

Jim I think we can.

Julie That's a beautiful theory but facts can't be changed.

Jim The trouble is we accept too many things *as* facts. Most everything we're afraid of is only a boog-a-boo that can be changed with a good jerk.

Julie I don't like jerks.

Jim Oh, they're fine. I *know* because I was pulled out of one thing and landed in the last place on earth I ever expected to be—and it's much bigger living than trotting along in the harness I was born in. There's nothing like a good hit in the head to make us see stars we didn't know were in the firmament.

Julie I don't agree with anything you say—but I wish I did.

Jim (*after a short quick laugh*) We never agree to anything till we've lived through it, then we *know*.

Julie When we know what we want and why we want it, and what we can't live without, what's the use of trying to live through any—

Annie (*going to* **Julie**—*having put the baby on the seat*) Excuse me, Miss—but the baby's asleep and it's the only chance I've got to get anything to eat. I haven't had anything today but an apple. If you wouldn't mind just keeping your eye on her in case she rolls off.

Julie Where are you going? (*Very dubiously.*)

Annie In the eatin' car to get somethin' to eat.

Julie Oh—*will* it roll off?

Annie No, Miss, I don't think so. I think she'll stay asleep.

Julie What would I do if she did?

Annie Just pick her up again.

Julie But aren't you afraid to leave it?

Annie Not if you watch 'er, Miss. If you'd be so good as to. I beg your pardon for askin' you, but I felt I had to have a little bite of somethin' *to*—(*Putting her hand to her head faintly.*)

Julie Yes, of course. I'll do the best I can.

Annie Thank you, Miss—thank you. You're very kind. I won't be any longer than I can help and I'm going to get this heated if I can. It gives her the colic to take it cold.

Holding the bottle of milk, **Annie** *goes out.* **Julie** *rises and looks at the baby— hesitates, then taking her book goes to sit in* **Annie***'s place.* **Jim** *from behind his paper watches her with the keenest amusement and interest.*

The baby begins to whimper a little, rapidly increases till it howls lustily. **Julie** *in consternation stands up.*

Julie Oh, what's the matter? Don't, baby! There—there! (*Patting it timidly.*) Don't cry. There, there! Oh goodness! What *is* the matter? What shall I do? Will you go and get the mother?

Jim Too bad to haul her back before she *gets anything to eat.* (*The baby gives a louder yell.*)

Julie It's choking to death! What shall I do?

Jim Take it up.

Julie Must I? (*The baby shrieks and* **Julie** *snatches it up in desperation.*) Oh, baby, please don't. What *is* the matter? Your mother's corning back in a few minutes. Oh, please don't cry so. What *shall* I do?

Jim You're doing pretty well seems to me.

Julie But I may be doing the wrong thing.

Jim The longer you stick it out the more the mother can eat.

Julie How can anything so little make so much noise? There! There! You poor little thing.

That's better. Why you're actually sort of pretty. What tiny hands! Oh, don't cry again. There! That's right! You must be good and wait for mother. That's a good baby. (*Wiping the baby's eyes with her own handkerchief.*) Do you think I could put her down again now?

Jim I think you'd be taking big chances. She seems to like this better.

Julie (*sitting stiffly, afraid of disturbing the young person*) Yes, she seems to have settled down for the evening. Nothing like taking things for granted, baby. You look extremely comfortable but *I'm* not. If you wouldn't mind handing me my book, I think I could read. (**Jim** *gives* **Julie** *the book. The baby whimpers.*) Oh well, never mind, I won't. (**Jim** *laughs and* **Julie** *laughs with him helplessly.*)

THE CURTAIN FALLS

Act Two

PLACE. *Same as Act 1.*

TIME: *Three days later—early evening.*

AT CURTAIN: **Mrs. Welch**'s *section is partially made up, but the curtains not hung.* **Leo** *is entertaining* **Annie** *and* **Mrs. Welch** *is with* **Mrs. Bay**. *There is a general air of intimacy and friendliness. The other passengers are not in the car.*

Mrs. Welch (*shouting to* **Mrs. Bay** *and elaborately polishing her fingernails*)   She's eating dinner with him *now* and I dare say he's paying the bill. I know why they went in so early—so there wouldn't be any of *us* there. You can't fool *me*. Any woman that will pick up a man on a train and let him pay for her ticket and then carry on with him like *this* is—well—you can't fool *me*.

Mrs. Bay   You don't think she's—

Mrs. Welch   Oh! I wouldn't be surprised. When you live in New York you're not surprised at anything.

Mrs. Bay   I won't let Lily talk to her any more.

Mrs. Welch   Oh, I don't *say* anything.

Mrs. Bay   The world is full of strange people. I'll be glad to get home where I know everybody. Our church circle is the salt of the earth—the backbone of the nation. I don't know any such people *any* place. You know the kind I mean.

Mrs. Welch   Lord, yes, I know 'em.

Mrs. Bay   What?

Mrs. Welch   Nothing.

Mrs. Bay   Dear me—Lily's out on the back platform with those two boys. I think I'd better go after her.

Mrs. Welch   Oh no, let her alone. She's all right. Let her have a little fun.

Mrs. Bay   They seem like very nice boys but I don't really know anything about them.

Mrs. Welch   *She* does. I bet she knows what kind of socks they like by this time.

Mrs. Bay   Lily was never bold.

Lily *bursts into the car with a scream—laughing and out of breath—***Charles** *close after her and trying to snatch the locket which she wears on a ribbon around her neck. Grandma's back is turned to them.*

Lily   I won't—I won't—I *won't!* You shan't see it!

Charles   Then I know it's some guy's picture or you wouldn't care.

Frank   Oh, let up, Charles—you're too fresh. She doesn't want you to see it.

Lily (*throwing herself into a seat*)   No I don't! Now please stop. Oh my hair! Goodness, I must be a sight.

Charles   You are—something terrible. It's all down your back.

Lily   Oh sakes!

Frank   It is not. It's all right. Shut up, Charles.

Lily   If Grandma sees it she'll have a fit.

Charles   You're losing your hairpins. (*Taking one out of Lily's hair.*)

Mrs. Bay (*contentedly to Mrs. Welch—not having heard the young people come in*)   Lily's just like I was when I was a girl—very quiet and lady-like and makes the boys keep their distance.

Mrs. Welch (*winking at Frank who looks at her*)   You bet—just the right distance, and she seems to keep some further than others.

Mrs. Bay   What?

Mrs. Welch   Nothing. Nothing.

Lily   Now, go away and behave. Oh, I must give this book back to that young lady. She loaned it to me and said "I'm sure you'll find it extremely amusing," but goodness I didn't see one funny thing in it. Not *one*. She and the man must be eating dinner. They act like real sure enough friends now. She laughs right out loud when he talks to her.

Charles   She ought to laugh at his jokes when he staked her to the ticket.

Lily   Isn't it funny. I keep wondering about her.

Charles   I've got a thirst. Want some water?

Lily   No, thank you. (**Charles** *goes out.*) Only one day more. I'll be home this time tomorrow night.

Frank   Four days is a pretty long trip? Isn't it?

Lily   Y-e-s.

Frank   This is the shortest it's ever been to me.

Lily   Is it? Why? (*With shy excitement.*)

Frank   Oh—I don't know. Kind—a—it's sort of –it helps—-along some to have a girl to talk to.

Lily   Oh—*any* girl?

Frank   N-o—not *any* girl. *A* girl. *YOU.*

Lily (*trying to cover her embarrassment by laughing*)   Oh!

Frank   I—I—may be—I might have to go through your town this summer—sometime. I—might stop and say hello.

Lily Oh—do. You—you must stay to supper if you *do*.

Frank Oh, I couldn't do that—thank you—but—

Lily Yes you could, too. The idea! Of course you could. You'd have to. You couldn't go through our town without coming to a *meal*. Mother would be—she'd be so glad to see you.

Frank How about you?

Lily What?

Frank Would you be glad?

Lily Yes I would. Of course, I would.

Frank I don't know many girls. I don't know any as well as I know you.

Lily Oh my! Don't you?

Frank I suppose you know a lot of fellows.

Lily W-e-l-l *some*, not such an awful lot. Not so awfully *well*. I mean—there isn't anybody in *particular* that I know so awfully well—you know. I mean—*You* know what I mean.

Frank How about the fellow in that locket?

Lily It isn't.

Frank Oh come.

Lily No, it isn't.

Frank How can you expect me to believe that?

Lily Don't you tell Charles and I'll show it to you. Promise?

Frank Sure.

Lily (*opening the locket*) It's the very dearest person in the whole world. See—it's mother.

Frank Oh—she's a peach.

Lily *Now* do you believe me?

Closing the locket.

Frank I guess I've got to. (*Gazing at her hands.*) Awfully little hands you've got.

Lily (*hiding her hands*) Oh no, they're not. They're *not*. Why I—I think I have *very* large hands.

Frank Let's see.

Lily No.

Frank Go on—please. Let me see.

There is a slight struggle as **Frank** *tries to get her hands.*

Lily   Oh don't. He's coming back.

Charles *comes back.* **Lily** *and* **Frank** *relapse into dignified silence for a moment. Then the three burst into laughter.*

Leo (*strolling down the aisle to* **Mrs. Welch**)   Here's a Kansas City paper. Like to have it?

Mrs. Welch   Do I *look* it?

Leo   Ouch! (*Slapping his own cheek.*) Have a paper? (*Going on to the boys.*)

Charles   No thanks.

Leo   You fellows going home from school, ain't you?

Lily   Why, how could you tell?

Leo   Oh, in my business you're on. I can hang 'em on the right peg every time. These young fellows go down East to school to spend a little of Father's money, and the clothes and the hair get a new cut. You didn't buy them pants in Squeedunk. You bet your life you didn't. (**Charles** *and* **Frank** *laugh and Leo joins in.*) Think you're the real thing now, don't you? Well, I came from the village myself, but I've never been back. Main Street wasn't wide enough for me.

Mrs. Welch (*rising and stretching her long arms*)   I'm so sick of this cubby-hole I don't know what to do. I'll be glad when I can sleep in a real bed again.

Leo (*genially, as he comes towards* **Mrs. Welch**)   I bet you like a good big brass one.

Mrs. Welch (*with a very grand air*)   Not at all. I got rid of all my brass beds ten years ago.

Porter (*coming in and stopping at* **Annie**'s *seat*)   How's the baby this evenin'?

Annie   Oh, she's all right. Would you get a cup of water for her?

Porter (*taking the cup* **Annie** *holds up*)   I sure would. I sure would do that for this young Lady. She's the best traveller I ever seen. Hello honey.

Mrs. Welch   Porter, make my bed up first tonight. I don't propose to wait forever like I did last night.

Porter   Can't do it all at once, lady.

Mrs. Welch   *No,* but you can do mine *first.* Don't forget.

Porter   Yes m'am.

Smith (*coming out of the drawing room*)   Porter, make my bed up first tonight before you start out here. I didn't pay for this infernal box of a drawing room to be kept waiting till you'd made up everything else on the train. Do you understand?

He struts down the aisle and out.

Porter Yes, sir. Yes, sir.

Going out after **Smith**.

Mrs. Welch Um! Nothing like thinking of *yourself*.

Leo (*to the boys*) If you want to see the golden rule shining at its brightest, watch the travelling pub. Not safety first—but *me* first.

Julie *comes in from the diner. Leo starts towards her. The motion of the train knocks her towards* **Leo**.

Leo (*catching* **Julie**) Going some! Pardon me. Did I grab you too tight? I thought you was going over.

Julie (*drawing her arm away*) It's all right. Thank you.

Julie *doesn't look at Leo as she sits but he stands by her contentedly.*

Leo I've got a good book down there. One that'll keep you guessing. Like to have it?

Julie Thank you. I have books.

Leo I never read except when I'm on the train and then I like something doing. Want your window down? Allow me. (**Julie** *starts and puts her hand over one eye quickly.*) Got a cinder in your eye?

Julie It's nothing.

Leo Must be *something* to make you jump like that. Hurts like the mischief, don't it?

Julie It will be all right in a minute.

Leo No it won't. Oh, that blowing the other side of your nose don't do no good. The only way to get a cinder out is to *take* it out. I'll do it for you.

Julie Oh no.

Leo Very glad to.

Julie Oh no—no. It will be all—

Leo No it won't. I know the trick. You mustn't monkey with a cinder. Quick action is the thing. Just hold your head back and keep still a minute.

Julie No, I don't want—

Leo I won't hurt you. Give me your hankie. Now, I just turn the lid back like that and—Hold still—just a—Hold still—There you are. No wonder you squirmed. That was a whale of a fellow. (*Showing the cinder to* **Jim**.) How's that for size, to get in a lady's eye?

Jim *has come in from the dining car in time to see the cinder extracted, and now as* **Julie** *looks at him they laugh in a very friendly and understanding way.*

Julie I'm very much obliged, I'm sure.

Leo Don't mention it. Don't rub it now. (*To* **Jim**.) Had your dinner?

Jim Yes.

Leo Pretty bum layout. Gettin' to the bottom. Try the chicken?

Jim I know better.

Leo I got stung for a dollar twenty-five for the toughest old bird in captivity last night. I'll be damned glad when I get out of this. That's the worst thing about my business—sittin' still in a train—no action. Can't sell no goods—just have to wait. It's hell.

Jim Why do you do it?

Leo Why do I *do* it? So's I can live when I get back to Broadway. See? I'm going to take a chance on a little food now myself. You're not the only one who's playing a twosome. I've got a date myself in the diner.

Winking and smiling intimately at **Jim** *he goes out.*

Jim I hope that first aid to the injured was a success.

Julie I think it must have been.

Jim But you didn't look grateful.

Julie I wasn't. Oh, you were going to tell me—

Jim Wait till these people go out to dinner.

Julie Isn't it a bore!

Mrs. Welch, *having heard this conversation, raises her eyebrows and deliberately marches down to* **Julie**.

Mrs. Welch Poor food, isn't it?

Julie Pardon me?

Mrs. Welch I say it's awful poor food. Aren't you getting sick of it?

Julie I suppose we can't expect anything else.

Mrs. Welch Oh I don't know. Lord knows we pay enough for it. That's one thing I'm awfully fussy about. (*Sitting opposite* **Julie**.) I pay my cook eighty dollars and I never go near the kitchen. That's one thing my husband *will* have—good food. Prices are fierce though—aren't they?

Julie I believe so.

Mrs. Welch But I say to Harry "Well, we've *got* to live and you might as well be dead as have nothing you like to eat." We go out a lot too. When I entertain friends I like to take them down-town, don't you know. I think they like it better. What's your favorite place?

Julie Oh—they're all dull enough.

Mrs. Welch Oh I don't know. Not if you aren't a dead one yourself. You have to know the ropes of course and where *to* go, and that's one thing I *do* know—I know New York and what's going on in it. Here's this old lady over here talking about *her* town—*her* church—*her* friends—thinking the sun rises and sets right there. Funny ain't it? Just laughable when you *do* live in the *real* world.

Julie (*taking up her book*) Yes, I suppose so.

Mrs. Welch You've got real friendly with the fellow who loaned you the money by this time—haven't you?

Julie I beg your pardon?

Mrs. Welch Why not? I'm broad minded. I believe in taking all that comes your way—within reason.

Julie I really don't know what you mean.

Mrs. Welch Oh, I don't mean anything. I think you were darned sensible to do it and of course you have to be friendly to him since you *did* do it. It's caused some talk—but then that don't matter to *me*. I'm not so straight-laced.

Julie Talk? How absolutely disgusting.

Mrs. Welch Well you know you can't keep people from having their opinions and saying what they please. Nobody's got a little wire fence around 'em in *this* day and age. It don't go. I'm going to eat. (*Speaking to* **Jim** *as she passes him.*) You went in pretty *early* tonight, didn't you?

She smiles at Jim and goes out slowly—humming insinuatingly as she goes.

Jim (*rising to get* **Annie***'s suitcase which she is struggling to lift*) Mustn't let our youngest passenger fall. She wouldn't like it.

Annie I guess not. If anything happened to her—Thank you. If anything happened to her I might as well never try to get to Bill at all.

Julie I guess Bill would be pretty glad to see you anyway—wouldn't he?

Annie (*with a long hopeless sigh*) I wouldn't risk it without *her*.

Jim Is there anything I can do to make things easier for you? Because if there is—speak up. Don't be foolish about thinking I'm a stranger or anything of that kind. Understand?

Annie You don't seem like a stranger somehow.

Jim I'm not. There's no such animal. *Is* there something I can do?

Annie No—there ain't. There's nothin' nobody can do. I've just got to get to Bill. (*Touching her chest with a tired hand.*) Somehow I don't feel as if I was ever goin' to, though.

Jim Train's ripping along in fine shape, putting you nearer every minute.

Annie Yes, but that ain't it. I just have a feelin'—I want to speak to that lady. (*She crosses to* **Julie**—*taking the baby with her.*) May I speak to you a minute?

Jim *goes out.*

Julie (*moving some things on the seat opposite her*)   Sit down.

Annie Thank you. I just want to thank you for mindin' her every day while I went out to eat.

Julie Oh, please don't.

Annie You've been awful good.

Julie Nonsense! I liked it. I really believe she knows me now.

Annie Of course she does. She—she's an awful good baby.

Julie Indeed she is. With very wonderful manners and a most engaging smile. Aren't you, baby?

Annie I mean she's healthy, an' I've always kep' 'er clean. I've always managed to do that.

Julie Yes, I'm sure you have. And that's so important. Isn't it?

Annie Yes—but it's hard. It costs an awful lot to be clean.

Julie Oh—yes, I suppose it does. (*Leaning over the baby.*) Baby, you've got the cunningest, most tinsy-weeny—adorable nose I ever saw in my life. Oh see—see how she curls her fingers around mine. Look! Isn't that too sweet!

Annie Un-hun.

Julie See—she won't let go. Think of there being any strength in those delicate little things. Hello, baby. You've had a beautiful nap—yes you have and your cheeks are like roses. You *are* wonderful—you blessed little—*little* thing. Do you know I've never really known a baby before. They *are* marvelous.

Annie Do you like her?

Julie Of course.

Annie What I wanted to say to you was—you don't happen to know anybody wants a baby, do you?

Julie What?

Annie I mean—to adopt one. There's a lot of it done, you know. Lots of people—rich people—is awful glad to get babies without going through the trouble of havin' 'em. An' it *is* a trouble, God knows. I used to be awful strong. I did, honest. *She's* strong and healthy. Nobody don't need to be afraid of that miss. You believe me, don't you?

Julie But—you don't want to give up your *own baby.*

Annie No. I don't want to. But somehow I kind a feel as if it might be better. I kind a have a feelin' I ain't going to last long.

Julie Oh, don't say that.

Annie An' I—I—ain't so sure about Bill nohow.

Julie Aren't you?

Annie I kind a' thought some of your swell friends might like her.

Julie My "swell friends" are a thing of the past—-and they aren't very keen about babies.

Annie Or I kind a' thought maybe you might like her yourself—seeing you took such a likin' to her—or you'd know *somebody*. Don't you, Miss? Honest, Miss, I mean it.

Julie There isn't a single being in the whole world I could ask to help you or one tiny little thing I could do for you myself.

Annie Oh—(*Looking at* **Julie** *like a hurt dog and lowering her head.*) Oh, I thought a lady like you could do anything—if she wanted to.

Julie "A lady like me" is a very helpless thing and more unhappy than you. You have your baby and you're going to Bill. I'm going to people who don't want me, and when I get to the end of my journey I'll have about ten dollars left in my pocketbook—a few clothes in—their last stages—and that's all. And my ticket must be paid for—somehow—some way.

Annie Oh my! That *is* bad,—ain't it?

Julie I'm telling you so you won't think me a beast. I'm sorry but—you—you'll be all right—when you get to your husband.

Annie I'm sorry for *you,* lady. You look like you ought to be awful happy.

Julie Yes, I think myself I *ought* to be—but I'm not. You—you'll never be alone—and quite unhappy—with *her*—will you?

Annie If I was only sure I could last long enough to pull her through till she's a big girl—that's all.

Julie But you will. You must.

Annie (*touching her chest*) It's here. I'm all gone here somehow.

Julie I—wish there was—something I could do.

Annie Thank you, Miss.

Annie *goes back to her seat with the baby.* **Julie** *sits absorbed in her thoughts.* **Jim** *enters, going to his seat.*

Lily Come on, grandma. Let's go to supper.

Mrs. Bay All right. I'm ready. But we mustn't eat as much as we did last night. It costs entirely too much. We could have got along without that poor soup just as well as not.

Charles Come on, Frank. (*To* **Lily**.) We can all sit at the same table.

Mrs. Bay Are the young men coming too? That's nice. Come along. I like young people.

Frank (*taking* **Mrs. Bay** *by the arm*) Be careful. She's hitting it up pretty high just now.

Lily Oh, don't tell her that.

Mrs. Bay What?

Frank (*very loudly to* **Mrs. Bay**) It's a nice evening.

Lily *goes out after* **Frank** *and* **Mrs. Bay**. **Julie** *rises and walks restlessly to the end of the car.* **Charles** *turns and goes back to* **Julie**.

Charles Here's the book you gave Lily. I read it too. I hope you don't mind.

Julie I'm delighted. Did you like it?

Charles Y-e-s.

Julie Oh, was it as bad as that?

Charles I spent most of the time wondering why *you* like it.

Julie Then it wasn't a success.

Charles Oh yes it was, only I'm not exactly "on."

Julie Don't try to put so much into it. It's only nice nonsense.

Charles Will you let me come and ask you about it, after dinner?

Julie I'll let you come and *tell* me about it.

Charles Don't think I'm fresh, but the girl in it seems—just like you.

Julie Goodness! Why?

Charles That's what I'd like to talk about.

Julie This is going to be *very* interesting.

Charles It will be for me.

He beams on her with shy adoration and goes out.

Julie (*going to lean over* **Annie**'s *seat*) Won't you go to your dinner now while the baby's so quiet?

Annie I would like to, if you don't mind, Miss. You sure have been good doin' it. I don't know how I could a' got on without you.

Annie *goes out.*

Jim Aren't you going to miss this new habit of your—minding the baby?

Julie (*going to* **Jim**'s *section and sitting opposite him*)   It's too bad you haven't a place for mothers and babies in your camp. That poor woman seems rather desperate.

Jim I'm going to have—a baby farm some day. When you catch the kiddies young enough you can bring up a fine crop. That's really better than making them over after they're grown up. You've struck my hobby now.

Julie Really? Then maybe you *could* take this baby.

Jim Wish I could. Nothing's ready yet.

Julie She doesn't seem to be any too sure that her husband wants her.

Jim Bill, you mean.

Julie Yes.

Jim I don't think Bill *is* a husband—at least not Annie's.

Julie What? What makes you think that?

Jim Just a hunch.

Julie Poor thing. Poor thing. (*A long pause.*) Haven't you anything to amuse you out there in your camp? It must be horribly desolate with just men.

Jim Not on your life. Turn a lot of men loose together out in the open and they're boys again. It's only when I get back where women are that I miss 'em. That's when a fellow's lonely—in a crowd—women to left of you, women to right of you, and none of 'em yours. They seemed prettier than ever in New York this time—and further away.

Julie And don't you know *any*?

Jim Not one. Not since *the* one. She hung on as long as she could while I was drinking myself into a beast and then—it all snapped. That was the jolt that sent me out there. That's how the camp happened—and the trying to pull up other fellows.

Julie I see. I wondered. And—are you satisfied with that?

Jim While I'm at it with my teeth in it hard I am. It's only when I come back that I want something more.

Julie Doesn't she know now what you've done?

Jim No.

Julie Why don't you let her know?

Jim What's the use? Too late. Married I s'pose.

Julie And isn't there anything to look forward to—but just your work out there?

Jim Nothing. That's enough. It grows like blazes.

Julie But how do you—the money—I don't see how—

Jim Oh, money's the easiest part of it. I just took a fellow back home now. That's what brought me East—a fellow that's been out there six months and got back the decency that was pretty nearly gone. I took him home to a heartbroken woman and they're both so grateful—that they've given me a big boost with money for the place. That happens every once in a while. Oh, I've got great schemes for the future. It's a live wire all right.

Julie Oh, but it's so far away from everything—the *real* world.

Jim The *real* world is life—and the same life runs through us all.

Julie Oh, nonsense!

Jim Real life—with all the layers of luxury and class ripped off-down to the bone. It takes a lot of living to *know* that.

Julie If you're trying to tell me that what I'm going through will make me over into something better you never were so mistaken in your life. Why pretend I can be good and noble just because I'm unhappy? Everything in the world I've lived *with* and *for* is gone. The aunt who took me when I was a little girl and lavished everything that was beautiful and exquisite on me—has suddenly lost her money and turned me off. There's not a single spot on earth where I can go—except out to my brother in this little town. He's a doctor and has seven children and a wife I've never seen and she'll hate me and I'll hate her—and it's all disgusting and sordid and no *ideas* nor *ideals* can change it. You might as well take a fish out of the sea and tell him he can live just as well on the land—and that it's *his* fault if he doesn't.

Jim You and the fish are a little different. If civilization *does* produce a higher breed its highness is only tested and proven *by the way* it *lives* when *life* is hardest. If you're going to let unhappiness smash you—then you're *not* the high product you think you are. You don't think I'm horribly impertinent, do you?

Julie No. What difference does it make? We'll never see each other again. (*Rising and going back to her own section and then suddenly letting herself speak with an intimacy and warm charm which she has not allowed herself before.*) I've talked *more—really talked* to you—in these three days than I've ever talked in my life.

Jim Of course—because all the silly little stickers of convention were knocked in the head when you lost your ticket and you *had* to take help from somebody.

Julie You make me out an awful prig.

Jim Well you are—aren't you?

Julie (*laughing a little*) I suppose so. Oh—this flying along through space—shut up tight with a few people—is a funny thing, isn't it?

Jim (*going to her section to sit*) I like it. It's got a sort of getting together feeling about it. The outside world stops.

Julie Yes. I used to hate it but I've been thinking all day how much easier it would be to keep on going then to *stop* tomorrow night.

Jim And you could keep on minding the baby.

Julie She's so sweet. She knows me now.

Jim And I could keep on talking to you. Lord how I have talked! I've spilled it all out.

Julie So have I.

Jim Oh, no, you haven't.

Julie A lot anyway.

Jim I haven't talked to a woman like you since—well—

Julie You're a strange person—aren't you?

Jim Not a bit.

Julie You seem to have all the nice things that—that—a—you know.

Jim You mean I don't eat with my knife?

Julie Yes—and yet you seem to be utterly and absolutely free from every convention on earth.

Jim You could be too.

Julie Never.

Jim Oh, yes. And you'll never draw a long full breath and get all the air that's coming to you till you *are* free.

Julie What do you mean?

They are leaning toward each other—drawn by a strong mutual attraction and giving way with a certain abandon.

Jim Outside things make you and control you. Even here—sitting here alone—cut off from everything—you're measuring things with your same old tape measure—not really approving of yourself because you're talking to me—

Julie Oh—

Jim You're tied up by thousands of outside things—and your *real* self—has never been let loose at all.

Julie I'm *not* tied up. *I'm—I'm—protected* by tradition—if that's what you mean.

Jim That's the polite way of saying you're frozen by a lot of damned nonsense.

Julie Good manners and good form are only the result of good sense. Because I observe them doesn't mean that my *mind* isn't free.

Jim You don't know what freedom means.

Julie Nonsense! Of course I do.

Jim No, you don't. *I'm* talking to *you* because I *want* to. Who you are—what you are—where you came from—doesn't matter. But you're talking to me over a very high fence—just taking a little peek at a queer animal out of sheer curiosity and because as you said, just now—It doesn't matter—you'll never see me again.

Julie But I'm not so—

Jim Oh yes, you are—much more so—

Julie Well at least you must admit *this*—*I'm* being much freer and much more wildly unconventional for *me* than *you* are for *you*. You're used to it. It's nothing at all for you to pick up a stranger and treat him like a friend. In fact, I heard you tell Annie there's no such animal—as a stranger.

Jim There's something in that but when you get off the train this little incident will close for you—but for me it will *stick* as something I've lost.

Julie I—I shall *remember*. Not only the money and the ticket but you've made these days interesting that would have been long and dreary.

Jim But nevertheless I *am*—an incident—to you.

Julie Y-e-s. But—what—you've done—and what you've been these three days will stand out all alone as something big and free and sweet—and—and different—apart from place and people-and anything I've ever known or ever will know again.

Jim Then why don't you keep it?

Julie It couldn't last if I ever saw you again. Every day life would kill it.

Jim Can't every day life have in it anything you *want* to put into it?

Julie Oh, you don't know—(*She draws back suddenly as the others begin to come back.*) Oh, these people—

Mrs. Bay, **Lily**, **Frank** *and* **Charles** *come in from the diner, all watching* **Julie** *as they walk by.* **Jim** *goes back to his seat.* **Mr. Smith** *comes in with a large unlighted cigar in his mouth. He struts down to the other end of the car and back—with the air of taking a constitutional—oblivious of the other people-and meets Mrs. Welch as he turns.*

Mrs. Welch (*as she comes in from the diner—seeing the cigar*)   Well! This isn't the smoker.

Mr. Smith No, but this is *my* cigar.

Mrs. Welch I thought you had it lighted. Excuse me.

Mr. Smith All I need is a match. Got one?

Jim *gives a box of matches to* **Mr. Smith**.

Mrs. Welch (*to* **Julie**)   Does he *own* the yacht?

Mr. Smith (*having lighted his cigar—much to* **Mrs. Welch**'s *horrified amazement*)   Don't be alarmed I'm not going to stay out here.

Mrs. Welch   I should hope not.

Mr. Smith (*giving the matches back to* **Jim**)   Much obliged! (**Mr. Smith** *and* **Mrs. Welch** *try to pass each other but find the aisle inconveniently narrow.*)

Mrs. Welch   *Well—I've* never had any trouble before in my life getting through an aisle.

Mr. Smith   I can't say I ever have either.

Mrs. Welch (*moving into one of the sections*)   I'll step in here if you'll be accommodating enough to walk by.

Mr. Smith   That's what I've been trying to do for some time. (**Mr. Smith** *waddles on into his drawing room.*)

Mrs. Welch (*to* **Jim** *and* **Julie**)   Don't he take the prize as a human swine? Wouldn't you think nobody else was on earth but him?

Julie   He's just a little more outspoken than most of us. I don't know that he's so very different.

Mrs. Welch   There may be *some* people just *exactly* like him. But I don't happen to be that kind. Porter, why haven't you got my berth made up? (*As the* **Porter** *comes in with sheets and pillow cases.*) Do it right away. (*She takes her bag and goes into the ladies' dressing room.*)

Porter   Yes ma'am.

Julie   How contented she is with herself! It's wonderful.

Frank (*to* **Lily**)   Here's an awfully pretty little piece of poetry in this magazine. Don't you want to read it to me?

Lily   Oh, I couldn't.

Frank   Yes, you could. Please.

Lily   Oh *dear!* I used to recite at school but I don't believe I could read this to you.

Frank   Come on, please.

Lily (*reading the poetry in a sing-song sentimental way*)

> Sweetheart, be my sweetheart
> When birds are on the wing
> When bee and bud and babbling flood
> Bespeak the birth of spring.
> Come sweetheart, be my sweetheart,
> And wear this posy ring.

> Sweetheart, be my sweetheart
> In the golden summer glow

Of the earth aflush with gracious blush
Which the ripening fields foreshow.
Dear sweetheart, be my sweetheart,
As into the moon we go.

Sweetheart, be my sweetheart
When falls the bounteous year,
When the fruit and the wine of tree and vine
Give us their harvest cheer.
Oh sweetheart, be my sweetheart,
For winter draweth near.

During this the **Porter** *brings in a step ladder from left and stepping upon it, hangs the curtains for* **Mrs. Welch***'s berth.* **Julie** *sits quietly looking out the window.* **Jim** *reads in his own seat.*

Mrs. Bay (*as* **Lily** *finishes the third verse*)   What is it, Lily? Read it to me.

Lily *sits forward and reads the last verse in a louder voice.* **Mrs. Bay** *leaning towards her and keeping time with her head*

Lily

Sweetheart, be my sweetheart
When the year is white and old
When the fire of youth is spent forsooth
And the hand of age is cold.
Yet sweetheart, be my sweetheart,
Till the year of love is told.

Charles (*as* **Lily** *finishes*)   Oh slush!

Jim (*going back to* **Julie**)   The thing I've been waiting to say to you is this—

Julie   What? Say it.

Jim   Why didn't you fight it out for yourself back there—since you hate coming out here so fiercely?

Julie   Fight it out? Make my own living, you mean? Because I don't know how. I'm going out here because it's the only place on earth I can go and I'll be a horrible burden to them, and still I haven't the courage to jump off the train. Ridiculous—isn't it?

Jim   Haven't you ever wanted to work with your hands? To take hold of a thing and *do* it—make it go because you *willed* and were making your own power?

Julie   No.

Jim   See here. It's all up to you whether you're beaten or not. You've got two things to choose from. Either to go back to this little town and shrivel up into a bitter old woman—or to live by giving what you've got to other people. If you *have* got something fine and precious which lifts you apart from the common her—then give it out to other people. Give it—give–*give*.

Julie I haven't anything to give.

Jim Then why didn't you marry somebody and stay back there where you say you belong?

Julie He only had six thousand a year. That isn't enough. Oh, you needn't laugh. It's true. He was right.

Jim Six thousand a year not enough for one man to make one woman happy?

Julie What do you think it takes to make one woman happy?

Jim Love—love and work.

Julie Oh yes—but the man!

Jim She must have the eyes to see him when he's there. The heart to love him—the hands to work with him. The courage to take him when he comes.

Julie (*coming out of the spell and drawing back from him*) Oh—we *are* flying through space—up in the clouds. Stern reality is waiting at the other end. Why don't I jump off the train now—now?

Jim I'll open the door for you—if you want to do it.

Julie Do you mean that?

Jim I do.

Julie Will you help me?

Jim I'll open the door.

Julie Would it be right?

Jim It's your right—if you want it.

Julie It would save a lot of trouble for other people.

Jim Well, are you going to do it?

Julie Yes. (*She starts to rise, he takes her by the arms.*)

Jim Some man was a coward not to keep you.

Julie You can't blame him.

Jim Did you love him?

Julie I would have married him.

Jim He was a fool and a coward.

Julie Oh, no.

Jim Oh, yes. Why didn't he hold you and fight for you?

Julie I'm not worth it.

Jim You are to me. (*Holding her by the wrists.*)

Julie Oh—

Jim Let me help you. Isn't that better than what you've started to do? Give yourself another chance. There's so much of life waiting for you. Don't do it. Wait.

Julie Oh, I—

Jim You've fallen out of the skies for me. You're what I've lost and what I've wanted every day—every hour. Your life is in your own two hands. Are you going to throw it away or let me try to make things right for you? Wait just a little. Give me a chance to make you know me. Don't end it now.

Julie If this were all—yes—to sit here—with you. But this isn't real—talking to you like this.

Jim It is.

Julie No. It's just a wild moment or two—when I'm letting go because nothing matters.

Jim They're *real* moments.

Julie No—no they are not. This isn't *me*.

Jim It's the *real* you.

Julie No. It's something new. I'm talking to you because I don't care—and because you're strange and wonderful and there's something in you I—I've been looking for in someone else. I wanted it so to cling to. To believe in. I don't want to live. I don't. I don't! Thank you—Oh thank you for all you've done for me.

Jim I haven't done anything—but I could—I could!

Julie It's so strange to be pouring out my heart to you like this.

Jim No, it isn't.

Julie I seem to want to tell you everything. (*She begins to sob—***Jim** *puts his hand on hers to stop her as* **Mrs. Welch**, *singing, comes from the dressing room at R. end in a flamboyant kimono. She stops near* **Lily** *and the boys.* **Julie** *puts her head on her arm on the back of her seat and Jim, remaining where he is, takes up a book.*)

Mrs. Welch Why don't you all go to bed? It's the best way to kill time I know of. Haven't you talked yourselves out yet?

Charles (*rising—looking* **Mrs. Welch** *over with a twinkle*) I've just thought of something else I *might* say.

Mrs. Welch What?

Charles I—won't tell.

Mrs. Welch Our friends down there are going to elope I think if the train ever stops. (*The boys and* **Lily** *turn to stare at* **Julie**.)

Mrs. Bay What's the matter? What did she say?

Lily Nothing, Grandma.

Mrs. Bay (*pointing to* **Julie**) Don't talk to that lady any more, Lily.

Porter (*coming to tap* **Mrs. Bay** *on the shoulder—with sheets and pillow cases over his arm*) I'm ready for you now.

Mr. Smith (*coming out of the drawing room in, time to hear this*) No, you don't. I'm waiting.

Porter (*hurrying into the drawing room*) Comin' sir. Comin'.

Mrs. Bay You boys scuttle away now. I'm going to get ready for bed myself. (**Mrs. Welch** *goes to her own berth and disappears behind the curtains.* **Mrs. Bay** *takes her suitcase and goes out.* **Leo** *strolls in from the diner at left, complacently using a toothpick.*)

Lily Oh, look. That's the first toothpick I've seen since I left home.

Leo (*stopping by* **Julie**) Well—one day more and we'll all get out of this box. You get off tomorrow, don't you?

Julie (*unnerved and desperate*) I don't know. Yes, I do.

Leo I guess you and me are the only Eastern parties in the bunch. The others are going home to roost. When you've seen as much of the country as I have you can spot 'em with one squint. This tall party here—turned in I guess—(*Nodding towards* **Mrs. Welch***'s berth.*) thinks she is putting it all over us. Funny, ain't it? (**Leo** *strolls back to his own section.*)

Mrs. Welch (*making violent movements behind her curtains and thrusting her shoes out*) Porter! Take those shoes and give them a good shine. A *good* one. Is that you, Porter?

Leo Guess again.

Mrs. Welch Well, where on earth is he? He's never in the right place. (*She throws shoes into the aisle—hitting* **Leo**.) Give him these.

Leo Here, do your rough housin' on the inside. There's passers by out here.

Charles (*coming down the aisle*) Is it safe to go by?

Leo I wouldn't risk it.

Mrs. Welch (*emerging from her curtains—finishing the braiding of her hair*) Oh, Lord! I've bumped my head so I can't tell whether I'm coming or goin'.

Leo Believe me your *goin' some.*

Mrs. Bay (*coming down the aisle*) Can I get by?

Leo Not if I was the judge. (*Looking at* **Mrs. Bay** *who has put on her night cap and dressing gown.*)

Mrs. Welch That reminds me. I lost my boudoir cap this morning and never did find it. I wonder if that blamed porter took it.

Annie (*coming in, in time to hear this*) It's under the seat, Missus. I seen it.

Mrs. Welch Why on earth didn't you say so?

Leo I'll get it for you. (**Leo** *dives for the missing cap and brings it out.*)

Mrs. Welch Well upon my soul! Wouldn't that jar you! Thanks. (**Mrs. Welch** *tucks up her braid and puts on the cap—a most elaborate affair of lace, ribbons and flowers.*) Now if anybody disturbs me tonight, they'll wish they hadn't.

Leo I promise I won't.

Mrs. Welch Good night everybody. (*She disappears again.*)

Charles Nightie-night.

Leo I don't know but that I prefer Grandma's. (*Indicating grandma's cap. He takes up a magazine.*)

Jim (*to* **Julie**) Don't be so unhappy. Don't.

Julie Oh, how white and big and soft that cloud is, and how fast it's sailing! I wish I could be caught up in it and disappear.

Jim We don't get off so easily. We only get what we have the courage to take. Throwaway the part that's been a disappointment and a failure. Look the new thing in the face.

Julie I can only see one thing-my own despair and I can't face it. I can't! I want to escape it and I only know one way. You said you'd open the door for me.

Jim I won't.

Julie Then I'm going anyway. (*She rises.*)

Jim (*catching her*) I won't let you go. (*There is a crash. The lights go out—wild shrieks and cries—the sound of glass breaking and wood splitting. Pandemonium and darkness. Gradually words are distinguished above the cries and groans.*)

Jim Are you alive?

Julie Yes! My head! I'm falling!

Jim Do you want to live or die?

Julie I want to live! Help me!

THE CURTAIN FALLS

Act Three

TIME: *Five o'clock the next morning.*

PLACE: *A hill top covered with stubby grass, low bushes and a few trees. A bleak bare place. Cold grey dawn is coming on.*

AT CURTAIN: **Leo** *appears dragging after him* **Mrs. Welch**. **Mr. Smith** *also emerges half pushing her from the back. The three are in an extremely dilapidated condition—their clothes torn and mud-stained—their hair wildly disheveled.* **Mr. Smith** *is in pajamas and a raincoat—and one eye is conspicuously black and bruised.* **Mrs. Welch** *wears the dressing gown of Act II with a blanket about her shoulders. Her hair stands out in wisps and bunches but the cap dejected and bedrabbled is still in evidence. Leo is ghastly pale with a long cut on one cheek. The three gasping for breath reach the top and look disconsolately about.*

Leo It's the top.

Mrs. Welch Thank God! Let me sit down or I'll drop. Anything to get away from these horrors! I'll never get over this night—never to my dying day!

Leo You want to be damn thankful it wasn't your dying *night*. (**Leo** *and* **Smith** *each holding* **Mrs. Welch** *by an arm manage to help her sit on a rock.*)

Mrs. Welch (*groaning elaborately*) Oh—oh—oh! I'm black and blue all over.

Smith (*much chastened by the ordeals of the night*) Are you comfortable now? I wish all our fellow passengers could come up to this place. I'd like them to share our blessings. (*Sitting laboriously near* **Mrs. Welch**.)

Mrs. Welch You're so kind.

Leo (*laughing*) You might chase down and get some of your fellow passengers.

Smith I'll make an effort.

Mrs. Welch No, you won't. You must be very tired. Let the other fellow do it.

Leo (*laughing still harder and looking at* **Mr. Smith** *and* **Mrs. Welch** *in amazement*) Misfortunes sure do make quick bed fellows.

Mrs. Welch Say, are you trying to be funny? Don't, it's too early in the morning.

Leo You're right, it's too early in the morning for anything, even for a sunrise. (*He goes up back, looking down and shouting as he sees someone below.*) Hey—hi—boys! Come on up. What? Yes, you can. Bring her up. Yes you can. Make a cat's cradle and carry her—like this. (*Showing how to make a cat's cradle.*) That's the idea.

Mrs. Welch Carry her? Carry who?

Leo The young girl. She's all right but she can't walk.

Smith Do you see any more of our fellow passengers down there?

Leo N—no. But I can see the engine. She must have just about turned a somersault.

Mrs. Welch Oh don't!

Leo The first cars are all on top of her—where she took the header.

Mrs. Welch I'll always ride in the last coach after this. That's what saved us.

Smith We have many blessings. (*Sneezing violently.*)

Leo Blessin's are loomin' up big now, ain't they? (*Looking down the hill again.*) And I can see that Jim West fella out there where they're mendin' the bridge—bossin' the job and workin' harder'n anybody with his busted arm and shoulder.

Mrs. Welch *And he broke it saving her.* More's the pity.

Smith Do you think it's a pity she's saved?

Mrs. Welch I don't go as far as to say that.

Smith It's very deplorable—she's rapidly getting worse. When I saw her last—she was in a very bad way—almost raving.

Leo That may not last long but you can't tell. Sometimes when you're hit in the head like that you go back to a certain time and don't remember anything else in between.

Smith It isn't a going back with her—rather a going forward. And she blurts it all right out in a kind of semi-sane—semi-insane—you can't really tell the dividing line as to which is which.

Mrs. Welch You bet you can't. She's got you fooled to a finish—you men. Lord, how a woman *can* fool men!

Leo You're fooled this trip as sure as you're born—She's nutty—clean gone.

Smith And a *very* strange case.

Mrs. Welch Oh you make me sick. Why she's just *slick.* That's all—no more *crazy* than I am. She's up against it. Hasn't a cent in the world. Doesn't want to *go* where she's *got* to go and she's going to get something out of *this.* She's going to get a *man* someway. Look out. (*Looking at* **Smith**.) If she don't get the other one she'll have you before you know it.

Smith (*much flattered*) Oh I'm afraid she wouldn't look at me.

Mrs. Welch *Wouldn't* she? She's not *straight,* I tell you.

Leo You're barkin' up the wrong tree.

Mrs. Welch Oh! You can't tell a woman anything about *women.*

Smith I don't know—I sometimes think, my dear Madam—

Mrs. Welch My name's Welch. For heaven's sake stop *madaming* me.

Smith I sometimes think my dear Mrs. Welch—

Leo You sometimes think a man's the only animal that knows a good woman when he sees one—and right you are, my friend. The lady in question is as straight as a die but as loony as a bed bug. What do you call this? She walked straight up to him—

before the whole push—and said (*Imitating* **Julie**.) "I would rather have lost my life a *thousand times,* than to have had you suffer like this for *me*. I only hope the beauty of what you have done repays you." Now you know that's not naughty—but bughouse—bughouse.

Smith   She said some very strange things to me, too. Something about how ridiculously clear it all is once one sees with the eyes of the soul. It's very sad—very.

Mrs. Welch   Rubbish! Don't tell me I don't know a crazy woman from a bad one. I'll put a question to him—West—that'll show her up before you all. She's trying to make *us* think he's asked her to marry him. *He* ought to be put *wise* to it and I'll do it. Oh Lord, I'm so cold and starving and ache so I could yell!

Smith   Would you be more comfortable if you leaned on me?

Mrs. Welch   I might. (**Smith** *turns about and* **Mrs. Welch** *leans on his back.*)

Leo (*calling down the hill*)   Good work! That's the business. Slick as a whistle. (**Charles** *and* **Frank** *appear carrying Lily in a cat's cradle. These three also show the ravages of the wreck.* **Lily** *is exhausted with fatigue and her head droops against* **Frank**'s. *One foot and leg are clumsily tied up in a sheet.*) Put her over here! Give me this, I'll fix it. (*Taking the blanket which is over* **Frank**'s *shoulders and spreading it on a log.*)

Charles   That's the stuff.

Frank   Be careful. (*As they put her down.*)

Lily (*faintly*)   Oh, what a lovely place.

Mrs. Welch (*shivering and hugging herself in her blanket*)   Yeh—beautiful! Might just as well be home in your own bed it's so warm and cozy.

Lily   You've all been so kind. Everybody. I wish Grandma could come up here. She isn't hurt a bit. Isn't it wonderful!

Smith   I might make the effort to go and get her.

Mrs. Welch *digs* **Smith** *violently with her elbow for him to keep still.*

Charles   She's all right. Miss New York's got her.

Lily   Miss Rutherford—her name is. Isn't she wonderful? A regular angel of mercy she's been all night. Helping everybody. She's done some perfectly marvelous things. The doctors say so.

Mrs. Welch   Oh, I don't know. I held one woman's head myself for about an hour. But when the doctor came along and said she was going to die anyway, I thought I might as well give that job up.

Smith   The Almighty has been very good to us and has watched over us. (*Sneezing again.*)

Mrs. Bay (*bobbing up at the back. Her hair is down her back—her bonnet on* one *side, her dress skirt over one arm, her petticoat very torn and bedraggled, but she is* *smiling and cheerful and extremely spry in her movements*)   Well, well, well, how did you poor people manage to get up that hill? It's quite a climb for you.

Lily   Oh, grandma, I thought Miss Rutherford was taking care of you.

Mrs. Bay   What? (*Coming down to* **Lily**.)

Charles (*hurrying quickly to speak in* **Mrs. Bay**'s *ear*)   She thought Miss Rutherford was taking care of you.

Mrs. Bay   Fiddlesticks! I ran away. I'm so sick of everybody trying to take care of me, I couldn't stand it another minute. Everybody's calling for her. They need her—I don't. (*Going to look at* **Mrs. Welch** *and* **Mr. Smith**.) Well—how are you? Trouble of any kind goes hard with fat people, but cheer up, you don't feel half as bad as you think you do. (*Crossing over to* **Lily**.) Lily, don't pamper yourself too much. You must walk on that leg pretty soon before it gets stiff.

Mrs. Welch   If anything could have made me feel worse, it's a dose of damn cheerfulness early in the morning.

Leo (*shaking hands with* **Mrs. Bay**)   You're the gamest little sport I ever did see.

Mrs. Bay   What? Oh yes, good morning, I didn't recognize you at first. I don't *know* your name.

Leo   My name is—Call me Leo.

Jim *comes up the hill. His left arm is in a rough sling.*

Mrs. Welch   Oh, here's Mr. West. Has anything come?

Smith   Any relief in sight?

Jim   Not yet.

Mrs. Welch   Isn't anybody doing anything?

Jim   Yes, I think everybody's doing everything. The bridge is mended. I came up to see if you people are all right. Oh, I say, it must be pretty cold for you women sitting on the ground, isn't it? Suppose you fellows pick up some wood and build a fire. That would be about the best thing that could happen, wouldn't it?

Frank   Let's go to it.

Charles   Right you are!

Smith   I might make the effort to go with them.

Leo   Yes, you might.

Mrs. Welch   No, you mightn't. (*Turning to* **Leo**.) You leave him alone.

Jim   It's going to be pretty hard to find any small stuff around here. Try pretty well over there, see? (*Pointing down the hill. Turning to* **Leo**.) I advise you to slow up. You've worked like a nailer. About all in, aren't you?

Frank   That's right, don't come.

Charles (*giving* **Leo** *a push*)   Lie down, Fido!

Leo (*dropping on the ground as though* **Charles** *had knocked him down*)   Thanks for them kind words.

Mrs. Welch (*groaning vociferously*)   Oh—h—h will we ever get out of this?

Mrs. Bay   What?

Mrs. Welch   Oh—h—h—h! (*Burying her head in her arms, unable to cope with* **Mrs. Bay**'s *deafness and cheerfulness.*)

Jim (*raising his voice to* **Mrs. Bay**)   We're pretty lucky to be here, aren't we?

Mrs. Bay   Indeed we are! When I was thrown out in the aisle and people began walking on my stomach, and I heard the howls and groans I thought I had died and gone to hell, and all my life passed before me, and I wondered why I was *there,* when I heard our baby cry, and recognized it, and I never heard anything so sweet in all my life.

Mrs. Welch   Well, I didn't think any great and noble dying thoughts. All I wanted was to get hold of those railroad officials and I will, too. If they don't pay for my new spring clothes, I'll know the reason why.

Leo (*sitting on a rock*)   When I took the header through the window and felt the glass flying, I said to myself, "Well, Leo, it's *come,* and you ain't got no accident policy." That's the first thing I do now when I get back to Broadway, take out a traveller's insurance policy. You hate to spend the money while you're alive, but when you do cash in, it would be a nice idea to be able to say to yourself, *"Somebody pays heavy for this."* I could see that last night when the bump came.

Jim   Yes, it's wonderful what we see in that last flash, isn't it? The things we wish we hadn't done and the things we think we would do if we only had another day to do them in.

Lily   Do your arm and shoulder pain perfectly terribly all the time, Mr. West?

Jim   Oh no, they're all right.

Lily   You broke them in such a perfectly beautiful way.

Jim   Yes, it was nice, wasn't it?

Mrs. Welch   Pretty expensive business for you—saving her life and breaking yourself to pieces.

Jim   Well, I guess it's worth it, when you think how many she's saved herself, since.

Leo   That's a good way to check it up.

Mrs. Welch   She's a new breed to me. Just what do *you* say she is, West?

Jim   That's more than I can even try to say.

Lily   There's something so strange about her now.

Jim Yes, do you see?

Mrs. Welch How could a child see? To put it in plain English, do you think she's off her head since she was hit, or do you think she's something else?

Jim (*with a slow, whimsical smile*) That depends a good deal on how you look at it, doesn't it?

Mrs. Welch Oh—you're not on—*yet*.

Lily Oh her mind couldn't be gone, could it?

Leo Certainly, it could. Couldn't it, West, dead easy?

Lily She said to me just a little while ago—

She stops as **Julie** *appears at the back carrying the baby.* **Julie***'s clothes are also torn and mud stained, her hair disheveled, her face pale—a man's handkerchief tied about her forehead but there is shining out of her, a sort of exaltation which radiates an intensity of energy, and rather a disconcerting honesty and simplicity—seeing things for the first time and expecting everyone else to see them the same way. There is a pause as they all turn to look at her and feel in her a subdued excitement.*

Julie (*in a breathless tone*) She's gone.

Mrs. Welch Who?

Julie Annie. (*Looking at* **Jim**) You thought she was going to live—didn't you—but the shock and the whole thing were—She's gone.

There is a pause and a sympathetic murmur.

Jim Yes, I thought she'd pull through.

Julie I believe she was glad to go—poor little woman. You were right. She wasn't married to Bill.

Mrs. Welch Who's Bill?

Julie The man she was going to. And she was afraid to take the baby to him—and afraid she couldn't take care of it herself and just afraid—afraid of everything—afraid to live.

Mrs. Welch She had no business to die. What's going to become of that child?

Julie That was the hard thing for her and she was so unhappy about it. I said I *knew* I could find someone to take her and love her—and the most beautiful look came into Annie's face—a sort of radiance and—she just closed her eyes and slipped away—into peace—with one hand still holding this little hand. So I brought the baby right up to you first, Mrs. Welch, because I know you are generous and kind and well off and would love to have her. (*Kneeling before* **Mrs. Welch** *with the baby.*)

Mrs. Welch (*drawing away in amazed alarm*) No! I can't stand children. Anyway Harry would have a fit. What are you talking about?

Julie Oh, I thought you'd think it was wonderful to get her like this.

Mrs. Welch You'll have to think again.

Julie Wouldn't you like her, Mr. Smith?

Smith (*gasping*) I'm an unmarried man, Miss.

Julie Well all the more splendid for you to get her like this.

Smith I—You—She—I'd like to accommodate you but it's really quite impossible.

Mrs. Welch Of course it is. Even if anybody wanted to adopt a kid, who wants an illegitimate one with all its mother's bad traits?

Julie What has that to do with this love of a baby? Besides her mother was a very wonderful woman.

Mrs. Welch What?

Julie Wasn't she, Mr. West?

Jim (*with an intense shyness before this new and compelling* **Julie**) What makes you think so?

Julie She understood and appreciated *you,* that was one of the reasons. She said, "Lady, that tall fellow is a great man." Don't you think that shows some great understanding?

Jim She just wanted to see something decent in people. Poor little woman, she trusted too much.

Julie And never a word of littleness towards Bill. She said she loved him and that love had made her happy and that it was worth it all just to have had the baby to love for a little while. There's something rather splendid about that you know.

Mrs. Bay What is it, Lily? What are they talking about?

Lily About adopting the baby. The mother died. Oh Grandma, couldn't we take the baby?

Mrs. Bay (*hopping up*) My stars child, no. Your mother's raised one family and I've raised two, that's enough. (*Going to* **Julie**.) What's the matter, do you have to find a home for it?

Julie Yes I do—I must.

Mrs. Bay She's a nice child. I'll see what our Church Society can do about it.

Mrs. Welch That's a good idea.

Smith Excellent.

Leo (*drawing near* **Julie** *to look at the baby*) She's a darned fine kid.

Julie (*turning to him with the baby*) Isn't she? A blessed, blessed little precious thing!

Leo (*backing away*) But don't wish her on me, she ain't in my line. If she was a boy now, I'd stake him to pants as soon as he was ready, but I ain't got nothing in her line at all.

Jim Don't worry, you'll find a place for her some way.

Julie Yes, I know, what we *want* to be, *can* be. That's true, isn't it? Every word you said has come true—more glorious than you know. Something great enough to make up for this has come. (*Laying her hand tenderly on his broken arm.*) At least I want it to do that. Do you know what I mean?

Jim (*lowering his eyes*) Perhaps! Don't say it and there'll be nothing to unsay. (*He turns away towards the path.*)

Julie Are you going down?

Jim Yes, and I'm going to see if any help has come. (*He goes down the hill.*)

Julie Annie was right, he *is* a great man and what's more, he's a good man, with something so big and sweet and revealing in him, that one sees God for the first time through him. Isn't that true?

Mrs. Welch He's an ordinary good-hearted man ridin' on a railroad train, if that's what you mean.

Julie You hold her, Mrs. Welch, for a minute. If you've never had a baby, you don't know how wonderful it feels to have her in your arms. You hold her a minute and you'll love her. Oh, you don't know how sweet you are sitting there. It makes you look so much warmer and happier. (**Julie** *walks about restless and exalted.*)

Smith Now, now, don't excite yourself my dear young lady. You ought to go off to some quiet spot and lie down.

Julie Lie down?—I couldn't. I never felt so strong in my life.

Leo (*going to* **Julie** *anxiously*) Has the doctor examined your head very carefully?

Julie Oh, it's nothing but a cut and a bruise. Was I unconscious long?

Smith (*going over to* **Julie** *very cautiously*) How do you—how do you—feel?

Leo Do you seem to—How do things seem to you—pretty much exaggerated, eh? You haven't gone to the Golden Gates, or anything like that. Things are just as they were before you got hit.

Julie Oh no, the whole world has changed to me.

Leo No—no –it's just everyday stuff, you know. A spade is still a spade.

Julie (*exaltedly*) Yes, a spade is a spade but one can do wonderful things with it. I watched those men down there at work, all using their hands and some of them were so strong and clever and lifted those great beams and put them where they wanted them. They have come to the real things and are all working together for the same end—men—brothers. It's wonderful. Haven't you felt it, the thrill of it? Hasn't it made you want to use your *own* arms and hands and strength and will to make life right? Hasn't it?

Leo   Does it pain you all the time? (*Pointing to her head.*)

Smith (*turning to* **Mrs. Welch**)   It's taken rather a religious turn.

Julie (*looking at Leo for the first time*)   Oh Mr. Stern, did you know you have a very long cut across your cheek?

Leo (*backing away from her*)   Oh no, no, you only think it.

Julie   The doctor gave me a few things and I've watched him till I can do it pretty well. You must let me bandage it for you. (*Taking a small bottle and a roll of bandage from the pockets of her sweater.*)

Leo   Oh no, I'm all right. Am getting along very well, thank you. (*Trying to get away from her.*)

Julie   No, you're not. Sit down here and let me do it right away.

Leo (*sitting very dubiously as* **Julie** *takes him by the arm*)   I'm getting along all right this way, but I don't think I could stand anything more.

Julie   Oh my, it *is* bad! You've got mud or something in the wound. (*Going at him with interested energy.*)

Leo   You don't say! How careless of me!

Julie   Fortunately I have this little bottle to wash it out with.

Leo   A bottle?

Julie   I mean with what's *in* the bottle.

Leo   Oh!

Julie   Now hold very still please.

Leo   I can't promise. (**Julie** *bathes the cut with alcohol.*) Jee-rusalem, is that pure alcohol?

Julie   Perfectly pure.

Leo   It's a shame to waste it. (*Writhing in pain.*)

Julie   Oh, does it hurt so? It *is* a bad cut. I'm glad I had these things. Hold still. The only way the bandage seems to fit is this way. (*Putting it under his chin and over his head.*) I haven't got any more of those pins. You don't mind, do you?

Leo   Just so I don't look untidy. (*Trying to move his jaw.*) And give me a little jaw action, if you don't mind, that's all I ask.

Julie   There, I hope you'll be more comfortable.

Leo (*as she allows him to get up*)   I hope so too. I'm much obliged anyway. I take it just as you meant it.

Julie   I haven't forgotten what you did to my eye, you know. I'm paying you back.

Leo (*keeping away from her*)   You win, I'm paid. I think I'll go down and see if those fellows have forgotten all about that fire. (*He goes down.*)

Julie (*taking the baby from* **Mrs. Welch** *and going to* **Lily**)   Wouldn't you like to hold the baby, Lily? Poor child, how sleepy you are! (*She puts the baby in* **Lily**'s *arms and tucks a blanket about them.*)

Smith (*rising, starting after* **Leo**, *turning back to glance at* **Julie** *and holding up a warning finger to* **Mrs. Welch**)   And be very cautious. I wouldn't irritate her.

Mrs. Bay   I'll put on my dress skirt now. You see I saved it by taking it off.

Julie (*sitting beside* **Lily**)   How do you feel?

Lily   Oh it hurts, but I don't mind. Are you—do—*you* feel—quite well?

Julie   Yes.

Lily   I mean—I—I think I ought to tell you. Some of them think you're out of your head.

Julie   That's wonderful! It's such a chance to speak the truth.

Lily   But you—you're not, are you?

Julie   I'll tell you a secret. If I am—I want to be *always*. He's fallen out of the skies.

Lily   You mean? (**Julie** *nods.*) But—aren't you afraid? (**Julie** *shakes her head.*) Don't you think we—we—we ought to know a man—a long time—before we—we—fall in love?

Julie   When the miracle happens, we *do* know him.

Lily   But oughtn't we to be friends first?

Julie   Oh no. One has all one's life to be friends. Why ask love to wait?

Lily   Yes, but I was wondering.

Julie   Oh, my dear little girl. He's a nice boy. Don't be afraid to let him know what you feel.

Lily   Yes, but grandma would be so—

Julie   Yes, I know but don't hurt him. You may never see him again. It's a little flower of sweetness, you've gathered out of the horror. Let it blossom all it can.

Lily (*a little awestricken at* **Julie**)   What made you like this now?

Julie   Suffering and love.—They brought understanding.

Mrs. Welch (*having gone to sleep and fallen over*)   Oh, oh, oh, my back! My back! *Grandma and* **Julie** *run to her.*

Lily   What is it?

Mrs. Welch   It's a cramp. It's killing me.

Julie Where is it?

Mrs. Welch My back, my back! Oh Lord, what shall I do?

Julie (*rubbing* **Mrs. Welch**'s *back vigorously*) Is that the place?

Mrs. Welch No, lower down, lower down, lower down.

Julie Is that doing any good?

Mrs. Welch I don't know that it is, but it might.

Mrs. Bay If I only had my good liniment!

Julie It's making me warm, anyway.

Mrs. Welch You needn't do it on that account. Oh—oh—oh—(*Groaning with satisfaction.*)

Julie Better? Better? Is that better?

Mrs. Welch I don't know but that it is. Much obliged.

Mrs. Bay That's very apt to happen to fat people.

Mrs. Welch I'm not fat.

Jim *comes back up the hill.*

Julie Couldn't you take a little exercise to get warm?

Mrs Welch Yes, I'd just love to swing dumbbells right now for my health.

Jim Get up. Walk about. The worst thing you can do is to sit still, on that rock.

Mrs. Welch Well, if you can show me anything better to sit on around here, I'll do it.

Jim Get up, get up.

Mrs. Welch I won't. Oh—oh—oh—oh! Must I?

Jim Certainly. (**Mrs. Welch** *rises with the help of* **Julie** *and* **Mrs. Bay**.) Now walk.

Mrs. Welch Don't boss me like that. I'm not used to it.

Jim The sun's trying to show itself out there. It can't get in here just yet. Go out on that slope. That's where it will start first.

Mrs. Bay (*following* **Mrs. Welch**) Where are you going?

Mrs. Welch (*shouting at* **Mrs. Bay** *and hobbling off*) To the jumping off place.

Mrs. Bay I'll come with you. I'm very surefooted. (*Trotting after* **Mrs. Welch**.)

Jim (*looking at* **Lily**) She's asleep. Aren't you going? I'll stay here.

Julie What is it? Have I done anything to displease you?

Jim Of course not.

Julie Or to disappoint you?

Jim No.

Julie I'm trying so hard to show you how grateful I—

Jim *Don't* please. You don't owe me anything. Nothing is different because I had the luck to save your life. Things are just as they were before all this happened.

Julie I know now that life *can* be all you said—big and sweet and wonderful—if *we make it*. I want to give all the rest of mine to you—to thank you.

Jim That's what you mustn't think. That's what I won't let you say. That's what you can't do.

Julie Why not?

Jim *You don't owe me anything.*

Julie But I—

Jim You haven't changed because of *me*. You see and know because you've seen death and suffering. You're cold and hungry now and close to humanity and you've made things better for others by giving of *yourself*. That's why you're glad to be alive. It's yourself—yourself—not me.

Julie It all came *through* you.

Jim No.

Julie But the things you said to me—

Jim The things I asked when you were throwing yourself away—I don't ask now, and the things you said out of pity and gratitude are all washed out. he bridge is mended and you'll go over it—strong and on your feet. We're two travellers who have touched hands and are the better for it.

Julie What have I done? What's changed you?

Jim You're reborn and further away from me than ever. When you're down there, on the level again (*Pointing down the hill.*) out of the heights—you'll see me as I am—a plain man, not fit to touch you—separated from you by every law of your world.

Julie (*looking steadily into* **Jim***'s eyes*) You said she must have the eyes to see him when he's there—the courage to take him when he comes—the hands to work with him—the heart to love him. I'm here.

She stops as the voices of the boys are heard. **Jim** *turns, about to go, when* **Frank** *appears—followed by Leo,* **Charles** *and* **Smith** *carrying wood for a fire.*

Leo Here fellows—here's a good place, over here.

The men begin laying the fire.

Frank (*going to kneel by* **Lily**) Wake up. We're going to have a fire.

Lily What? Oh goodness—where am I?

Frank Up at the top of the world.

Lily Oh—I had the most wonderful dream.

Frank I guess you've got plenty of time to tell it before breakfast—so it'll come true.

Lily I wish it would. I dreamed that I was never going to see you again.

Frank Oh say!

Lily Wait, it was nice. I mean Mother didn't want me to write to you or have you come to see me—but it—it was sweet anyway—because I had *known* you.

Frank Oh! Is *that* all!

Mrs. Welch (*hobbling back with Grandma*) Where's that grand fire you were talking about?
You've been gone long enough to burn up the whole mountain. (*She sits on the rock at left above the spot where the men are making the fire.*)

Mrs. Bay It's more beautiful out there. You must all go out and look.

Mrs. Welch Thank you. I've had enough scenery to last for the rest of my life. Why in the name of common sense don't you light the fire?

Charles Who's got a match?

Leo I have, but *only one* and it's got to do the business. Now don't breathe anybody and make a draft. (*Taking* **Smith**'s *cap and handing it to* **Frank**) Hold this hat, Kid.

Charles Hold it lower down so it'll catch quicker.

Lily Oh, wouldn't it be awful if it doesn't light?

Mrs. Welch For Heaven's sakes don't fool with it.

Julie Shall we all stand around and keep off the air?

Leo No—keep away—keep away. Don't talk.

Charles Turn it the other way, Frank. (**Frank** *turns the cap.*)

Leo No you don't. Put her back.

Charles I tell you the wind's coming from this way.

Leo Maybe she is but this is *my match*. Turn that hat round the way I told you, Kid. Now hold still.

There is a breathless pause as **Leo** *strikes the match and they all watch.*

Mrs. Bay What's the matter? Why don't they hurry and light the fire?

Leo Tell the old lady to stop her conversation.

Julie, **Lily** *and* **Mrs. Welch** *motion to* **Mrs. Bay** *to keep quiet. They all watch the match tensely.*

Mrs. Welch   Oh Lord, it's going out!

Leo   Hold that hat still.

Charles   Turn the match up.

Leo   You shut up!

Frank   Wait—she's coming. Look out—there! Careful, there she comes.

Leo   Don't move. *Ah* there we are. Oh,—blast it! (*They all groan as the match goes out.*)

Jim   Wait, there's a spark. (*They blow the fire until it blazes up. There is a chorus of delight as the flame comes.*)

Leo   How's that for a blaze?

Julie   It's too good to be true! Oh, isn't that splendid!

Mrs. Welch   Thank Heaven! I couldn't have held out much longer.

Leo   Come close, ladies, and get next. (*They all talk at once as they seat themselves round the fire—stretching out their hands and feet to it with grateful groans.*)

Mrs. Welch   Why didn't somebody think of this before? Say, do you know what the best thing in the world would be right now?

The Others   What?

Mrs. Welch   A cup of coffee. (*They groan again—the mere mention of coffee making them lose their moral courage.*)

Charles   I could walk all the way home if I had some food.

Mrs. Welch (*getting up stiffly*)   You wouldn't be so spry about walking if you were in bedroom slippers. My feet will never come back to their natural size—never! Look at that—just look at it! (*Holding up one foot, swollen and bruised.*) I don't see for the life of me how I stand it at all. I honestly do *not* see how I stand it.

Julie (*stretching her hands to the fire*)   I know. Isn't it funny how we're doing all the things we thought were the very ones we could *not* do.

The **Porter** *appears at back carrying a large basket filled with bread and ham—cups, a bottle of milk, and a coffee pot—a bucket of water and a package of coffee. He can scarcely carry his load from exhaustion and a lame knee and shoulder. His clothes are in a deplorable condition. They hail him with delight.*

Charles   Look who's here! You're the hero of the day.

Leo   Welcome to our fireside!

Mrs. Welch   My God, he's human. He's even brought coffee.

Porter   Yes *ma'am!* You couldn't git nowhere without that.

Mrs. Welch (*taking the coffee pot and coffee*)   This must go right on the fire to boil.

Jim   Here's a place for it.

Mrs. Bay We mustn't spill it. Every drop is precious.

Porter (*taking a man's tan shoe out of one pocket and a black one out of the other and holding it out to* **Mrs. Welch**) Here, lady, I heard you whinin' for shoes all night. These is the best I could do.

Mrs. Welch (*seizing the shoes*) You angel! Now isn't that sweet!—Oh let me get 'em on quick. (*Hanging on the porter's arm she kicks off the slippers and puts her feet in the shoes with many groans of pain.*) Oh, Lord, how it hurts!

Porter (*holding her up and helping to put the shoes on*) They don't exactly match, lady, but they're the best I could do.

Mrs. Welch Match your granny! I'd give you the biggest tip you ever had but I haven't got anything left but the gold in my teeth.

Porter That's all right lady. I ain't out for graft this trip.

Mrs. Welch *Everything* lost. All my jewelry gone, but I know you didn't take it, you're a *very* honest man.

Porter I ain't stole nuthin' but them shoes.

Mrs. Welch You'll go to Heaven for that. Any sign of that coffee boiling?

Jim Not yet.

Mrs. Welch Well, don't sit there watching the pot or it will never boil. (**Frank** *and* **Charles** *have emptied the baskets.* **Frank** *is cutting the bread and* **Charles** *the ham.*)

Julie (*bending over the baby*) Here's some milk for you, precious. Isn't she the most angelic baby in the world not to cry? Here dearest—Oh, see, she's starving. You blessed, blessed little thing. (*The women all coo to the baby.*)

Frank Here's a nice piece of bread and ham for everybody.

Jim She's boiling! (*They sit about the fire helping each other with a new and exaggerated kindness.*)

Leo I've got mine. Here's a sandwich.

Porter (*modestly and very grateful for the sudden attention*) Oh, I'll sit over here.

Julie No—no, sit over here by the fire.

Leo Gosh, smell that coffee! Is that the same brand I've been kicking about for four days?

Mrs. Welch (*leaning forward eagerly*) Keep on pouring—keep on pouring!

Leo You can pour mine right down my throat if you will. (*Deep grunts and groans express their comfort as they eat and drink and talk with their mouths full.*)

Mrs. Bay We have a great deal to be thankful for. 'Spose we offer up our thanks in a little hymn of praise. Lily you start it.

Lily Oh, Grandma, I couldn't!

Mrs. Bay Well, then I will. (*In a sweet quavering voice she begins "Praise God from whom all blessings flow."* **Charles** *and* **Frank** *laugh.*)

Julie Oh, don't laugh! (*She sings softly with* **Mrs. Bay** *and gradually they all join in—at first lamely and then with honest thankfulness as the feeling grows. It swells into some discordant notes and into strains of real harmony. As they finish there is a long pause in which they gradually come back to self-consciousness.*)

Julie (*very quietly*) I've found a place for the baby.

The Others Where?

Julie I'm going to keep her myself.

Mrs. Welch What?

Julie Oh, you don't think I'm fit to take care of her, but I love her—and after all, love is the greatest thing in the world that can be given to her, isn't it?

Smith Oh, we mustn't allow her to do this.

Mrs. Welch (*hushing* **Smith** *with a gesture and speaking to* **Julie**) Don't you fool with a thing like that. Why, you don't know what you're letting yourself in for. It means everything you're not used to—*sacrifices* and *hard* things you hate. My God, it's an awful job taking care of a baby. How on earth can *you* do it?

Julie I don't know—but I just know I can. I *must* do it. It's the reason I'm alive myself. I know that now. Think of it, Mrs. Welch, she'll need me. I'm the only thing in the world she'll know—(*Getting to her feet.*) and I'll have to learn to take care of us both.

Mrs. Welch She's bluffing—and fooling with a pretty serious thing. And what's more, if it comes to a showdown that kid belongs to all of us as much as it does to her, and we've got a right to know what's going to become of it.

Julie But I know this—whatever I am, however worthless and weak, I *have* got the strength to take care of this baby. Oh, let me try—I can do it and I will.—Don't you believe me?

Mrs. Welch (*with a sudden conviction and a catch in her throat*) You bet I believe you. But I want to laugh. (*Looking at* **Jim**.) I was going to show her up to you. I thought she'd fooled you. But now I think you'd be pretty lucky to get her.

Jim I would be—the luckiest man in the world—but I haven't the slightest right in the world to ask her. (*Shouts from below.*) That means the relief train is here. Come on, Mrs. Bay. I'll take you down.

Mrs. Bay What's the matter? I don't want to go down. I want to know what's going on.

Leo What's the matter? Why isn't he going to marry her?

Mrs. Welch Oh, shut up! Stop talking about something you don't know anything about. (**Mrs. Welch** *takes the baby from* **Lily** *and puts it in* **Julie***'s arms—turning to* *the others*) Look here—it's just as much our business to help take care of that kid as it is hers. I'm going to give five hundred a year. Smith, you can do better than that, how much do you say?

Smith Why, whatever *you* say, of course.

Mrs. Welch A thousand will do for you to start with.

Leo Now you're shouting.

Mrs. Welch Now go on down everybody, we'll come in a minute. (**Leo**, **Smith**, **Charles** *and* **Frank** *gather round* **Lily** *and the baby.*)

Mrs. Welch (*to* **Julie**) I'm going to take you to ma's till we get things straightened out. She's got a big house and it will do her good to open up the windows and let in some fresh air.

Julie Oh—

Mrs. Welch Don't try to talk. I know everything you want to say. Come on down. That's the first thing to do.

Julie I want to sit here alone just a few minutes—till I—

Mrs. Welch I know, till you get a grip on yourself. I'm just going to take you under my wing. I don't often take a fancy to anybody—but when I *do* I stick.

Charles I'll stay with her. (*To* **Leo**.) You help Frank with Lily, will you?

Leo Sure. (*Going quickly to help* **Frank** *make a cat's cradle for* **Lily** *and turning back to* **Julie** *as they start down the hill*) I'll see you later . Don't you be lonely, Julie. You've got lots of good friends and little Leo's right on the job.

Smith May I offer my help in any way?

Mrs. Welch Now the kindest thing you can do is to go on down the hill.

Smith But I wish to say that—

Mrs. Welch You'll have plenty of time to say it. *I* need you now. *Go on.* Oh, these blessed shoes! Hey, don't go so fast, I'm no little fleet foot.

Smith (*turning back to help her*) Be very cautious. Let me go first and you put both hands on my back.

Mrs. Welch I will. Go on. Take good care of her, Charlie, and come down in a minute. I'll be waiting for you, Julie dear. Oh, go on! Go *on!* (*Giving* **Smith** *an impatient push.*)

Charles (*after a pause, kneeling beside* **Julie**) I wish there was something I could do.

Julie You're all so good.

Charles I'd be so proud to marry you and help take care of the baby if you'd only let me.

Julie You dear boy!

Charles I'd cut college and go to work right away. Won't you think about it? I'm not so young as I look.

Julie You dear, dear boy! How sweet you are! How kind the world is.

Charles Do you want *him*? (*He turns as* **Jim** *appears again at the path.*) Oh—I guess I'll go down. You don't need *me*. (**Charles** *goes off slowly down the path.*)

Jim You will let me help you with her—won't you?

Julie Oh—no—That won't be necessary.

Jim You mean you don't want—

Julie I shan't need you.

Jim But if there's anything—anything in any way I *can* do—will you let me—(*She looks at him and moves up toward the path.*) I won't come near you—if you don't want me to—but just to know that a friend is over there behind that range—that's the way I can stay in your life a little, isn't it?

Julie (*turning*) *I'm* not separated from you by anything in heaven or earth. I love you.

Jim You can't. It's life—not me—you love.

Julie Then you are life—I love you.

Jim (*closing his arms about her*) Be sure what you are doing.

Julie I love you—I love you!

Jim Oh, I'll take care of you. I don't just love you—I worship you.

Voices call to them as

THE CURTAIN FALLS

Mary the Third

A Comedy in Prologue and Three Acts

Characters

Mary The First/ Mary The Second/ Mary The Third
William/ Robert/ Lynn
Richard/ Hal
Mother
Granny
Father
Bobby
Lettie
Max
Nora

Prologue

Mary The First

TIME: 1870.

The stage is hung in dark curtains, the center is lighted and the figures which walk into the light are framed by darkness.

An old mahogany sofa, upholstered in black hair cloth, is the only furniture in the scene.

A girl of twenty sits on it—dressed in an evening gown of the period. The skirt voluminous with ruffles and lace. Her arms, bosom, and shoulders are bare but the fashion of her hair is demure and maidenly with the proverbial curl and rose.

She fans nervously with her diminutive fan, waiting and watching. She is soft and pretty and flower-like. Her voice is sweet. Shyness and modesty are her manner. Her movements are graceful and coy and mincing—full of a conscious charm.

An orchestra from a seductive distance is playing an enticing polka. A tall goodlooking fellow of twenty-five—in the evening dress of the period—comes quickly into the scene.

Mary Good gracious! How did you know I was here?

William You told me you would be.

Mary I didn't! The idea of you thinking such a thing!

William (*heavy, honest and simple minded*) I thought you said as soon as you finished that dance with Hiram, you'd come in here.

Mary I may have said I *might* but I didn't say I *would*.

William Well, I hoped you would.

Mary Where's Lucy? I didn't suppose you'd be looking for *me* when you were dancing with *her*.

William I finished.

Mary Aren't you going to dance this one with her? It's your favorite polka and *now* no one in the world dances the polka so well as Lucy, of course.

William No one but you.

Mary Oh, that's what you *used* to say. But you can't say that any more. Go on. Don't keep her waiting.

William Who's waiting for *you*?

Mary I won't tell you.

William It's Hiram. How many times have you danced with him?

Mary How do I know?

William Every other dance. Is this his, too?

Mary I'm not dancing with anybody this time. I'm just sitting here resting. It's so sweet and quiet. Listen! Isn't the music sweet? I shall always think of you, William, when I hear that music. We've danced to it so many, many times. Oh, I oughtn't to have said that.

William Why not?

Mary I mustn't say those things now. And you must go. There mustn't be any more of these sweet little stolen moments under the stairs. This is really good-bye, William, isn't it?

William No, it's not. Unless *you* want it to be.

Mary Oh, *me*! Don't say me. What have I to do with it?

William Everything. It all depends on you whether it's good-bye or not.

Mary Then of course it's good-bye. Dear, dear little Lucy! I hope you'll be happy with her, William. Good-bye. (*Giving him her hand daintily, and drawing it away at once.*)

William What are you goin' on like this for? Nothing's going to be any different for you and me.

Mary Oh, do you suppose for a minute she'll ever let you dance with me again?

William She can't help herself.

Mary Oh, you don't know her as I do. I love Lucy very, *very* dearly. She doesn't mean to be –

William What?

Mary Nothing. I ought not to have said that.

William Said what? What are you hiding?

Mary Oh, I'm not *hiding* anything about Lucy. Good gracious! I wouldn't have you think *that* for *any*thing. Oh dear. Oh dear! Rather than have you think that, I'll tell you right out what was on my mind. I only meant that under her sweet little purring ways, she's very, *very* strong and stubborn and always gets what she wants. She won't let you be my dear old friend any more. She's been very cold to me lately and there can't be any reason for it unless it's because she doesn't like you to like me—even a little bit.

William She can't stop that.

Mary You mustn't say that. It's all over now.

William It never would have been over if you hadn't preferred Hiram and his money.

Mary Oh, don't blame me. But it *is* over. So let's not talk about it. Let's just be happy for a moment here . . . in this sweet little corner where we've sat so many, many times.

William We'll sit here again sometimes, too. (*Trying to take her hand which she finally allows him to do after a modest struggle.*)

Mary Oh, never, *never*! I'm not that kind of a girl. You ought to know that, William. You ought to know that I will be loyal to Lucy always—above everything. Nothing shall ever dim my devotion to her. Dear, dear little Lucy! I must be true to her.

William What about being true to me? You can't throw me away like an old shoe—just because I'm getting married. I'm not going to throw you away, let me tell you.

Mary Oh, but you're a great, big, strong man. You can do as you please and still control your feelings. I'm only a weak little thing. I wouldn't dare try to go on seeing you after you are married. I might not be able to hide my feelings.

William Hide what feelings? What kind of feelings have you got for me, Mary?

Mary (*turning away and brushing a tear from her cheek*) No kind. Good-bye, William! You must go.

William I won't go until you tell me just what you mean and just how you're feeling.

Mary No—No—it's too late.

William It's not too late. I'm not tied up yet. We can change things.

Mary Oh, no—no—Lucy!

William I've got more money than Hiram has now. More than he ever will have. Granddad left me rich, Mary. I'm a rich man now. If I thought you still cared for me the way you once did—nothing could hold me back from getting you.

Mary Oh, William—William, you mustn't say that. (*Taking the rose from her hair, smelling it and holding it to her lips*) Take this and keep it and look at it sometimes when it's faded and think of me. Perhaps I'll be faded, too. Isn't it pretty?

William Not half so pretty as you are.

Mary Oh!

William Your cheek is much softer and pinker.

Mary How can you say such a thing! It couldn't be. See. Look! (*Holding the rose to her cheek and bending near him. He kisses her cheek.*) Oh—how could you! How could you, William! Oh—you're hurting my arm! You're going to make it black and blue. There, look at that red spot. Kiss it and make it well. Oh no—I mustn't say that. (**William** *kisses her forearm, her elbow, her shoulder and her throat.*) Oh, William—you mustn't!

William   I won't let anybody else have you. Are you engaged to Hiram?

Mary   Oh, what does it matter?

William   I never have loved any other girl. I never will.

Mary   And do you think I've ever loved any other man? Oh, I ought not to have said that. But I will say it, just this once before we part forever. I loved you as no girl ever loved a man.

William   God! (*Bending over her hands and holding them to his lips.*)

Mary   We must be brave, William, and say good bye.

William   (*kneeling before her, his head bowed in her hands*)   I can't—I can't—don't ask it.

Mary   It's too late. You're pledged to another. You must be true to her and live a beautiful life, William.

William   I ain't going to do it. You're my fate. I'll blow my brains out if you don't marry me. I'll kill anybody else that gets you.

Mary (*sobbing*)   But fate is parting us.

William   Look here. I'll have the horses ready in an hour. You go home and put on your riding habit and meet me at the cross-roads in an hour.

Mary   No, no, William. I couldn't—I couldn't.

William (*still on his knees*)   You've got to. We can't let life treat us like this. We've got to take hold of things. Nothing can stop us. This is meant to be.

Mary   Then it would be wrong to let anything separate us. It's stronger than we are, William. Eternal and beautiful like the stars. But, oh, I can't do it, William. Never—never in this world can I do it. I'm not sure that it would be right. I'll be behind the oak tree. It's bigger than the maple.

William (*getting up*)   You angel!

Mary   Don't you bring Fleetfoot. I'm afraid of her. Bring Silver Star. Will you love me forever?

William   Forever and ever.

Mary   In this world and the next?

William   Longer than eternity.

Mary   There never has been a love as great as this. I feel it. I know it. Oh, William, I love you so! I love you!

They are locked in each other's arms; their lips pressed together as the light fades.

Mary The Second

TIME: 1897.

The light comes on again and shows the same sofa with a tall, fair, rather æsthetic looking boy standing by it.

He wears evening clothes of the period and is examining closely a dance program, checking off numbers with a small pencil.

An orchestra is playing Sousa's "Washington Post" twostep with great swing and pomp.

A dark boy, more sturdy in appearance, also wearing evening clothes, comes into the scene quickly.

Robert (*as he comes on with smiling self-assurance*)   Hello, Richard. Who's the dude dancing with Mary?

Richard (*with injured dignity*)   I thought she was dancing with you.

Robert   No, I have this next one with her.

Richard   Oh no. *I* have it, It's mine.

Robert   You're off your trolley.

Richard   You're mistaken. She has it with me.

Robert   You better go find her, then. I think I'll wait here (*Throwing himself on the sofa.*)

Richard   You seem to be very sure of yourself.

Robert   You bet, I'm sure.

Richard   You're not going to stay here and make a scene, are you—over a little thing like this?

Robert   I haven't anything to make a scene about. I'm just waiting to dance with Mary. If that's painful to you, why not *withdraw* so you won't suffer so much?

The orchestra changes to "Daisy Belle" and **Robert** *sings a verse with a gaiety intended to madden* **Richard**.

> Daisy, Daisy, give me your answer true,
> I'm half crazy all for the love of you.
> It won't be a stylish marriage—
> I can't afford a carriage,
> But you'll look neat—upon the seat—
> Of a bicycle built for two.

Richard   Oh, don't! It's bad enough to have to dance to anything so vulgar—without hearing the words.

Robert I'm stuck on the words.

Richard You probably are. They're just about suited to your vocabulary.

Robert What's the matter with my vocabulary?

Richard Nothing. I dare say it expresses everything you think—very adequately.

Robert Meaning my intellect is not so colossal as yours.

Richard I couldn't be so rude as that.

Robert Suppose you clear out then before I say something so rude you won't care to hear it.

Richard You're making a fool of yourself.

Robert (*rising quickly*) I'll show you who's the fool!

Mary (*coming into the scene out of breath*) Oh, I'm nearly dead! Mamma *made* me dance with that old man.

Mary *is the perfect* **Gibson** *type-in dress and hair and figure.*

Robert He's got cheek asking you. He must think he's a young masher. Come on, this one is ours.

Richard It's *mine*, Mary.

Mary Oh—which one *is* it? Isn't it?

Robert and Richard The tenth—a twostep.

Mary No, this is an extra.

Robert No, it isn't. Let me see your card.

Richard Let *me* see it.

Mary (*hiding her program*) No!

Robert (*showing her his*) Look at this. There it is—the tenth—perfectly plain.

Richard (*showing his card*) Nothing could be plainer than this.

Mary That's funny. Well—the *next* one is an extra. One of you can have *that*.

Robert It's mine, anyway.

Mary I'll tell you what let's do. Let's divide *this* one. I'll dance the first half with you, Robert, and the other half with you, Richard.

Robert I don't see why I should give up half my dance.

Richard Oh, give it all to him. You're wasting time talking about it.

Mary NOW boys, don't be silly. I'll stay here and sit it out. The first half is Richard's. Go on Robert. I want to talk to Richard.

Robert Rats! I make myself pretty tired doing this.

Mary It's a sweet thing for you to do. Ta-ta.

She turns her back to **Richard** *and blows a small kiss to* **Robert**.

Robert I'll be back in a jiffy. (*He goes out.*)

Mary (*sitting on the sofa*)   Now we can talk.

Richard How *could* you?

Mary How could I what?

Richard I don't care anything about the old program. (*Going to her and tearing the program in two*) I want to know what you said you'd tell me tonight.

Mary I'm not going to tell you anything when you're in that kind of a humour.

Richard What kind of a humour did you expect me to be in?

Mary The kind you were last night—when you're different and not like anybody else.

Richard You were different—too—you made me believe you *would* marry me and tonight you've hardly looked at me.

Mary But I'm thinking every minute.

Richard What are you thinking?

Mary Life is wonderful. I want to live it wonderfully.

Richard We'll live it wonderfully—together. Our souls are like one soul.

Mary Yes, but our dispositions aren't. Sometimes we feel alike. When you read poetry to me we're awfully high and exalted, but when we're just going along in an everyday way we aren't a bit alike.

Richard Well, it's better to be alike and feel alike on the heights than in commonplace things that don't matter.

Mary But I believe they do matter. I wonder which matters the most.

Richard Which are the more important in the world—the great things or the little things?

Mary Oh, of course, of course—but the trouble is when you do ordinary little things that I don't like, I forget the great ones and I could just –

Richard Just what?

Mary Just kill you.

Richard But that's your fault, dearest—not mine.

Mary I wonder. I wonder if it *is* my fault when I hate you and yours when I love you. I do love you sometimes—Richard.

Richard Oh, Mary, we belong to each other. We were *meant* for each other—in our *real* selves.

Mary But I'm not sure which *is* my real self. You see, Richard, it's this way. Now listen and see if I can make you understand. Sometimes you're the most wonderful thing in the world. You say things that no one else says-and you think and feel and understand—and then sometimes—

Richard It's you who don't understand. Listen dearest—

Robert (*dashing in*) Time's up. Slide, Kelly, slide! You must have said everything you ever thought of by this time.

Richard Oh, time doesn't matter. (*Rising slowly.*) A minute—or eternity are all alike.

Robert You don't say! I'll take mine done up in sixty-minute parcels, thank you—and you've had more than your share. Skip.

Richard (*looking at* **Mary** *as he goes*) Eternity.

Robert (*after* **Richard** *has gone*) Dick's got' em again. What in the name of Heaven, do you scrape up to talk to him about?

Mary Oh, lots of things.

Robert Does he spout poetry to you *all* the time?

Mary It wouldn't hurt you to have a little poetry, too.

Robert (*laughing and sitting beside* **Mary**) All right. I'll get some. Anything you say. What more do you want me to have?

Mary You don't think much about—

Robert About what?

Mary Oh, about things that aren't just *things*.

Robert What?

Mary You see, you don't even know what I'm talking about.

Robert How can I tell what you're thinking when you don't *say* anything.

Mary That's just it. You ought to be able to.

Robert Well, all right. I'll find out how it's done if that's what you want.

Mary Oh!

Robert What's the matter, little girl? I'll give you anything on earth and the moon and stars thrown in. Honest, Mary, no man ever loved a girl the way I love you. And I'll never change. *That's* the point.

Mary What if you did? It would be horrible.

Robert But I wouldn't. I couldn't. How could I? You're meant for me. You're mine. We suit each other. Don't you trust me, Mary?

Mary Oh yes, I trust you—but getting married is forever and ever and ever.

Robert Of course.

Mary And Oh—unless two people *do* love each other—Oh, in the most wonderful way—that *nothing* can change—

Robert Like us.

Mary Now listen, Robert. I want to make you understand.

Robert (*taking her in his arms*) You don't need to. I do understand. I know all about it. (*He covers her face with kisses.*) I'll make you the happiest girl in the world. I love you. And we'll never change. Never.

Mary (*clinging to him*) Oh, if it could be that way, Robert!

Robert Of course it will be that way. Nobody ever loved anybody the way I love you. You're going to marry me, aren't you? You know you are! *Say* it!

Mary Yes.

Robert Do you love me?

Mary Oh, I do, Robert—and we must make it the most wonderful love that was ever in the world.

He folds her in his arms as the light fades.

Act One

TIME: 1922. *Summer.*

PLACE : *The living room in the Robert Hollister house.*

It is the conventional room of conventional success — filled with a certain amount of beauty and comfort produced by money rather than individual taste. The walls are made by the same draperies used in the first two scenes – with the frames of the doors and windows set in. The furniture is a mixture of old and new – brought into harmony in dull tones. The sofa that is seen in the first scenes is now upholstered in chintz.

Late afternoon in summer.

AT CURTAIN, **Mary** *the First at 75, and* **Mary** *the Second now 45 are in the room.*

Granny – **Mary** *the First—sits on the sofa, still somewhat the pretty and spoiled darling—still a trace of coquetry in her soft blue frock. She is knitting a blue woolen scarf on large needles.* **Mother***,* **Mary** *the Second, grown into a handsome full-blown rose—wears a gown and hat in good style and unobtrusive prettiness. She comes in by the long window—a little warm, a little bored and tired.*

Mother Hello, Mother.

Granny Back?

Mother Oh—It's hot! (*Sitting listlessly in a comfortable chair.*)

Granny (*after an elaborate search for her ball of wool*) Who was there?

Mother Oh, everybody.

Granny Did you have a good time?

Mother Not very.

Granny You're a funny woman, Mary. I don't see why you ever go to a party. You're so indifferent about it.

Mother What else is there to do?

Granny When I was your age, I never missed a party. Euchre was a much better game than bridge too. Much more sociable. You could talk all you wanted to, and I usually took the prize.

Mother I'll bet you did, Mother.

Granny Did you play for money?

Mother Yes.

Granny How much did you win?

Mother I lost.

Granny Serves you right. Ladies and gentlemen didn't act like professional gamblers when I was your age. Mary, let me tell you something. From something I heard Mary drop the other day I wouldn't be at all surprised if *she* plays for money too—sometimes.

Mother   I shouldn't be surprised if she does.

Granny   Do you know she does?

Mother   How can she help it, Mother? Everybody else does.

Granny   You could put your foot down hard and forbid it.

Mother *smiles again and reaches for the afternoon paper on the low table near her—and opens it indifferently.*

Granny   I know Robert doesn't know. Aren't you going to tell him?

Mother   I don't think so.

Granny   You ought to. At least he'd try to put a stop to it. Robert certainly does *try* to make his children what they ought to be. He certainly tries harder than you do, Mary. Don't you think he'd try if you told him? (**Mary**, *reading, doesn't hear.*) Mary!

Mother   Un? What? I beg your pardon, Mother.

Granny   I say don't you think Robert would try?

Mother   Try what?

Granny   Try to put a stop to Mary's playing cards for money, if he knew.

Mother   I expect he would. He's tried to put a stop to almost everything else she does.

Granny   You don't help him much. You're certainly not bringing your children up the way I brought *you* up.

Mother   And do you think you did a good job on me?

Granny   At least I did a better one than you're doing on *her*. Look here! (*Drawing a box of cigarettes out from under one pillow and a box of matches from another*.) Look here! It isn't enough to have them laid out on every table in the house. They're stuck under everything you touch. I expect to find them in my own bed some night. Why she hasn't set the house afire long ago I don't see for the life of me.

Mother   I don't either.

Granny   And look at *this*!

Mother   What?

Granny   A hole burned right through this sofa by one of those abominable things.

Mother   Oh, that's a shame.

Granny   I should think it is. It's my *sofa*, too, you know. It came out of Aunt Fannie's house. I sat on it in her house the night I told your father I'd marry him.

Mother   Well—that was a great moment for us all, wasn't it?

Granny Yes, it was. You needn't be sarcastic. And here's Mary abusing it. Sitting on it morning, noon and night with boys—boys—*boys*. Do you know how many boys she *has* sat on it with?

Mother No, I don't. I served my time at sitting on it, myself.

Granny That's what I say. All sorts of things have happened on this sofa and here she is treating it like—with no respect at all.

Mother Were you taking care of the sofa when you were sitting on it?

Granny Of course, I was. And so were you. I didn't *allow* you to abuse it. You were *taught* to take care of things.

Mother I don't seem to remember that.

Granny Seems to me you're forgetting a great many things you ought to remember. Seems to me you're getting very hard and worldly as you grow older.

Mother Nonsense, Mother! There's nothing hard about *me*. I wish there were.

Granny You wish there were! There you are! That's a hard thing to say. You're getting more like everybody else—callous—just *callous*. You let things slip and you're not holding up strict enough standards to your children.

Mother Yes, I know. Let's not start that, *please*.

Granny There you go! You don't care a fig about what I say. There was a time when people thought what I said was of some importance, and listened to it—too.

Mother Oh, Mother dear, I *do* listen.

Granny You have no more respect for my opinion than that. (*Flicking her fingers.*)

Bobby (*dashing in from the outside*)   Mother are you through with the car?

Mother Y-e-s-but what do you –

Bobby I left my racket out at the club. I want to dash out and get it. (*He starts out and turns back.*) Oh Granny, another button's busted off this coat. Will you sew it on please? (*Putting it on the table.*)

Granny Yes, dearie. Don't put it there. Give it to me. You can't put anything down in this house if you ever expect to get it back.

Bobby (*going to give her the button*)   See—it came off here and it sort of took a chunk of the coat with it.

Granny You bad thing! I s'pose I can darn it. Here, you keep it. I mended sixteen pairs of socks for you this morning.

Bobby Thanks.

Mother Mind you're back in time for dinner Bobby. Your father will probably want the car tonight.

Bobby I'll hurry.

Mother And don't drive too fast Bobby.

Granny I'll never go with you again if you drive the way you did yesterday.

Bobby Oh, you think anything over five miles an hour is too fast. (*He hurries out.*)

Granny Bobby's a sweet child but he's getting to be a ripsnorter, too – just about as bad as Mary. Both of them are as wild as colts.

Mother Well—after all they're my children and if I don't mind the things they do I don't know why you should.

Granny Your children! Anybody would think I hadn't brought up a family of children of my own.

Mother I expect you were a much better mother than I am, dear.

Granny I *know* I was. You're shutting your eyes to things that are right under your nose. Robert does try. I will say that for him. Robert's peculiar in some ways, but I must say he does try to bring up his children right.

Mother (*seeing a letter on the desk and opening it to read*) Robert is always right.

Granny I don't say that. But he certainly is as right as most men are. As men go, he's a very fine man. You're a very fortunate woman.

Mary As women go, I suppose I am.

Granny I sometimes think you don't appreciate him, Mary. I sometimes do.

Mother I've spent my life appreciating Robert.

Granny I don't know why you wouldn't . . . a man who has succeeded as he has and put you in this beautiful house.

Mother (*sitting at the desk to write a note*) He certainly did *put* me in it.

Granny Un? What do you mean by that? You're getting so sort of nifty and highty-tighty lately I don't know what you mean half the time.

Mother Well, I don't mean much of anything. I wouldn't worry about that.

Granny You're not living up to the principles I brought you up with.

Mother Mother – if you'd only acknowledge that what you brought me up with hasn't any more to do with the case now than I have with the North Pole – and stop stewing about it—you'd be a much happier person.

Granny Why Mary McDougal Hollister! That I should live to hear you say that! What's happened to you? You're different lately. What is it? Is anything wrong?

Mother Everything's just exactly as it always was.

Granny I should hope so. You're a happy woman. If you're not, you ought to be ashamed of yourself. When I was your age, it was the fashion to be happy. Women loved their husbands and appreciated their blessings. Or if they didn't they didn't air it from the house-tops.

Mother No – they just lied along and covered things up.

Granny Well land knows *you* haven't anything to cover up. That's one sure thing. (*A pause.*) Have you?

Mother (*sealing her letter and getting up*) Of course not.

Granny Then what's the use acting as if you had? The thing for you to think about is your children and how to keep them from being contaminated by the terrible things that are going on. You aren't half strict enough with Mary. I tell you she's in danger – actual downright danger, and you don't seem to see it at all.

Mother We're *all* in danger. You're in danger of becoming a fussy old woman. I'm in danger of being swamped by the hateful ugliness of – respectable – everyday life. If Mary's got anything more dangerous than that to face, she'll wriggle through somehow, I s'pose. (*Taking her hat and going to the hall door.*)

Granny And make a muddle of it. *She* doesn't know what's good for her. It's your business to make her see who's the right one for her to marry, and make her marry him.

Mother Did your mother make you marry Father?

Granny She didn't have to. I *knew* he was the best and I took him. Didn't I help you to take Robert?

Mother No, you didn't, and I didn't take him—I was taken. Mary won't be taken – and she won't take. She wants something different.

Granny Wants? Wants? What does she want?

Mother Something that *comes*. Something you nor I ever had.

Granny I think you're out of your head lately! I'm going to take Mary in hand myself.

Mother No, you won't, Mother. I must ask you, please to let Mary alone.

Mary (*coming in quickly through one of the long windows*) Mother – I've got a great scheme.

Mary *is twenty – slender and straight as a boy. She wears a slip of a frock—which leaves her free—and she vibrates with vitality and eagerness – rather dynamically interested in her own affairs. She pitches her hat into a chair as she comes in.*

Mother Have you, dear? What?

Mary Some of us are going camping—Lettie and Max and Lynn and Hall and I —and do all our own cooking and cleaning up and everything—and see how really awfully well and decently we *can* do it. We think we know, in fact – it's the best way in the world—the only way to really know each other—you know – to see each other all the time – in a sort of messy way – doing things we don't like to do – and sort of getting right down at realities you know vital stuff.

Mother   I see. But why do you want to know each other so well? Why take such risks?

Granny   I think as much! It's hard enough to like anybody when they're all dressed up and on their good behavior, let alone when they're all dirty and eating bad food.

Mary   That's just it, Granny. That's the point exactly. It's a magnificent test.

Mother   But why not let well enough alone?

Mary   Because you see some of us—all of us, in fact—are in love with some of the others—and we're going to take this way of finding out—just what kind of love it is, and what we're going to do with it. See?

Granny   You take my advice and pick out the best one and stay at home with him, and wear your good clothes every day.

Mary (*going to* **Granny** *to chuck her under the chin*)   I bet you were the worst kind of a vamp, Granny.

Granny   I was a very modest maidenly girl, through and through and *through*.

Mother   Who's going with you? Who are the chaperones, I mean.

Mary   That's the point. We're not going to have any.

Mother   Oh –

Granny   What?

Mary   It would be the same old thing if we did and put the whole scheme on the blink.

Mother   But you don't mean—

Mary   Nobody would be natural. It would be the cut and dried conventional stuff and that's just what we don't want. We want to see each other as we really *are*.

Granny   You mean go way off alone—boys and girls *together*— without any older people?

Mary   Yes.

Granny   Are you stark staring crazy?

Mary   Not at all. I think it's a great idea. People don't *know* each other before they're married. That's why most marriages are merely disappointing experiments instead of lifetime mating. That's why the experimenting ought to be done *before* marriage.

Mother   We'll talk about it after while, dear.

Mary   Oh Mother—why wait to *talk*?

Granny Yes, *why*? Tell her now that it's an unheard of, immoral, *disgraceful* idea to have even come into a nice girl's head. Tell her that—this minute.

Mother Wait, Mother.

Mary Immoral? Disgraceful? Why, pray? Why?

Granny Because it outrages all the decencies. What would you do at night, I'd like to know?

Mary We'd go to bed and sleep—as decently as we do at home in our own beds.

Mother Now, now, dear.

Mary If you can't think of anything but *that* Granny, you *have* got an evil mind.

Mother Mary!

Mary We aren't going away just so we can sleep together. We could stay right at home and do that, let me tell you.

Mother Mary!

Granny (*rising in shocked excitement*) Are you going to *do* something? Don't you know *now* you must do something, or are you just going to go on sitting still?

Mother Mother, will you *please* let me—

Mary If I could just talk to Mother alone once, Granny, without you interfering, I might be able to make her understand something.

Mother Mary—be quiet! Aren't you ashamed to speak to your Grandmother like that?

Granny No, she's not. There's no shame in her. She's brazen and disrespectful and you *let* her be.

Mary She isn't *letting* me be *any*thing. I'm myself, Granny. Can't you understand that? And I'm talking about something very important to me which you don't understand at all.

Mother Mary—that will *do*, I say. Tell your grandmother you're sorry, and don't let this happen again.

Mary (*going to* **Granny** *reluctantly*) I'm sorry, Granny. I really am. I didn't mean to be disrespectful. Will you forgive me?

Granny (*bursting into tears*) No, I won't. You're an impertinent little minx, and I don't want you to speak to me.

Mother Oh, Mother dear, don't take it that way.

Mary I said I was sorry.

Granny Don't touch me! Nobody loves me. Nobody appreciates me.

Mary Please forgive me.

Granny Let me alone. You've broken my heart. (*She goes out into the hall sobbing.*)

Mother Now see what you've done.

Mary (*closing the door*) Grandmother's the limit. She really is.

Mother She's dear and sweet, and you have no business to say wild things you know will shock her.

Mary What's wild about what I said?

Mother You know as well as I do. Decent people don't *do* those things.

Mary (*throwing herself on the sofa*) Because they don't is no reason it wouldn't be a darned good idea if they did.

Mother Oh—*dearest!*

Mary If nobody ever did anything that had never been done before we'd be a sweet set of dubs. People are dull enough as it is, goodness knows—without setting that up as the law to live by.

Mother You're talking from very lofty heights. Unfortunately, we have to live in the valleys of common sense.

Mary That's the way you always get out of everything, Mother. I want to *try* things. What else is life for?

Mother You can't try things the whole world knows have nothing but danger and disaster in them.

Mary Do you mean to say I couldn't go any place with anybody and not stay *myself*—just as I am now—unless I *wanted* to be something else? And then if I wanted to why of course I *would*, and that would be my own affair anyway.

Mother Mary! Stop it. If I thought for a minute, you *meant* that stuff, I'd be terribly frightened. But you don't.

Mary Certainly I mean it. And I've just about decided that free love is the only solution to the whole business anyway.

Mother What on earth are you talking about?

Mary I don't know that I *could* live all my life with one man-however much I loved him. Of course you and Father are satisfied with each other because you've never had anything else. But you don't know *what* you might have been, Mother, if you'd lived with a lot of men. Experience—constructive experience is the only developing progressive thing in the world.

Mother There's nothing new about the relations between men and women and there's nothing true or right but the same old things that have always been true. I'm afraid you've been reading too much new stuff—trying to be clever and advanced. Don't, dear—don't.

Mary Gosh, Mother—you don't suppose anything I've read in a book cuts any ice? I'm talking about *me* myself, and how I feel and what I want. Hal and Lynn both have qualities that attract me enormously—and I want to find out if I want to marry either one of them. I wouldn't be satisfied to be happy just in the way you and Father are happy. I want something that is beautiful, and beautiful all the time.

Mother Nothing is beautiful *all* the time. If you're going on a quest for that you might as well stay at home.

Mary Mother, are you and Father really happy?

Mother (*startled*) Of course! Why on earth do you say that?

Mary Lots and lots of times I—Nothing.—

Mother What do you mean?

Mary There isn't anything really wrong, is there? You do love each other, don't you?

Mother (*evading* **Mary***'s eyes*) Don't be silly. Of course, we do. Now see here, Mary—you can't expect me to take your scheme seriously. . . .

Mary But I do. What if I must do it, Mother? What if I must to *express* myself to find myself? After all, it's my life, you know.

Mother Mary, if you'll promise me to stop thinking about this nonsense I won't tell your Father, but if you don't—I will—and he'll—I don't know *what* he will do.

Mary I do. I know every snort and gesture but that won't make any difference if I think my happiness – (**Lynn** *comes through the lower window followed by* **Hal**. **Lynn** *is the prototype of* **Robert** *Hollister* **Hal** *of* **Richard**, *seen in the prologue.*)

Lynn Hello, Mary! Hello, Mrs. Hollister!

Mary Hello, Lynn!

Mother Hello.

Hal Hello.

Mary Come in—come in. Pray do.

Hal What's the matter?

Mary I've just told Mother the scheme.

Lynn It doesn't seem to have made a hit.

Mother It's too silly to talk about. You two boys ought to be men of the world enough to make Mary realize how impossible it is—instead of putting such ideas into her head.

Mary They didn't, Mother. I put them into theirs.

Mother Then get them out. I trust you, boys, you know, and when I come back into this room I expect you both to give me your word of honor that the whole thing is off. (*She goes out—closing the door.*)

Mary Mother's difficult because she's so nice. Give me a light—somebody. (*Going to sit on the sofa and taking a cigarette. Both boys strike matches and sit – one on either side of her, lighting their own cigarettes.*)

Mary (*going on after a long puff and throwing back her head to blow the smoke—crossing her legs and folding her arms*) It's almost impossible to talk to her or get anywhere with her, because she's a perfectly happy inexperienced woman, the most dangerous kind.

Lynn Dangerous? I wouldn't exactly call your mother dangerous.

Mary She's dangerous because she's contented, and therefore not progressive—stupid.

Lynn Oh.

Hal (*slowly and importantly*) Of course – I get that.

Mary And she represents such an awful lot of women. They haven't moved an inch for ages.

Lynn Your mother's a peach, though.

Mary Of course she is – a perfect darling. I'm crazy about her. That's why this thing is so hard.

Lynn Then give it up. Hang it, I'm not so mad about it, you know.

Mary I knew you'd be the first one to back out.

Hal So, did I.

Lynn I'm not backing out.

Hal Yes, you are. Give it up, old man. It's not your gait anyway. Just drop it.

Lynn And let you stick? Not much. Don't worry about my gait. I'll keep up all right.

Mary Is the first thing that Mother says going to knock it all out of you?

Lynn No—but people are going to talk like blazes and I can't stand to have you talked about, Mary.

Mary Oh Lord, Lynn! Do we have to begin all over to convince you?

Hal You see, old man, you're not really with us. You're only going because you don't want to be left out. You don't see it as something important to the improvement of the whole question of love and marriage.

Lynn Take it from me, Max and Lettie aren't up in the clouds the way you two are – you're fooling yourselves there—*hard*.

Hal I don't agree with you. I think Mary and I have succeeded in making them see that—that—

Lynn That what?

Hal That if they haven't the courage to lead their own lives regardless of other people's moth-eaten convictions—they will never get anywhere or be any further along than their fathers and mothers.

Mary Of course, to me it's thrilling—positively thrilling. I've never done anything in my life that I like so much. It's so simple—so absolutely simple – merely to go off and live naturally and freely for two weeks—doing a thing we know in the bottom of our souls is *right*, and knowing perfectly well the whole town is going to explode with horror. Then we'll march back again with our heads well up and prove that we're finer and more intelligent people than we were before we went away. I think it's big—you know.

Lynn Y-e-s-but what if it never was understood and accepted. It would be terribly hard on you two girls.

Hal Even so—it would be worth it. They'd both be doing something great. Wreckage of the individual doesn't count in the world's work.

Lynn Not so long as the *other* fellow happens to be the wreck.

Mary Now listen. We've all reached the point where we think it's worth doing. I've even decided I *must* do it—in spite of mother. But if we're going to get away with it, we've got to do it quickly before the others back out and spill the whole business. I think we'd better go tonight—after the party. We'll all be out late—anyway—and nobody watching the time and expecting us. I'll get word to Letitia, and we can pack now and put the stuff in—in your garage, Lynn, and all start off together.

Hal Great!

Lynn No—we've got to be foxy getting out of the garage—not get together till we're out of town—then when we're out on the road, let ' er go.

Mary I can hardly wait! And now—you boys have to promise me utterly and absolutely—that you won't make love to me the whole time we're gone. It's going to be a square deal for everybody, and don't forget this—I may not want to marry either one of you—and you may not want to marry me after all. You *do* understand—don't you?

Hal *I* do. Certainly. You're magnificent, Mary. If we haven't enough of your spirit in us to rise to this we're rotters. If you *do* find that Lynn's the one to make you happy I shall understand and if I can't take you by the hand, old man, and wish you luck—I shall be horribly disappointed in myself.

Lynn And if the same thing happens to *me*, I hope I'll have the guts to clear out and not stop to wish anything on anybody.

Mary (*getting up and standing between them*) You're splendid both of you. Shake. (*The boys clasp hands and she puts hers over theirs.*) Skip now before Mother comes back—and avoid the issue. Bye-bye—see you tonight. (*The boys go.* **Mary** *goes to the hall door-about to open it.* **Hal** *comes back.*)

Hal (*in a whisper*) Mary!

Mary Oh!—I thought you'd gone.

Hal Just a minute.

Mary What do you want? (*They go to the sofa and sit.* **Mary** *turns on the light in the lamp which is behind the sofa—the rest of the room is in shadow – with the same effect as in the scenes in the prologue.*)

Hal I just want to say this, dear—that whatever happens—I'll be with you and you can count on me and my love – and above all on my *friendship*.

Mary I know I can, old dear. I know that and it gives me such a wonderful feeling of security—your understanding, I mean.

Hal That's what I wanted to be sure of. That you *do* feel that.

Mary Oh I do—I do.

Hal Of course I know your soul belongs to *me*, Mary—whatever happens. We may get lost from each other, and confused and entangled—but *that* will remain through eternity—that our souls have found each other and understood.

Mary Yes, I know dear. I know.

Hal And I'm sure of *you*—*now* in reality. No love as great as mine could fail to find its completion. *You* will be sure too. I'm not afraid. I love you, Mary. I love you as no man ever loved before.

Mary If I were sure of that!

Hal You *will* be. Will you kiss me, Mary, as a consecration to our ideal?

Mary Of course. (*She kisses him with a very honest and unfeeling smack on the lips.*)

Hal (*rising with a sigh*) That will live through eternity. (*He goes.* **Mary** *goes to the door again.* **Lynn** *comes to the other window.*)

Lynn Mary!

Mary Oh—I thought you'd gone.

Lynn (*coming in*) I waited. I knew Hal would come back to say something. Just a minute, Mary. Come here. (*They sit on the sofa.*) I came back to say this—that if I wasn't *dead sure* I'm going to get you, I wouldn't go a *step* on this tom fool expedition.

Mary Now –

Lynn Listen! I'm going to take care of you and pull this thing off *right*, and you're going to come back engaged to *me*.

Mary Now if you're going with any fixed ideas you can't go at all. It's going to be growth and freedom.

Lynn I don't need to grow. I *know* what I want. I love you.

Mary But that isn't enough. You don't know that it will last forever.

Lynn Of *course* it will. When people love the way *I* do, it's *got* to last. You *do* love me, don't you?

Mary Yes – I do—in a way—very, very much. But not in *all* ways. It isn't the great love that embraces everything—that envelops and sweeps one away—so there's no doubt about anything.

Lynn Tell me how much you do love me and I'll take a chance on the rest.

Mary I think – I *think* I'd rather you were the father of my children than any man I ever saw.

Lynn Well then what difference does anything else make?

Mary But that isn't everything.

Lynn What else *is* there?

Mary Beautiful—mystic—far away things. Please go. I'm afraid Mother will come and spoil everything.

Lynn (*catching her hand*) Kiss me.

Mary No!

Lynn Why not?

Mary I don't want to.

Lynn Well if I've got to act like a dead man for two weeks—you might kiss me once—now.

Mary No.

Lynn (*taking her by the arms*) You've *got* to!

Mary If you do I'll hate you.

Lynn Did you kiss Hal?

Mary None of your business.

Lynn But *did* you!

Mary (*pulling away from him*) Do you want Mother to catch you here? Don't! I'll run around the house and get upstairs.

She darts out the upper window and Lynn the lower. After a moment **Mother** *opens the hall door and comes in—turning on the lights. She hesitates, is about to go back into the hall when* **Bobby** *comes in quickly through the lower window.*

Bobby Mother—have you got seventeen dollars? I need it quick.

Mother No. Why?

Bobby   I ran into a fellow and smashed his fender. He'll settle for that and keep quiet and I can get 'em at the garage to fix our car tonight—if you'll keep Dad from wanting it.

Mother   Oh Bobby—*again*! This is awful.

Bobby   It's hell. Have you got the seventeen?

Mother   I don't know. I don't think so.

Bobby   Go see—please, Ma, and it'll be all right. The fellow's waitin' ' round the corner.

Mother   But I don't believe—

Father (*coming in through the window*)   Bobby, a fellow out at the gate asked me if you'd just come in here. What does he want?

Robert *Hollister is fifty—a solid successful man with a very agreeable manner when he is agreeable, and a man who, not so successful and sure, might have been a very delightful person.*

Bobby   Oh—he—just—He's got a car out there he wants to show me.

Father   Indeed! That will be profitable to him.

Bobby   Well—I guess I can *look* at it—can't I?

Father (*going to the desk, where he sits turning on the light and opening his paper*)   I guess you can. Why don't you go out and look? You can't see it in here, can you?

Bobby   I'm going. (*He looks expressively at* **Mother** *and she starts to the door as* **Granny** *comes in.*)

Granny (*her pride and her feathers still somewhat ruffled*)   Is that child in here? Because if she is, I won't come in a step.

Father   What's the matter with you, Granny?

Granny (*sitting on the sofa*)   A good deal. I want to talk to you, Robert.

Mother   A—don't talk to him now, Mother.

Granny   Why not? Can't I even *talk* when I want to?

Bobby   Mother! Ahem! (**Mother** *looks at* **Bobby** *who nods frantically for her to go.*)

Mother   Robert's tired now. Wait till after dinner.

Father   Let's get it over with now—whatever it is. I'd like to rest after dinner. I want a long ride. Bobby, you get the car out and have it here so I won't lose any time. We'll all go for a long ride in the country.

Bobby   Yes, Father.

Mother   Oh—that's too bad, Robert.

Father   What's too bad?

Mother   I promised the car to someone else this evening.

Father   You did? And what in the name of common sense did you do that for when you know it's the only recreation I have? The only way I can cool off and get a good night's sleep.

Mother   But it's for a poor sick woman who has *no* way of getting out.

Father   She *hasn't*? Well, I haven't either. I'd be a poor sick man if I didn't have *some* little outing. You don't seem to have thought of that. Is the poor sick woman going to drive my car herself?

Mother   No—Bobby's going to take her.

Father   Then take her for half an hour, Bobby, and be back here sharp—understand?

Bobby   Yes, Father. (**Mother** *starts to the door again.* **Granny** *snivels.*)

Father   Now, Granny, what is it? Out with it.

Granny   She—

Mother   Bobby, bring me a handkerchief out of my top bureau drawer—in the box in the right-hand corner. You know, you can get it. (**Bobby** *suddenly understanding starts to the hall door.*)

Father   How about that fellow waiting out there?

Bobby   I'll see him as soon as I get Mother's handkerchief.

Father (*to* **Granny**)   Has Mary been doing something to upset you again?

Granny   She–

Mother   Oh, she didn't mean to, Mother. She didn't mean to hurt your feelings.

Granny   Oh, never mind my feelings. I'm used to that. I think Robert ought to know things and I think it's my duty to tell him. You're so slack yourself. Mary's very slack, Robert.

Father   What have you been slack about now, Mary?

Mother   Mother doesn't realize that girls can't be just the way they were when she was a girl.

Granny   Fiddlesticks! Right and wrong haven't changed a bit and no amount of angling and twisting and dodging can get away from facts.

Father   Well—well—what are the facts in this case? Come to the point.

Granny   Mary's got—

Mother   Please, don't talk about it *now*. I'll tell Father at the right time.

Granny   The right time! The right time is *now* this minute, before any harm's done. Putting things off is your worst—

Father   For heaven's sake, what *is* it? (*They both start to talk.*) Now don't both talk at once. Christopher! It's enough to be in court all day without hearing cases all night, too. What is it? Now you first, Mary. Wait, Mother.

Granny   Oh yes, I can wait. I'm used to that.

Mother   It's only a very foolish idea Mary has in her head, and I know I can get it out if I go at it in the right way—without making a row about it. I'm used to that.

Granny   That's what you always say, Mary,—and it don't very often succeed, so far as I can see. This time it's too serious to fool with. It's got to be nipped in the bud.

Father   There's a good deal in what your mother says, you know, Mary. You *are* pretty soft and undecided. That's your besetting sin.

Mother   If anybody's *hard* with her now it *will* be serious. It's got to be handled very carefully. She believes she's right with all her—

Granny   Shucks! She doesn't anything of the kind. It's a dangerous—

Mother   That's why we must avoid the danger and—

Father   Now see here Mary. Tell me what it is and I'll settle it without any squeamish nonsense. What danger is she in?

Granny   That's the way to talk, Robert. I knew you'd settle it. You tell him the truth Mary, or I will.

Father (*looking at* **Mother**)   Well—

Mother   It's already settled.

Father   Un?

Mother   It's all right. She won't do it.

Father   Won't do what?

Granny   How do you know she won't?

Mother   Because I know. I trust her.

Mary (*coming in quickly from the hall*)   Mother, will you hook me, please? (*She wears a charming evening gown—very simple. Her lovely young body is free and somewhat exposed. An evening cape is thrown over her arm.*)

Mary   Hello, Father.

Father   Hello, daughter.

Mary   I got all my bills straight, Dad—and I haven't overdrawn my allowance a penny for three months. Pretty good—un?

Father Yes, I must say you do pretty well in that line. You've got a good mind if you'd just use it—instead of throwing it away.

Mary What makes you think I'm throwing it away?

Father I wouldn't have to *think* much to see that.

Mary I think you have a perfectly corking mind, Father—but you don't always use it the way I think you ought to.

Father And what's this I hear about some new idea you have in your head?

Mother Robert-*please*! (**Father** *shrugs his shoulders and goes back to his paper.*)

Mary Mother, your hands are shaking. Can't you find the hooks?

Granny I don't know why she couldn't. There's nothing to the whole dress *but* the hooks.

Mary Are you still cross at me, Granny? I'm awfully sorry. I'll be good.

Granny I don't know how you can expect to be good in that dress.

Mary What's the matter with this dress? It's a love. Isn't it, Mother?

Mother It's very pretty, dear.

Granny Yes, you uphold her in her nakedness, instead of making her put on clothes enough.

Mary Oh Granny!

Granny I'll wager you haven't got a sign of a petticoat on.

Mary Of course, I haven't.

Father (*looking over his paper*)   What's the reason you haven't?

Mary Heavens—nobody wears a petticoat, Father.

Granny I do. Look at her. She might just as well be stark naked for all the good her clothes are doing her.

Mary You needn't talk, Granny. I think it's much better to show my back than the way you used to show your front. Thanks, dearest. (*As her mother holds the cape.*)

(*A whistle is heard from outside.*) That's Lynn. Good night, everybody. Good night, Granny. (*Kissing* **Granny**'*s cheek.*) Good night, Dad. (*Kissing the top of his head.*) Good night, Mother dear. (*Putting her arms around her mother.*)

Father Where are you going?

Mary To Lettie's for dinner and a dance at the club afterwards.

Father What time will you be in?

Mary Why—I don't know.

Father I don't want it to be so late as it was last night, mind you. Understand?

Mary   Yes Father.

Father   And listen to me—if you've got any *new* kind of daredevil recklessness in your head, you get it out or you'll reckon with me. Understand?

Mary   Yes Father.

Granny   Aren't you going to put anything over your head?

Mary   Goodness no, Granny. It's roasting.

Granny   Mary, are you going to let her go out in the night air without putting anything on her head?

Mary   Oh—

Father   Put something over your head. Do you hear?

Mary   I haven't anything to *put*.

Mother (*snatching up the scarf* **Granny** *was knitting*)   Here, dear.

Granny   My fascinator! You'll ravel it all out.

Mother   I'll fasten it, Mother. It won't hurt it a bit. Good night, dear.

Granny   How do you know she won't take it off the minute she's out of sight?

Mother (*holding* **Mary**)   Because I trust her—always—anywhere.

Mary   Good night, Mother dear. You are a darling. (**Mary** *starts out. She comes back impulsively throwing her arms about her mother.*)

Mother   What is it, dearest?

Mary   Nothing. Good night. (*She kisses her mother and goes out quickly.* **Bobby** *has come back through the upper window during this scene and sits sprawling in a chair.*)

Granny   Where's your mother's handkerchief, Bobby?

Bobby   Oh—I forgot. I went out to see the fella.

Granny   I'll wager it wasn't a handkerchief she sent you for at all. I expect it was something else—something you ought not to have.

Father   What's that? (**Mother** *moves a chair up to the desk and sits with her back to* **Father** *as she reads.*)

Granny   I say I expect—

Father   I heard what you said. What have you been doing, Bobby?

Bobby   Nothing.

Father   What about the fellow's car? What did you think of it?

Bobby   Oh—I didn't think much of it.

Father (*still looking over the paper*) I got the repair bills today on *my* car and by Jove if they aren't cut in two this next month, I'll sell the damn thing. I never saw anything like it.

Bobby Well, I don't make the bills, Father.

Father Oh no. The car just walks out and gets itself out of commission. I'll sell it I tell you. I'm not made of money, you know. All the bills were terrific this month, Mary. Something's got to be done.

Granny Well, I don't run up the bills. I'm a *very* little eater if you mean *me*, Robert.

Father I don't mean anybody. But you might control things, Mary, and keep them within bounds.

Mary Oh, I do try to, Robert—I do.

Granny You're not as careful a housekeeper as I was, Mary.

Mother No—and eggs aren't ten cents a dozen now, either.

Father We've got to cut down. That's all there is about it.

Bobby That's what you always say the first day of the month, Dad.

Father The whole country's going to collapse if we don't look out—with this reckless extravagance. Everybody's living beyond their income—everybody. Same wild looseness there is in every other direction. There's a general lowering of standards and ideals that is undermining society and civilization.

Granny That's just what I was saying to Mary this afternoon. She don't see it. She don't see it creeping into her own children.

Father Creeping in—striding in, you mean.

Granny Yes, that's it.

Mother You can't expect your own children to be different from other people's, you know.

Father I do expect it, by Jove. If I had my way they would be. If I had my way they'd all be at home this evening.

Granny That's what I say. It certainly is a lovely, *lovely happy* home, and they ought all to be in it.

Nora (*a neat maid-opening the hall door*) Dinner is served.

Mother There's dinner and you two aren't ready. Run along, Bobby and get ready for dinner—and *hurry*. Why *will* you two *always* wait till dinner is on the table before you move? Hurry, Bobby, *hurry*. (**Bobby** *rises and shambles out.*) Come Robert.

Father It might wait a little for me.

Mother You simply *cannot* have decent food and keep it waiting. You've done it all your life and it's terribly irritating.

Father (*rising reluctantly*)   I have to rush all day. I would like peace and relaxation at home.

Mother   Here's your hat, Robert.

Father (*as he goes into the hall*)   I don't want it.

Granny (*trotting after him*)   We're going to have chicken tonight, and I declare it is a shame we aren't all here to eat it. I do believe in a family all being 'round the table together when night comes. (**Mother** *ends the procession-going out with* **Father***'s hat as.*)

THE CURTAIN FALLS

Act Two

Scene I

SCENE: *The scene is dark, showing a motor, a roadster, facing the audience. The whir of the motor is heard.* **Lynn**, **Mary**, *and* **Hal** *are in the car.* **Lynn** *is driving.* **Mary** *sits next to him and* **Hal** *beside her.*

Mary   She's only going forty. Step on her Lynn.

Lynn   Are Max and Lettie right behind us?

Hal   Yes, they're sticking.

Mary   Oh, isn't it wonderful! I never was so happy in my life!

Lynn   We're ten miles out now. Ought to do it in three hours.

Mary   Easy! Isn't it wonderful driving at night when nobody gets in the way!

Hal   Everything's wonderful when nobody gets in the way.

Mary   Now she's sixty! Gosh, isn't it great!

Hal   You can't keep this up, Lynn.

Lynn   What's the reason I can't? She's just beginning.

Hal   For God's sake, don't stop or turn. They're right behind us.

Mary   I hope you're not afraid, Hal.

Hal   Of course I'm not. But there is a limit, you know.

Lynn (*bending over the wheel*)   No there isn't! Gee, it feels good to let her out!

Mary   It's marvelous! I never was so alive before. Isn't it glorious to know nothing can stop us! We're free! I feel as if we were part of the wind and sky. I think we're going right on up, through the sky, into the stars.

Hal   Yes, we may do that sooner than you think. For Heaven's sake, let up a little, Lynn. You've lost your head.

Lynn   Not a bit! She's a good little wagon. This is easy for 'er.

Mary   Don't spoil it, Hal. This is the way everything always ought to be—going with all we've got and nobody saying "*don't*." Oh, aren't you glad we did it? Don't you know now we're right, Lynn?

Lynn   *This* part of it's all right.

Hal   Of course we're right. But let's go slow enough to enjoy it.

Mary   But, Hal, I thought this was what you wanted, moving swiftly, alone, leaving the world behind. The world's asleep and we're running away from it out into the unknown.

Hal   This isn't spiritual exaltation. This is just reckless foolhardiness. Not what *I* came for.

Lynn   Do you want us to let you out?

Hal   Don't be funny.

Mary   Buck up, Hal. You're *free*! For the first time in your life.

Hal   There goes my hat!

Mary   Never mind. What's a hat?

Hal   You're doing everything you can to queer the whole idea.

Lynn   I'm taking you *to* the idea as fast as I can. Do you want to go back and get your hat?

Mary   Shut up, boys! This is glorious! Doesn't everything we've left seem a thousand times worse and more ordinary and piffling than it ever did before? Oh, there's a rabbit ! Don't hit him, Lynn. Oooo! (*Screaming and hiding her face against* **Hal**.)

Lynn   Look out, boy! Whew! Never touched him.

Hal   Stop it , Lynn! I can't stand it!

Lynn   Nothing to be afraid of.

Mary   He can't help it. Shut your eyes, Hal, and put your head on my shoulder.

Lynn   Here, here, none of that. Where's your nerve, Hal?

Mary   He's got a great deal more nerve about some things than you have. Gee, if you were both mixed up together into one man you'd be pretty good. See the stars. We *are* going up—up—right into them. This is life! Go on, Lynn! Step on her!

Lynn *bends lower over the wheel with a set face.* **Hal** *is holding on, sick with fear.* **Mary** *sits between them, her head thrown back, ecstatically happy.*

CURTAIN

Act Two

Scene II

TIME: *4 o'clock the next morning.*

PLACE: *The living room again.*

AT CURTAIN : *The light of early morning comes through the windows. After a moment five figures are seen crossing the upper window outside. They come to the lower window. Hal opens it cautiously and comes in quickly, carrying Mary's suitcase which he puts on the floor above the chair at left C. Lynn carries Mary in. Letitia and Max follow. Letitia is a pretty girl of the flapper type. She wears Max's topcoat over her evening gown and his cap on her bobbed hair. Max is a rather flamboyant and good-looking youth. The three boys are in evening clothes.*

Hal Put her over here, Lynn. (**Lynn** *puts the limp* **Mary** *in the armchair at the left. The others come close, bending over her.*)

Letitia (*kneeling beside* **Mary**) How are you now, honey?

Hal Don't try to talk, Mary. How do you feel?

Letitia Thank goodness we got her home! I never was so frightened in my life. I thought you were going to die, Peaches.

Hal How is the pain now, dear? Just as bad?

Lynn Mary, I'm going to call a doctor.

Mary No!

Lynn Then I'm going to call your mother.

Mary No!

Letitia Yes, we will. We must, honey. It's perfectly awful to see you like this.

Mary No!

Lynn Then how *is* the pain?

Mary (*suddenly sitting up*) There never was a pain.

The Others What?

Mary I didn't have a bit.

The Others What?

Letitia She's out of her head. Don't you know me, lamb? It's Tish.

Mary I wanted to get you home. I knew I must do something desperate, so I had appendicitis.

Letitia You wanted to get me *home*?

Mary Yes.

Letitia After raising heaven and earth to get me to go? Oh, she *is* out of her head.

Hal No, she isn't. She's arrived at something important. Speak to us freely, Mary. We must be honest or it's all futile.

Max She needs a drink.

Lynn Shut up, Max. What do you mean, Mary?

Mary Sit down just a minute and I'll tell you. Ssh!

Letitia Oh don't push me. (*There is a general commotion.*)

Mary Do be quiet. Don't wake anybody up – for heaven's sake. I suddenly knew I'd been all wrong – that the only thing to do was to get you back.

Letitia Do you mean it was all a joke?

Lynn Ssh!

Letitia Did you never intend to—

Mary No, no—no! Listen! Sit down, all of you – please.

Letitia Nobody wants to sit down.

Hal (*sitting on the floor near* **Mary**) Yes, we do. Yes, we do. Don't be so emotional, Letitia. You have no mental poise at all.

Letitia No, and I don't want any. I'm sick of trying to act like a highbrow. I'm not one. I'm a human being.

Hal Well, you might control your human feelings long enough to see what Mary's mental attitude is now. This reaction is very important.

Max (*lying on the floor in front of the others*) What the devil's it all about, anyway?

Lynn Well, listen—listen, and you may find out.

Letitia We listened enough while you were working us up to *do* it, Mary. I don't want to listen while you *un*work us again.

Max Come on, sweetie. Sit down. Don't be peevish!

Letitia I think it's just too awful to come home in this perfectly flat way. (*Sitting with a flop.*)

Hal Wait, Lettie, till you find out how it is. This may be the beginning of something greater. I'm sure it is, Mary.

Max Stop chewing the rag, Lettie.

Lynn Oh for heaven's sake, be quiet. Go on, Mary.

Letitia Yes, do. We're all sitting at your feet as usual—waiting for you to tell us why you changed your mind.

Mary   I *didn't* change my mind. It was something much bigger than that.

Max   Must have been *colossal* to make you turn turtle like this. (*They are all sitting on the floor in a circle about* **Mary**. *Each has lighted a cigarette.*)

Mary   The whole world and life and what it means suddenly flashed before me, and—

Letitia   I thought that flashed before you long ago. I thought that was why we—

Lynn   Sh!

Hal   Wait, Lettie, wait.

Mary   I knew that we were wrong. destroying something—hurting something.

Lynn   You bet we were! I'm darned thankful we're back. We're well out of a nasty mess, let me tell you.

Mary   Oh, *you* don't understand, Lynn. It isn't that at all. I mean that we were absolutely right in what we believed but we've got to be big enough not to hurt other people with it.

Hal   Oh, Mary that is so weak.

Mary   I never *wanted* to do anything so much in my life, but I just suddenly saw it the way Mother and Father would—and knew how it would seem to them.

Max   You knew that in the first place, didn't you?

Mary   No—not actually—in the real way. None of us thought of it from their side.

Hal   Oh Mary, their side doesn't count. We know we're thinking way beyond the general level of thought and if we don't act on it we're not advancing. (*He hits* **Letitia** *'s nose with a gesture.*)

Letitia   Oh, Hal, my nose! (*There is general noise and confusion.* **Mary** *hushes them.*)

Lynn   I don't see any use advancing so far that everybody thinks you're a *lunatic*.

Mary   But because we *do* see further than other people—we must be a— magnanimous. They can't help it—you know—these deep prejudices, and after all— they *are* our parents.

Hal   Personally, I think parents are much overrated—and given entirely too much importance in the general scheme. Though I believe if my father had lived he would have been a great man.

Lynn   I suppose *you're* very much like him.

Hal   They say so. (*The others laugh.*) We're the next generation and the *next generation must go on*. We know that marriage *as is* – is a failure—a gigantic human failure—and we also know that it's getting worse.

Max   You don't have to do much profound thinking to know that. Look at our own crowd. Every damned one of ' em divorced or ought to be. What's the use of being married at all?

Letitia Yes—love—yes—but we've said all that long ago and often. The discussion in hand at the moment is – was it a mistake for Mary to bring us back or not?

Mary The point is—we have no right to make our parents suffer.

Letitia Suffer! Mother does anything *she* pleases—regardless of me. She's been married twice now and it isn't at all impossible that she will be again. She won't hesitate to rip things up – in spite of the fact that I've just got used to calling this one Father, and just got so—I sort of can stand him. I don't see what I owe to them—and anyway, I don't think they'd suffer a darned bit no matter what became of me.

Hal My mother is entirely sympathetic with our idea—of course. She knows Father would have left her sometime without a moment's notice, if he had lived. He wouldn't have vulgarized it with a quarrel or a divorce. *He* was *way* in advance of his time.

Max My father and mother are so old school—it would do them good to get a shock. If I want to try out Lettie in a *new* way—it's none of their business.

Letitia Try *me* out? I'm trying *you* out. Don't forget that, my lamb.

Max (*kissing her hand*) Excuse me darling.

Hal If we never did anything except what our parents want us to do the world wouldn't move much.

Mary Yes, but we've got to begin all over again and *make* them understand, and *tell* them what we're going to do. It was the sneaking away I couldn't stand.

Letitia (*getting up*) You certainly have put me in a sweet hole. I wrote a note and stuck it on Mother's pin cushion. I'm going to feel clever when they find me in bed in the morning in the same old way.

Mary Oh Lettie, I *am* so sorry.

Letitia Oh don't mind me. Come on, Max. I might as well marry you *first*. Why not? You've got more money than anybody I know. (*Going up toward the window dragging her coat after her.*)

Mary Oh Tish, don't give up like that. We aren't through yet—we're just beginning.

Letitia I'm afraid you'll have a hard time inflating me again, Mary. I feel as though I had started off on wings and come back in a wheelbarrow. Are you coming or staying, Max?

Max You bet I'm coming. (*He hurries to the window.*) So long! This is all right you know. Good luck, fellers—I've got *my* girl. (*He goes after Letitia.*)

Lynn Of course it's all right. It's turned out the best thing in the world. And you were a brick – a brick, Mary, to do it.

Mary It isn't all right. I've made it worse than ever—and nobody really understands what I meant at all.

Lynn *I* do.

Hal Have I ever misunderstood you, Mary? But I do think you were weak, dear girl. I do think you let sentiment—pure sentiment—run away with you—after you've been so strong and done such good—*individual* thinking.

Lynn Oh, cool off and let's get down to solid rock.

Hal Oh yes, solid rock! That's what we're all chained to. I don't expect you to feel this as I do, Lynn. You couldn't.

Lynn I *hope* not.

Hal I'm not going to pretend that I'm not disappointed in you, Mary. But this isn't the end. You *will* do it yet—and in a still wider, fuller way. Anybody who's got the idealism you have, can't go back to the sordid conventional old rut.

Lynn Start the car, old man, I'll be right out.

Hal Thanks. I'll walk home.

Mary Hal—you're not angry with me?

Hal No—not angry, but hurt and horribly—*horribly* disappointed. You were thinking with distinction and now you've gone back to the ordinary level of the average girl. Of course, I'm disappointed. (*He goes out.*)

Lynn It's turned out the best thing in the world. I love you more than ever, Mary. And you love me—don't you, dear?

Mary Don't ask me now—please. I'm just beginning to find out something.

Lynn You needn't expect me to believe for a minute that you hauled us off on this wild goose chase and then hauled us back again, because you got afraid of public opinion, and hurting people—and that stuff.

Mary You don't—

Lynn You say you had a sudden flash—well, it must have flashed on you which *one of us* you wanted to marry, and God knows it couldn't have been Hal—I give you credit for that—so, in all modesty, it must have been me.

Mary I can't talk about it now. I want to think. The thing that brought me back is more important than *that* just now.

Lynn Just what *did* bring you back? Tell me.

Mary I will try to make you understand – sometime.

Lynn I'll stop on my way downtown in the morning.

Mary Then hurry. I want to lock the window.

Lynn Well tell me this. Even if you haven't found out yet, you want *me*—aren't you *dead sure* you don't want Hal?

Mary Please go.

Lynn But I want *you* and I want you harder than ever. Talk about going up into the stars! I went up and I'm still there and I'm going to stay. When you sat there close to me—making me go faster—when your hair blew in my face—I didn't care whether we smashed into eternity or not. We were together—alone.

Mary We weren't. Hal was there.

Lynn Same thing. You weren't the only one who got a flash of what it all means. It was only you and me and space—that was *life*, all right—and I'm going to keep on living it—*up there*—in the stars.

Mary But we can't. It's too high.

Lynn Not with *you*.

Mary We had to come down.

Lynn Well, what of it! When I think what you went out to find—and that you even let me go with you to try to find it—I—my head swims. I can't say it, Mary—but I *know* what you want—because I've found it. I couldn't wish anything more wonderful for you than for you to love someone the way I love you.

Mary Oh Lynn! I wanted to go on with you for I wanted to push Hal out of the way and go on and on—and never stop—with *you*.

Lynn Mary!

Mary I wanted to get inside your coat—close to you—away from everything else in the world.

Lynn And that's right where you're going to stay.

Mary And then I got afraid—of myself—of you —of everything.

Lynn Dear!

Mary And then I wanted to come home—and now I don't know what I want. We've lost that wild sweet something. It's gone and I'm afraid it will never come back.

Lynn You wanted to come home because you knew that you loved me. All that wild stuff's over. We don't need it. I love you, and I'm coming over the first thing in the morning, to tell your father and mother.

Mary Oh-I s'pose you might as well. There's nothing else to do.

Lynn What's the matter dear? Aren't you happy?

Mary I was—out there.

Lynn And you will be here. We've got the star dust and we're going to hold on to it—tight.

Mary Do you think we can?

Lynn Certainly we can—nothing as great as this can get away from us.

Mary We mustn't let it, Lynn—we mustn't let it. Go now—please. (*He holds her a moment—kisses her—and goes out quickly.* **Mary** *fastens the window—starts to the hall door and sees* **Bobby** *asleep on the couch.*) Bobby, what are you doing there? (*She goes to the couch and shakes him.*) Bobby! Wake up. I bet you're just pretending to be asleep. I'll bet you heard everything. Bobby—*get up!*

Bobby Un?

Mary What are you doing down here this time of night?

Bobby (*half waking*) I came down to unlock the window for you—and I want to give you a tip.

Mary What about?

Bobby They're on the war path. You've done it once too often. What the devil do you mean staying out so late? A girl can't get away with stuff like that—chasing 'round all night.

Mary Oh a girl—a girl! What's the reason I can't come in when I please? (*Sitting on the couch beside* **Bobby**.)

Bobby Because you *can't*. Dad's foaming at the mouth. Gramma told him about your dope for goin' campin'.

Mary She didn't!

Bobby She did.

Mary If Grandma could only hold her tongue *once* in a while!

Bobby I wish she'd let me hold it for her once in a while. I'd pull it out.

Mary What did Father say?

Bobby He's going to send you away.

Mary What? Where?

Bobby Oh—just away. (*Waving his arm.*) Anywhere out of this pernicious town with its pernicious influences.

Mary Lordie, doesn't it make you tired?

Bobby You were a chump if you thought you could get away with that. You never would have had the nerve to do it anyway.

Mary We *did* it. We were there at the place where we were going to stay.

Bobby When?

Mary Tonight. We went sixty miles an hour some of the time. It was marvelous.

Bobby You're a queer nut, Mary. What in "h" did you get yourself into that kind of a—

Mary Because I'm *tired* of doing just what everybody else does because they think anything different is wrong. I came back for Mother and Father's sake—but if they're going to act up about it, I wish I'd *stayed*.

Bobby Well, gosh—you can't blame them much. Your rep won't be worth two cents if it gets out. Dad hit the ceiling so hard he hasn't come down yet. Honest, Mary, he is going to do something. Don't let 'em know you *did* go. He'll sizzle you. You'll have to dope up some reason why you stayed out all night.

Mary I *won't*. Why should I? The way Mother and Father *make* you lie is sickening. Why can't they let me alone? I don't say anything to them about the things *they* do.

Bobby Wouldn't you *like* to, though?

Mary *Wouldn't* I? Just to let go and tell 'em a few things.

Bobby I'd like to shoot a few at Dad—square in the eye—what I like about him and what I don't.

Mary Exactly.

Bobby If I could just once let him know that I'm *on* to him I could listen to his favorite remarks about my character with more equanimity.

Mary I know. *We're* always wrong. They *never* are.

Bobby And the worst of it is you can't tell 'em.

Mary Tell? You might as well try to tell God He's wrong.

Bobby If Dad didn't take it as a matter of religion that I ought to give him the paper! If once in a while, he'd say, "Here, Bob, you take it" —I'd be crazy about giving it to him.

Mary Of course. And if I could only *talk* to Mother. I did try. I did try to make her see. She doesn't know at all what I want and what I think and feel. I know a great deal more about life and what's going on this minute than she does. They've never done anything thrilling or had any fun themselves and they don't expect anybody else to.

Bobby (*with a chuckle*) Oh I don't know. They must have been pretty devilish—buggy-ridin' Sunday afternoons.

Mary Yes—looking for wildflowers. Mother never had any beau but Father, I s'pose, and she just married him and settled down and there you are. Anything *I* do is wrong because *they* haven't done it. (*Giving* **Bobby** *a poke to make him move over and sitting closer to him.*) Listen, Bobby. I came back for *them*. I wanted to do this thing more than I ever wanted anything in my life—but just as I was the happiest and the surest I heard Mother say—" I trust you—always—anywhere" —and she stayed right there with me—nearer than she's ever been before and I—well—I came back.

Bobby Darn good job you did too. I could have told you before you started your idea was bunk.

Mary Oh of course it all seems silly to you. You aren't old enough to know what it means.

Bobby Slush! I'm eighteen—you're only twenty.

Mary Yes, but those two years make all the difference in the world. –

Bobby Ho—o—Don't you fool yourself—I know a thing or two. Those fellows are big chumps if they were goin' off to let you size them up like that and take your choice.

Mary Well—anyway—here I am—back—as Lettie says—in the same old flat way. You see—I began to think about Mother and Father somehow. They're narrow and old- fashioned, but they're *good*.

Bobby Yea—they're all right—even if they do—scrap sometimes.

Mary Sometimes I'm sort of worried about them.

Bobby I know. Sometimes it's rotten.

Mary But home and the family and you and me are the most important things in the world to them. After all we're awfully lucky to have such parents. Lots of them are running around on the loose, you know.

Bobby You bet your sweet life they are!

Mary And a really, truly home like ours *is* wonderful—and I just couldn't do anything to hurt it. They're good and they love us, and they *do* love each other. I guess I *will* just sneak upstairs and tell one more lie to keep them happy. Don't you ever really peep that I really *did* go. Don't—for their sakes, old man.

Bobby I'm with you. Go to it, Sis. (*She takes up her suitcase.*) St! They're coming!—Beat it ! (**Mary** *starts to the hall door.*) Look out! You can't do that.—You're caught. (**Mary** *drops the suitcase.* **Bobby** *turns out the light and rolls under the sofa.* **Mother** *comes in quickly from the hall—runs to the lower window and peers out. She wears a negligee—her hair disordered.*)

Father (*From the hall*) Are they there?

Mother No.

Father (*coming in – in bath robe and slippers*) I told you so. He's gone after her then. They're in cahoots. He knew all the time where she was.

Mother I hope so.

Father You do? You hope he lied to me steadily for hours?

Mother Yes—if he knew where she is.

Father (*he paces about restlessly irritable with apprehension*) There you are. No wonder they lie.

Mother They don't lie.

Father   They don't lie—don't they?

Mother   No, they don't.

Father   No they don't. They just go on deceiving you and getting away with it because you shut your eyes to it.

Mother   You wouldn't telephone any place again, would you?

Father   What good would that do? We've tried every place. Lettie's gone. Those good-for-nothing boys are gone. Of course that's what it means. She's bolted,—right under your nose.

Mother   I won't believe it. She *couldn't*. She wouldn't do it without telling me.

Father   Telling you? She *did* tell you.

Mother   She only said she was *thinking* about it. She was honest enough to tell me that—and I could have persuaded—

Father   Honest your foot! She's fooled you—deceived you. She does all the time.

Mother   (*coming away from the window*)   Do you think Bobby *has* gone after her?

Father   He must have. He must have gone . . . to warn her that I know and that I'm going to punish her. I think he's gone to tell her that and bring her back.

Mother   Listen! I thought the 'phone was going to ring.

Father   I tell you I'm going to change things. I'm through. I won't be made a fool of by my own children. What's the matter with 'em? Where do they get it anyway? I sometimes think it's something in *you* they get their looseness from, Mary.

Mother   I expect it is.

Father   (*his voice rising*)   I don't believe you *try*. You're not firm enough. If you'd kept *at* it—day in and day out, since they were born—impressing the principles of—

Mother   Don't yell so! I'm not deaf. You'll raise the neighbors.

Father   I'll raise the roof. I'll raise heaven and earth. I won't *have* such children. What *do* you teach them—anyway?

Mother   (*going back to the window*)   I don't teach them anything. What difference does it make? I want to *know where she is*.

Father   She's *gone*. That's what she is. She's disgraced us.

Mother   I don't believe it.

Father   No—you never face facts. That's what's put us where we are. She's *gone off just the way she told you she was going to*.

Mother   Try to get Lettie's house once more.

Father   No use getting that maid out of bed again. She's told us *fifteen times now* there's nobody at home. Of course that blatherskite of a Lettie—has chosen a time to go off when her mother and father are away—but yours did it right before your eyes.

Mother (*going back to her chair again*)   Don't keep on saying that. *Do* something.

Father   Why didn't *you* do something at the right time? Why in the name of heaven haven't you controlled her?

Mother   Because *I don't know how.*

Father   Why don't you know how? It's your job. Why can't you run your house and your children as well as I run my office? Good Lord, she's only a young girl. You're more than twice her age. Why can't you manage her?

Mother   You're more than *three* times Bobby's age. Why don't you manage him?

Father   I do.

Mother   No, you don't.

Father   Besides, he's a boy. He's got to have experience. It wouldn't hurt him to go off on a spurt like this.

Mother   It would. It would. I couldn't *bear* it.

Father   You undermine everything I say to him anyway-with your softness. *I* don't know what's the matter. It's not *my* fault. What in the name of heaven *is* the matter? Why have we *got* such rotten children? (*He sinks into a chair-putting his head in his hands.*)

Mother (*after a pause*)   We don't know what kind of children we have.

Father   What?

Mother   We don't know them. We don't know how to take care of them. We don't come any place near it.

Father   Speak for yourself. Don't blame *me* because *you've failed.*

Mother   Of course *you* haven't—in *any* way.

Father   No—I don't think I have.

Mother   You're always *right* about *everything.*

Father   Well, what am I wrong about *now*? Haven't I told you from the beginning all the things you've let her do would—

Mother   Yes—yes—yes—you have!

Father   It's because you haven't done what I wanted that—

Mother   You're only thinking about what *you* want—and not about what's right for them at all.

Father   Well, is this right? This and everything that's led up to it?

Mother   No—but you wouldn't have made it any better by being hard and pig-headed.

Father (*getting up*) Have you made it any better by being so weak and sloppy you let this happen?

Mother She didn't mean any *harm*. (*Beginning to cry with quiet heartbroken tears.*)

Father Oh no—no harm—just disgraced us. That's all.

Mother Poor child! She was trying to find the unfindable thing—a perfect love. I went through it myself floundering around in the dark—trying to choose.

Father I think you did pretty well for yourself—choosing.

Mother Oh yes—it was wise choosing—

Father You regret it—do you?

Mother Don't you?

Father If I do, I've got the decency not to say so.

Mother If you could have seen what we'd be like in twenty-five years—would you have chosen *me*?

Father If you feel that way about it—*whose* fault is it?

Mother Or even *ten*. Did we have ten years that were worth *anything*?

Father Are you blaming *me*?

Mother At the end of *five* we were a failure—jogging along—letting out the worst side of ourselves for the other to live with.

Father You're saying a lot of wild things. You haven't had one of these spells for years.

Mother No—because I've just about given up *trying* to tell the truth to you about *anything*.

Father That's so all right. You certainly are not any too keen about telling the *truth*.

Mother Because you can't stand it. Your nature can't stand the truth.

Father Oh don't excuse your lies and deceit and weakness by *my nature*.

Mother Don't think I wouldn't be glad to be honest—to honestly be *myself*. You think I'm weak. Well, you couldn't *stand* my strength.

Father What?

Mother We *can't* speak the truth to each other. We haven't anything to speak it with.

Father I'm flabbergasted at you. You seem to have lost what sense you did have. You disappoint me terribly.

Mother (*with a sudden outburst as her suffering gets beyond her control*) Of course I do. Don't you think you disappoint *me*?

Father You haven't come along the way I thought you were going to. I can't *count* on you. You aren't *there*. Sometimes I think you aren't the woman I married at all.

Mother And sometimes I think you're a man I *couldn't* have married. Sometimes I loathe everything you think and say and do. When you grind out that old stuff I could *shriek*. I can't breathe in the same room with you. The very sound of your voice drives me insane. When you tell me how right you are—I could strike you.

Father Mary!

Mother Oh! (*She screams as she suddenly sees the suitcase.*)

Father My God—what's the matter?

Mother Her suitcase! That wasn't here when I was in this room before. She *is* here. Mary—my darling—where are you?

She rushes out of the room. **Father** *goes after her. After a pause* **Mary** *comes slowly from behind the curtain-stricken white and dumbfounded.*

Mary Bobby! They hate each other.

Bobby Un.

Mary How can they ever speak to each other again!

Bobby D'know.

Mary I didn't know it was like this. And you can tell it's been going on—sort of smothered.

Bobby It sure has busted out now.

Mary It makes me—all gone—inside.

Bobby Nothing to hang on to.

Mary Father and Mother! I wish I hadn't come back.

Bobby I'd like to light out myself.

Mary *Our* father and mother! I can't believe it!

Bobby (*going close to* **Mary**) We can't let 'em know we know.

Mary How can we help it?

Bobby I guess plenty of parents fight.

Mary But *ours*! I always thought they were so *good*! Oh Bobby! (*She drops her head on his shoulder and is shaken with sobs.*)

Mother (*calling from the hall*) Mary—Mary—where are you? (*Rushing back into the room.*) Oh my dearest—where were you? Where have you been? What have you been doing?

Father (*having come in after* **Mother**) Now young lady! This is the last time! Where have you been? What have you been doing?

Mary Nothing wrong.

Mother How *could* you? Do you know what time it is?

Father It's morning. That's what time it is—and you've been out all night. This is the last time you're going to do a thing like this. And I know your *new* idea—what you were planning to do.

Mother Robert—wait.

Father I almost thought you'd done it tonight. If you're reckless enough to have wanted to do it at all—I almost thought maybe you'd started off tonight.

Mary I did.

Father What?

Mother Oh no—Mary—you didn't. You didn't do that.

Father You what?

Mary I—went—tonight—all of us, to the place we were going to stay.

Mother Mary—

Mary And then we came back.

Mother You don't mean you went to *stay*? You didn't expect to do that?

Mary Yes, I did.

Father I'm not surprised. This is the *end*. You've gone too far. I'm going to send you away.

Mother Oh Robert—no you're not. Wait!

Father Why should I wait? I've waited too long. I'm going to send you where you'll live a decent normal life till you come to your senses. The thing you planned to do is a brazen outrage.

Mother She didn't do it. She came home.

Father Much *home* means to her! You've abused it all—everything your Mother and I have taught you to respect and hold sacred—thrown it away. Why you came back at all I don't see.

Mary I came back for a very silly reason.

Father I'll bet you did—nothing with any good in it.

Mary No—not a bit.

Mother My dearest—don't say that. You came back because you love us.

Mary (*breaking a little but controlling herself quickly*) Yes—I did, Mother.

Mother Because you were sorry and didn't want to hurt us.

Father Hurt us! You've wounded us so we'll never get over it. You've destroyed everything your Mother and I have held up to you as right—all our standards—the sanctity of the home.

Mary Oh *rot*, Father.

Mother Mary! Stop it! You're out of your senses.

Mary I came home for that and found it was a joke.

Father What do you mean?

Mary We heard you—Bobby and I. We were here in this room.

Father Heard us what?

Mary Heard you say things to each other that makes everything you're talking about now *disgusting*.

Mother Oh, my child!

Father You heard us discussing *you* and what you've done. You heard us say how pained we are.

Mary We heard you *fight*.

Mother Mary—don't—don't! You don't understand, dear child. Your Father and I were only excited. I honor and respect your father above everything on earth.

Father Your Mother and I have had a lifetime of devotion—with the highest ideals of married life. We didn't think we'd live to see our own children desecrate all that we've lived for.

Mary Oh don't! We heard. We know. You told each other the *truth*. What's the good of trying to plaster it over for us?

Father There's nothing left. This is the result of the wild life you've been leading.

Bobby Why do you keep going on about *her*? It's you two that have smashed everything up.

Father Stop! She's disgraced us.

Bobby She's not the one that's done the disgracin'.

Mary I don't see how Bobby and I can ever hold up our heads again.

Mother Don't child—don't.

Mary What's the use of anything when everything we ever thought and believed about *you* isn't true?

Bobby We *know we're rotten*—plenty of times—but we always thought you were—

Mary We always thought you were good.

Father How *dare* you! Is nothing sacred to you?

Mary A lot of things used to be. We always thought there was something between you and Mother, sort of holy—and different—that most people didn't have at all. How do you s'pose we feel when we know that it isn't so? I don't see that it makes much difference what *we* do—anyway—when everything's all wrong with *you*.

She goes swiftly out of the room as her sobs begin to come. **Father** *turns away to the window.* **Mother** *sits helpless and dazed.* **Bobby** *lowers his head—ashamed to look at either one of them as*

THE CURTAIN FALLS

Act Three

TIME: *Three hours later. The dining room. The same curtains are used for the walls—with the same doors and windows placed in a different arrangement. The table is set for breakfast.* **Father** *sits at the Right, holding the newspaper so that it completely hides him from* **Mother** *who sits opposite, trying to drink her coffee, and making a pretense of reading a few letters.*

Mother (*forcing herself to speak*)   We must make them know it was never—quite so bad before.

Father   Oh, I guess they've come to their senses by this time.

Mother   No matter *how* you feel towards me, make them think—

Father   I don't know that it makes much difference what they think.

Mother   It's the only thing that *does* make much difference.

Father   The point is, what are we going to do with her. And I've made up my mind.

Mother   To what? What are you going to do? (*A pause.*) You wouldn't do anything without telling me. You—

Nora *enters from the pantry with a small platter of scrambled eggs. She puts the platter on the serving table.*

Father   Thank you, Nora.

Nora *looks from one to the other—scenting something wrong—removes the fruit plates and serves the eggs. Mr. Hollister takes some, Mrs. Hollister refuses,* **Nora** *goes out.*

Mother   You wouldn't do anything without telling me?

Father   What good will it do to tell you?

Mother   But you can't—

Father   *You* didn't tell *me*. And it's because you didn't that this whole thing has come about. You've shown you haven't the strength and decision to compete with your children. There's nothing left but for me to take hold and—

Mother   Be careful.

Granny *enters from the hall cheerful and chipper. She wears an agreeable little lavender frock and a pink fluffy shoulder shawl.*

Granny   Good morning.

Mother   Good morning, Mother.

Granny   I said good morning, Robert.

Father (*from behind the paper*)   Oh—good morning.

Granny (*opening her napkin with cheerful fussiness*) The paper must be even more entertaining than usual. Didn't I get any letters, Mary?

Mother No—nothing.

Granny Who are yours from?

Mother Oh nobody in particular.

Granny They must be from *somebody*. Pass me the sugar, Robert, please. Isn't there anything you want me to read, Mary?

Mother Oh—here's one from Cousin Maria.

Granny Funny she didn't write it to me. She owes me one. Sugar—sugar, Robert. (*Poking Robert's arm, then opening the letter.*) I don't see why Maria *will* use this paper. I've told her twice I don't like it. (*Robert passes the sugar to* **Granny**.) Thank you, Robert. (*Patting his hand and smiling at him in her most irresistible way.*) Feel a little grumpy this morning? Didn't sleep well, I expect. Mary, are you going to give me any coffee or not? Is your coffee all right, Robert? Nobody's paying any attention to you. I believe in petting a man a little in the morning till he gets the creaks out, and sort of warmed up. I'm always sorry for a man when he has to leave his comfortable home and start off for the day. Goodness! Maria's writing gets worse and worse. I can't read a word she says. Read it to me, Mary.

Mother I will after breakfast, Mother.

Granny You aren't eating a thing. At least you do come down to the table. I'm glad you're not like the lazy women who lie in bed and have their *own* breakfasts and let their husbands come down to the table. I think breakfast is the nicest meal of the day and the time people ought to be the cheeriest. Where are the children? You certainly do let them lag behind, Mary.

Mother They were up late. I'm letting them sleep.

Granny It wouldn't hurt them to come and see their father. I know a man likes to see his family 'round him before he starts off for the day. Does Maria say anything about coming?

Mother Um—sort of a hint.

Granny Well, just don't you take it. I love Maria dearly, but I can't stand her in the same house. There's nothing she hasn't got her nose in—(**Nora** *enters.*) just boss, boss, boss. Maria's got money. Let her stay at home and spend it. Don't you say so, Robert? Do put down that old paper, Robbie, and eat your breakfast. What's the news?

Father Oh—nothing.

Granny I never saw a man in my life who found any news in the paper after having his head stuck in it for a week. (**Nora** *serves the eggs to* **Granny**.) Oh! Scrambled eggs again! I wonder if she stirred cream in these? Did you tell Lizzie what I said, Nora?

Nora Yes m'am.

Granny What did she say?

Nora Well—

Granny Lizzie's a mule. It's the only way they're fit to eat. (**Nora** *goes out.*) See how tough these are? (*She takes a bite of egg complacently and looks from* **Mother** *to* **Father**.) What *is* the matter? What's the matter, Mary?

Mother Why nothing, Mother.

Granny You two had a tiff? What if you have? This is another day. You have to begin all over again.

Father It looks like rain.

Granny Does it? (*A pause.*)

Father We need rain. The country needs it badly.

Granny Yes, I s'pose it does.

Father (*after another pause*) It's been the driest spell we've had for some time.

Granny (*with a chuckle*) Robert's doing pretty well, Mary. You might say *something*.

Mother I have a headache, Mother. I can't talk. (**Nora** *enters, with more eggs and toast.*)

Granny If I'd stopped talking to your father every time I had a headache many a thing would have happened that didn't. I hope you two haven't quarreled over Mary. You have to stand *together* to control her. That's the only way you'll ever—

Mary *comes in from the hall—solemnly followed by* **Bobby**.

Mother Good morning, dear. Good morning, Bobby.

Bobby AND **Mary**. Good morning.

Granny Good morning. Good morning. Good morning. (*They seat themselves.*) Aren't you going to kiss me good morning?

Mary Do you want me to?

Granny No—I don't especially want you to—but I think you ought to.

Mary I don't see why.

Granny I'm not so anxious to be kissed, young, lady—but I believe in keeping up appearances.

Mary I don't.

Granny Um—you'll get over that—the longer you live.

Mother Eat your breakfast, dear.

*As **Nora** serves the eggs again.*

Mary No thank you, Nora.

Mother Oh—

Mary No—just some coffee, Mother.

Father No thank you, Nora.

Bobby *falls upon his breakfast eagerly.* **Mother** *pours two cups of coffee.* **Nora** *serves the coffee to* **Mary** *and* **Bobby** *and goes out.*)

Granny You're all awfully silly. I don't know why you can't go on eating, just because there was a little—*discussion* last night. You needn't be nifty at me, Missy, because I told your father. I did it for your own good.

Mary Oh, that's a very small thing, Granny. Forget it.

Granny Then what *is* the matter? Why can't you start off the day like a happy family ought to?

Mary Because we're not a happy family.

Mother Mary—

Granny Then why don't somebody tell me what's the matter?

Mary I should think you'd know.

Father That will do. We won't discuss it now. But I've come to a decision.

Mary About you and Mother?

Father About you. I'm going to send you where you will learn the important things of life and learn to conform to the opinions of those who know.

Mary Where am I to learn that?

Father At a school I know of—a very fine one.

Mary And are you and Mother going on in the same way?

Father What do you mean?

Mary I'm perfectly willing to go away to school place or any old place if it will help. Bobby and I talked it all over. If you and Mother want a divorce, we'll see you through.

Granny She's out of her senses.

Father Don't put me and your Mother in the same class with the rotten set you've been running with. We don't tear up the ties of a life time just because we've had—a—hard places—sometimes.

Mary Do you mean you've patched it up? We won't *let* you.

Father *Stop* I say.

Mary Mother, do you prefer to stick together and hate each other?

Mother You have a wrong impression. We were only wrought up over—

Bobby *starts to leave the table.*

Mary Bobby, for heaven's sake, speak up. Tell them what *you* think.

Father (*shouting at* **Bobby**) Are you a part of this rubbish?

Bobby I know how you feel, Dad. I used to feel that way about it myself. But I changed my mind last night—after I saw how things are. We'll buck up and do anything—so long as it's got to be. Don't mind us.

Father This is *insufferable*.

Mary Go on, Bobby.

Granny I can't stand it!

Bobby There's nothin' the matter with a divorce—it's the havin' to have it that's rotten—and when you do—why you just *got*-a. So let's get at it and get done with it.

Father You leave the room. Go upstairs. (*to* **Mary**.) Tonight I'll try to make you see straight. I can't say anything more now.

Mother (*shaking her head at* **Nora** *who starts in from the pantry*) No—Nora. Don't come in at all. (**Nora** *goes out.*)

Mary I won't go away a step—to school or any place else—till you and Mother are settled.

Father You'll do as I say.

Mary And leave Mother wretched like this?

Father Your mother is *not* wretched.

Mary Yes, she is, and so are you, Father.

Father I'm not.

Mary Mother, do you want to go on living with Father or *not*?

Mother *bursts into tears.*

Father You've made her hysterical. She can't speak.

Granny Well, *I* can! Hold up your head, Mary, and tell us you're a happy woman. (*to* **Mary** *the Third.*) You ought to thank your lucky stars your father and mother get along as well as they do. Life's not all skittles and beer, let me tell you—and you ought to be put to bed on bread and water till you get over this romantic notion of wanting to be *happy* every minute.

Mother You don't understand, you children. Your father and I are sorry we quarreled last night, but you're making too much of it entirely. Stop it. It's over and ended.

Mary You're crawling out of it, Mother. Now's your chance. We all *know*. You can't go back to the same old thing, because we *do* know.

Father If reason won't control you something else will. You've made it impossible for us to let you stay at home. You've outraged everything that goes to make a home.

Mary That's what *we* think *you've* done.

Bobby There isn't any home when you and Mother are like this.

Father Do you set yourselves up against us?

Mary Say something, Bobby.

Bobby What more is there to say? We've told you we don't want you to go on tryin' to keep up the bluff for *our sakes*. And you surely don't want to for yourselves. So what is there to it but to get together and quit? We're only tellin' you that we want you and Mother to be happy, and go to it. (*He goes out of the room.*)

Father If it comes to defiance—you'll both go away.

Mary Very well. We'll meet you half way. We'll go if you and Mother get a divorce.

Father I'll settle you tonight. (*He goes out.*)

Mary Oh Mother, don't cry.

Granny What do you expect her to do? It's the awfullest thing I ever heard of any child doing to any parent—*ever*—*any*where.

Mary Oh Lord, I don't see anything to cry about. Let's get some action.

Mother I think the best thing to do *is* for you to go away for a while, dear. Till we get over this.

Mary Mother—do you actually mean you *want* to go on living with Father?

Granny Listen to her! Who *else* would she live with?

Mary Granny, will you keep out of this—*please*? I'm trying to help Mother.

Mother Oh, don't you two quarrel. I can't stand any more.

Granny We're not quarreling. Come here, honey—come here. (*Drawing a chair out from the table and sitting.*) Now listen, dearie. I know more in a minute about men than you and your mother put together. It won't be necessary for you or anybody else to go away—or upset our peace and comfort, if you'll just use your wits. A little tact and wheedling goes further with a man than all the storming in the world. You can get anything on earth out of your father if you'll just manage him. Let him *think* you're giving up to him, and you'll get your own way every time.

Mary I think that's perfectly disgusting, Granny.

Granny Now—now—don't be saucy. I'm trying to help you.

Mary I don't need to be helped. It's Mother.

Granny Well, the only way you can help her is to calm your father down. Rub him the right way till all this blows over.

Mary Blows *over*? If you don't know how it is you ought to. They don't *love* each other. Bobby and I found it out last night, and we can't stand this twaddle and mush about home and the family when we know Mother and Father ought not to even be in the same house. Is that the truth, Mother—or isn't it?

Granny It's new-fangled nonsense. Modern selfishness. That's what it is. A man and woman have no right to expect to be happy *all* the time—every minute—day and night. You *have* to have a good fight now and then to clear the air. Your grandfather and I had plenty. You women now-a-days don't know how to manage men. That's what's the matter with you. Of course, they get the best of you because you're trying to make 'em think you know as much as they do, and they won't *stand* it. You're such simpletons. You oughtn't to let 'em *ever* see how smart you are. Why I had my way about everything on earth. The madder your grandfather got the more I cried and the softer I was. I just twisted him round my finger—like that. And he thought I was right under his thumb.

Mary Oh Granny—how can you! Mother isn't Father's mistress you know.

Granny (*putting her hands over her face*)   Oh! I never used that word in my life!

Mary It's a perfectly good word. Mother and Father undertook the greatest relationship in the world and it hasn't been a success—so the only thing for them to do is to start another kind of life entirely. Isn't that so, Mother?

Granny No, it's not! What would become of the rest of us?

Mary *Us*? What have we got to do with it? It's their own inner closest life. It's not *right* for them to live together. It's not decent. It's absolutely *immoral*.

Granny I won't listen to such talk! It's Godless and heathenish! (*Going to Mother.*) Mary, you come upstairs and I'll help you. I can help you to bear anything you've got to bear with Christian fortitude as a good and noble wife should. I never dreamed you were silly enough to *let* yourself be unhappy. Heaven knows, you've got enough to be happy with—and if you're as clever as you ought to be you'll take the bit in your own teeth and he'll come trotting right along. There ain't a man on earth as smart as a woman if she just uses what God gave her—and there's no young chit can teach *me* any tricks! (*She goes out with her head well up, closing the door.*)

Mary Now Mother—let's decide what to do.

Mother Mary, you *must* stop this. You're making a tragedy out of just a little hard place that your father and I have to get over in our own way.

Mary *Was* there someone else you ought to have married—or just the ideal man of your dreams?

Mother Oh, we always like to think it might have been different with someone else—when we fail. I *have* failed—utterly.

Mary (*kneeling quickly by her* **Mother** *and throwing her arms about her*)   I adore you Mother. I didn't know till last night how much I loved you. I'm lots older than you are. Really I am. You're just a little girl and I'm going to take care of you.

Mother   I wish I were.

Mary   But still I *am* awfully sorry for Father. You do get on his nerves. He's bored. Father's bored to death with you, Mother. You're disappointed and disillusioned in him—but I do think it's more your fault than his.

Mother   Oh—Mary—Why?

Mary   Women will have to change marriage—men never will. At least you've come a long way ahead of Granny. Her marriage was on a very *low plane*, of course. You haven't stood up to Father and looked into his eyes—levelly—without conditions and silly compromise because he's a man and you're a woman.

Mother   Go on.

Mary   The interesting side of you—as a *person*—you haven't given to Father at all. He said last night 'You don't come through. You aren't there.' He *is* there in his way. There's *his* side, too.

Mother   Oh-h—don't think I don't know that.

Mary   But you *are* going to stand up now and keep a stiff lip and come through with *this*.

Mother   I don't see anything but blankness before me. And there's Mother. She has to have a home.

Mary (*looking deeply at her mother*)   You mean you haven't any *money* without Father? That you and Granny are dependent on him? (**Mother** *nods*.) All that is so horrible . . . so disreputable!

Mother   *Mary*!

Mary   It *is*! It's *buying* things with *you*. Don't let it go on, Mother. We'll fix it some way. I'll help you.

Mother   I'm not young. I can't go out and make my own living.

Mary   But you *ought* to be able to. That's the point to the whole business. I shall *have* my own money. I'll *make* it. I shall live with a man because I love him and only as long as I love him. I shall be able to take care of myself *and* my children if necessary. Anything else gives the man a horrible advantage, of course. It makes the woman a kept woman.

Mother   Oh you—

Mary   Why it *does*, Mother. The biggest, fairest, most chivalrous man on earth can't feel the same towards a woman who lives with him only because she has to be taken care of—as he does to one who lives with him because she loves him. Unless it's love and only love—

Father (*coming back into the room*) I want to speak to your mother.

After a slight pause **Mary** *goes out.*

Father The boy's hard hit. He's taken this thing terribly seriously. We've got to do something about it.

Mother And the girl?

Father Oh—She's excited—but *he* is actually suffering. As you say we've got to make them see they're mistaken. . . .

Mother But *are* they?

Father Then you meant everything you said to me last night?

Mother And you meant everything you said to me.

Father We were all stirred up.

Mother Yes—enough to speak the truth.

Father Well—what are you going to do? Let them go on—thinking what they think?

Mother They've made their own solution.

Father You mean . . . (*She nods.*) You don't think for a second we . . . (*A pause.*) We haven't done anything people get—divorces for, Mary. (*His voice growing a little hoarse.*)

Mother We've done the worst of all things.

Father What?

Mother We haven't made it a success—and it *might* have been.

Father Oh—we've been careless. We need more self-control I s'pose.

Mother Self-control is a poor substitute for love.

Father It's impossible to think of you and me—not together. It used to be all right. We've got to go back and begin all over again.

Mother Go back to what?

Father See here, Mary—some of the nonsense that child spouted has got hold of you. Don't let any of her silly . . .

Mother She isn't silly. She's brutal because she's so young—but she's honest and—

Father She's the product of this damnable modern loose-thinking.

Mother And she's thinking nearer the truth than *we* ever did. She's got something dangerous and ridiculous in *one* hand and something big and real in the other.

Father Oh, you can't take her seriously?

Mother You say we must go back. Go back to what? Our accidental love affair—when we didn't know each other at all ? We *do* know each other now. How can we go on after this? *I* can't.

Father What about me? I've got something to say about this—too—you know. I won't have my home broken up. Good God, Mary! Nothing means anything to me but you and the children! I won't have—

Lynn (*coming in from the veranda quickly*) Good morning. Good morning, Mrs. Hollister. I'm glad you haven't gone yet, Mr. Hollister. I want to say to you both that I've come back to my senses good and hard. Mary's up in the clouds about the whole business but I've come down with a thud and know where my feet are. I know the good old way is the *only* way—like you two did it . *You* didn't need any experiments to make you know you loved each other for good and all, did you ? You *knew* you'd stick to the end, and be crazy about each other forever—didn't you? And you've proved it. And that's what got Mary, you know. She sort of seemed to realize for the first time what marriage means, and she came back for your sakes. (**Mother** *and* **Father** *turn away.*) Honest, I'm—not stringin' you. I know you want to kick me, Mr. Hollister, but I've come to you in the good old way to say I'd like to marry your daughter and ask your *consent*. I *know* I can make her happy—and I *know* we were meant for each other, and I know we'll make a go of it the same way you have, and I hope you'll back me up and help me to get her. (*He forces Mr. Hollister to give him his hand and shakes it vigorously and confidently.*)

Father (*to* **Mother**—*trying to get his hand away while* **Lynn** *shakes it*) Bring Mary down here and let's get at this thing. (**Mother** *goes out closing the door.*) Has she promised to marry you?

Lynn Yes. Don't you think I'd make her a good husband, Mr. Hollister?

Father How do I know what kind of a husband you'd make?

Lynn But with your experience, don't you think if a girl marries a solid practical man who can take care of her—

Father I don't think that has anything to do with the case.

Lynn But if we're—

Hal (*coming in from the veranda*) Good morning, Mr. Hollister. Hello, Lynn.

Lynn Hello.

Hal I was going into your office this morning, Mr. Hollister, to see you.

Father *Indeed*!

Hal I want you to know that I'm sorry we didn't go through with it last night.

Father Ah!

Hal Because it *looks* like a failure, doesn't change *me* in the least.

Father That's important.

Hal   I *know* we were right.

Lynn   Oh, cool off, Hal. It's all over now and Mr. Hollister doesn't care anything about what *we* think.

Hal   Excuse me—it *isn't* all over. And what I think is more important than ever. I want you to know, Mr. Hollister, that I love your daughter too much to marry her in the old blind accidental lottery that *your* marriage was.

Father   What?

Hal   It *was* a lottery, wasn't it? Just good luck that it turned out as it has? It might have gone the other way for anything you really know about each other, mightn't it? You've just had the luck of one in a thousand that you've loved each other devotedly and continuously all these years—haven't you? I'm sure you're a big enough man to acknowledge *that*.

Lynn   I think Mr. Hollister's bored stiff with us, if you ask me.

Hal   I suppose he is. But you've said your say, I'll bet, and I want him to know—

Father   I don't want to know *anything*.

Hal   But it's only fair to let me say that I'll stand up for my convictions before the whole town, if necessary. I know that unless we change the entire attitude of men and women towards each other—there won't be any marriage in the future. Unless we open our eyes to what happiness and decency really are—unless we lift ourselves to another plane of thought entirely—

Father   Oh, shut up about your plane of thought! You don't know any more what you're talking about than an unborn baby. Until you've *lived*—until you've gone through the mill—you don't know *yourself*, let alone anybody else. You don't know what kind of a fool you may be, or how you may ball things up.

Hal   That's just why we ought not to marry till we know—

Father   It's not the damned ideas that will get you anywhere—it's yourself. If you're ever lucky enough to have a woman love you, you take care of that *one love*—and don't be so cocksure of yourselves. If you—(**Mary** *comes in from the hall.*) Now see here, Mary, which one of these boys do you intend to marry?

Mary   Neither.

Father   You didn't start off on that outlandish idea last night without intending to marry *one* of them?

Mary   I hoped it would be one of them, of course. That's what I was going to find out.

Father   You couldn't have found that out by staying at home, I suppose, in a normal natural way?

Mary   I admit I found out a great deal more about it after I got home than I could have any other way.

Hal How, Mary?

Father Never mind that. You can't go as far as this with the most important thing in your life and drop it as if it was nothing at all. You can't go as far as this without having some indication as to which one of these boys you *prefer*. Now which one *is* it? What are you hesitating about?

Mary I'm not hesitating at all. I know now if I'd gone off with each one of you *alone* for a year—we wouldn't have *known* each other. Now I know it takes most of one's life to do that.

Hal Then we were right. I can't talk to you here, Mary, before other people—but you know I'd rather lose you than have you make a mistake.

Mary (*taking his hand quickly in both of hers*) Thank you, Hal. (*He goes out.*)

Lynn Mary, what's changed you since last night? What are you going to do?

Mary Father, listen! This is what I've just told Mother. When I got home I told Lynn I loved him—and I do. I love him so much I can't live without him. I was going to marry him—quick. But now I wouldn't marry him for anything on earth.

Father Why not?

Lynn What do you mean?

Mary Marriage is a disgusting sordid business affair that I wouldn't go into for anything.

Lynn Mary!

Mary But if you want me to, Lynn, I'll live with you till we're *sure* what we really mean to each other, and when we *know* we'll either be married or quit.

Lynn Good heavens, Mary! You don't know what you're talking about.

Father Is this the kind of muck and filth you've been thinking about?

Lynn Why you never even dreamed of such a thing.

Mary I didn't think I'd actually do it, 'till I found out how horrible a perfectly good and respectable marriage can be.

Father Haven't you any decency about anything?

Mary I'm sorry, Dad, but Lynn's got to know. He's got to know why I won't marry him. It's because of Father and Mother, Lynn. I don't believe in marriage.

Bobby (*coming in quickly*) I've got Mother to say she'll do it. (*He stops, seeing* **Lynn**.)

Father Do what?

Lynn Do you want me to go?

Mary Don't go 'way. Wait on the porch. (**Lynn** *goes out onto the terrace.*)

Father (*to* **Bobby**)   Do what?

Bobby   Leave you.

Father   You—(*He tries to speak but stops helplessly*)

Bobby   I've bucked her up to that and I'm going with her and take care of her, Father. You needn't worry about that part of it. But don't spoil it now—will you? Don't say anything to make her lose her nerve.

Mary   You won't, will you, Father? That's splendid, Bobby.

Father (*broken and unbelievingly*)   Your mother didn't tell you—she'd leave me, did she?

Bobby   Yes, she did.

Father *goes slowly to the other end of the table and sits.*

Mary   You won't do anything to stop her—will you?

Bobby   I'm thinking about you, Dad, just as much as I am about Mother. I know you want her to go. You just hate to come straight out and say so. Now's your chance—*do* it.

Father   Are you children blaming me for the whole thing?

Bobby and Mary   No!!!

Mary   Of course not, Father!

Bobby   You bet we're not! I can see that it's hard livin' with a woman. Imagine one man living all his life with Gra'ma.

Father (*getting hold of himself again and rising*)   You're acting like lunatics—both of you. If you've made your mother think I want her to leave me—

Bobby   If *I* have? I like *that*! You mean if *you* have.

Father   You don't know *anything*—you young whippersnapper. Your mother's the finest woman in the world. I'd lay down my life for her. Your poor dear mother!

Bobby *and* **Mary** *look at each other surprised and slightly disgusted at* **Father***'s sudden sentiment.*

Mary   For goodness sake, don't get sentimental *now,* Father—just as Mother's getting some spine.

Bobby   I think as much. I worked like the devil to get her to come to the point.

Father (*quite himself again*)   Now see here. If you think for one minute anything you say is going to—(**Mother** *opens the door and comes slowly into the room.*) Mary—you haven't let anything these children have said influence you?

Bobby   If you don't do what you said you were going to Mother—I'm going to clear out. I won't live here.

Mary And you know what I'm going to do, Mother. I've told Father, too.

Father Be quiet—both of you. Now Mary dear—tell them there's nothing in this nonsense. Tell them they've kicked up a fuss over nothing and we're going right on with our customary happy life. Assert yourself—and tell them they're entirely mistaken. (*A pause.*) Come—come—go on—dearest.

Father *tries to be sure of himself and assumes a slightly affectionate gaiety.* **Mary** *and* **Bobby** *look at each other, half disgusted, half ready to laugh.*

Mother I'm going away.

Father You're not. I won't have it.

Bobby Go on, Mother.

Father Be quiet, I say. What in the name of common sense do you think life is anyway? Your mother and I haven't done anything to get a divorce for.

Bobby Of course you haven't beaten her or broken the eighth commandment—or any—

Mary The *seventh*, Bobby.

Bobby Un? Well—but what you have done is a thousand times rottener, and if you're going to keep right on I'm leavin'. How about it, Mother?

Mother They're rebelling against the ugliness—and meanness—the cruelty and pettiness. They think it doesn't have to be. They're saying very foolish things—but they're true—they're true. I'm going.

Bobby And I'm goin' with you.

Mother No. I'm going alone. It's the only way we can find the truth about ourselves, Robert, or anything else. Where's Lynn?

Mary Out there.

Mother Call him in.

Mary (*going to the window*) Lynn !

Lynn *comes in.*

Mother Mary, I don't ask you *not* to do what you say you're going to—for I know I haven't given you anything better—but I ask you to wait. It isn't our marriage that was wrong—it's what we've done with it.

Lynn I'm not afraid, Mary—I'll make you happy.

Mary How do you know you will?

Bobby That's what. I thought the thing you were up to was all hot air and bunk—but I begin to believe there's a good deal in it. I know one thing, by golly—*I'll* never take a chance. I'll never take a chance of being where you and Father are. If you two couldn't make a go of it, I'd like to know who *can*. I don't see why men and women don't stop *tryin'* to live together anyway. (*He starts to go.*)

Mother (*stopping* **Bobby** *with her hand and going to the door*)   Oh no—that isn't it. It's we—ourselves and what *we've* done—that are wrong. (*She goes out.* **Bobby** *follows.* **Father** *goes to the door.*)

Mary (*putting her hand on* **Father***'s arm*)   Let her go, Dad. Let her go.

Father   But I'll bring her back.

Mary   Do you mean you love her?

Father   You've got an awful lot to learn, little girl.

Mary (*suddenly throwing her arms about his neck*)   Make her love you, Dad. Make it all over. If you could! If you could!

Father—*too moved to speak holds her close for a moment and goes out—closing the door.*

Lynn (*going down to* **Mary**—*after a pause*)   Gosh, I'm sorry. It's the last thing in the world I would have expected to happen.

Mary   Why didn't they know in the first place? Can anybody ever know?

Sitting in her father's place at the table.

Lynn   *We* know. (*Sitting in* **Mother***'s place at the table.*) We were *meant* for each other. No man ever loved a girl the way I love you.

Mary   I bet that's what Father said to Mother. I bet that's what *everybody* says. It makes me sort of sick.

Lynn   But we're different. We *know* what we've got.

Mary   How do we know we do? What if *the* very things you like in me now—you'd hate sometime. What if the things I think are strong and stunning in you now I'd think were pig-headed and kickable after awhile?

Lynn   How could we? People couldn't be better suited to each other than we are.

Mary   I suppose they thought that too . Twenty-five years Mother and Father have been looking at each other across the table. And most of that time they've wished they were looking at somebody else.

Lynn   Oh Mary, you don't—

Mary   If they hadn't been married, if they hadn't been *tied* to each other, or if Mother could have walked out and taken care of herself at any minute, they would have had to *please* each other in order to *hold* each other.

Lynn   I know. You're dead right. But what if they hadn't been married? You and Bobby wouldn't have thanked them much for bringing you into the world without any name or anything to put your feet on.

Mary   I don't see that they've given us so darned much to put our feet on now. They've smashed everything I ever believed about love and marriage.

Lynn   Oh—your mother said it—there's nothing the matter with marriage—it's what people do with it. What's the use trying to bust up the best thing we've got? Why don't we begin to make marriage better instead of chucking it? Why don't we make it honest and decent and fair—and if we have made a mistake we'll *quit*.

Mary   Lynn—you're *marvelous*!

Lynn   You angel!

Mary   Oh *don't*! I bet Grandfather called Granny an angel—and knelt at her feet while he was saying it.

Lynn   Well old pal—we're going to be side by side—both on the same level—both on the square.

Mary   And just as free as though we weren't married at all.

Lynn   Absolutely.

Mary   No hold on each other but love.

Lynn   None.

Mary   And the minute that's gone—we're through.

Lynn   That's the stuff.

Mary   Give me your hand on that old man. (*They clasp hands.*) *But* Lynn, I wouldn't marry you if I didn't *know* that ours is the love that will last forever. There *can't* be any doubt about a love as great as ours, can there, dear?

Lynn (*drawing her onto his knees*)   You *bet* there can't.

Mary   I *do* think we're safe because we've been intelligent about it. I adore the way your hair grows at the side, dearest.

Lynn   Your eyes are the most beautiful things in the world. They have in them *everything* I want.

Mary (*putting her arms about his neck*)   I love you.

Lynn   I love you.

Mary   And we must make it the most wonderful love that was ever in the world.

She kisses his lips.

THE CURTAIN FALLS

Let Us Be Gay

Let Us Be Gay was first produced by John Golden at the Little Theatre in New York City on February 21, 1929. The play was directed by Rachel Crothers.

Characters

Kitty Brown
Bob Brown
Mrs. Bousicault
Dierdre Lessing
Townley Town
Bruce Keen
Madge Livingston
Wallace Grainger
Whitman
Struthers
Williams
Perkins

DESCRIPTION OF CHARACTERS

Kitty *is twenty-five—small—delicate—vivid.*

Bob *is twenty-eight, tall refined and handsome.*

Perkins *is a neat, substantial maid of about thirty.*

Whitman *is gray and venerable, English and imposing—and only enduringly tolerant of other people and their shortcomings.*

Williams *is a well set up chauffeur, with a slight Irish brogue.*

Mrs. Boucicault *is seventy-six—half Victorian—half ultra-modern—an enormous amount of dominating personality radiating from her hardness and her insatiable thirst for life. Her hair—iron gray—is worn rather high in puffs. Her voice is warm and dep and her sense of humor dry and sharp. She has one slightly stiff knee.*

Struthers *is a good-looking footman.*

Dierdre *is a tall, dark, exotic creature of twenty.*

Townley *is forty—tall, plain and charming—not very vivid—not very weak—indestructible in his inscrutable agreeableness.*

Bruce *is young, tall and good-looking in a fresh straightforward way.*

Madge *is possibly thirty-eight—looking younger—tall and frail and beautiful in a pale patrician way.*

Wallace *is about forty. A man with a great deal of manner—the perfection of which seems trying to make up for lost enthusiasms.*

Prologue
Kitty Brown's Bedroom. Some place in California.

Act I
Mrs. Boucicault's place in Westchester. Three years later.

Act II
Scene 1—Two evenings later.
Scene 2—One hour later.

Act III
Next morning.

Prologue

Time: The present. Twelve o'clock—a night in spring.

Place: Kitty Brown's bedroom—in the Brown house —some place in California. Only a corner of the room is seen—showing the bed with canopy—and a small bed table with lighted lamp. A toilet table at Left—an arm chair below the table and in the chair a woman's small traveling case.

A door at Right opens on stage. A single chair is below the door.

The appointments are feminine and charming. The dim light falls across the bed— leaving the rest of the room in shadow.

At Curtain: The room is empty. After a moment **Kitty Brown** *opens the door, slowly. She controls a smothered sob—closes the door—locks it and goes slowly and lifelessly to the dressing table where she tries in a dead hopeless way to put some of the toilet things, which are on the table, into the bag.*

Kitty *is twenty-five – small – delicate – vivid. She wears a soft dressing robe over her night gown. As the knocking goes on she stares at the door in helpless agony – holding herself tensely.*

Bob (*as he knocks outside*) Kitty—open the door! Kitty—open this door! *Open* it! (*After a slight pause.*) I've read it. I've read the damned thing. You don't mean a single word you've written on this piece of paper. Open the door.

Kitty No!

Bob. If you don't I'll break it open.

He knocks violently.

Kitty Go *away*.

Bob *Open* it then.

Kitty Go away. Everybody in the house will hear you.

Bob (*as he stops knocking and pleads*) You didn't mean it. If you do you've got to say it to me. *Say* it to me. Don't shut me out like this, Kitty.

Kitty (*speaking with great effort*) I never want to see you again as long as I live.

Bob Please, dear – *please*. This isn't fair. I've got to talk to you. I've got to *see* you. Kitty, are you getting up?

Kitty No.

Bob You know you've got to see me. Why not do it now? Kitty, *are* you up?

Kitty No.

Bob Well, get up and come here and open this. If you don't – I'll –

He pounds on the door and rattles the knob. **Kitty** *goes to the door – unlocks it and moves backwards quickly till she stands against the bed – staring with dread in her eyes.*

Bob (*throwing the door open and coming in quickly – with an open letter in his hand*)   Why did you do this? Why didn't you wait and talk to me?

Kitty (*pointing to the letter*)   I've said it all there.

Bob   But you didn't mean one word of it. Kitty – dear girl – you've got to listen to me. You've got to let me tell you.

Kitty   It's *true* – isn't it?

Bob   No!

Kitty   What?

Bob   Yes – the bare facts – but –

Kitty   That's all that matters. It's *true*.

Bob   But it *isn't* all that matters. The fact is the least important thing *in* it. I'm not in *love* with her. I'm in love with *you*.

Kitty   Don't!

Bob *speechless a moment at her agony, stares at her.*

Bob   Kitty – I – I'm sorry. I wish I'd told you – myself. Who did tell you?

Kitty   She did.

Bob   Not Alice?

Kitty   She said she wanted to be honest. She couldn't do anything that wasn't open and fair.

Bob   How did she –

Kitty   She says it's right – that something of you belongs to her – that she won't let anything cheat her.

Kitty *sits on the bed quickly with a low moan.*

Bob   It's all over and I – I'm sorry. You – Good God – don't take it like this! – *It has nothing to do with you* – nor what I *am* to you. That's what you've got to *see*. That's what –

Kitty   Go away – out of the house – till I get my things together. I'm going to take the children to mother, and I'm going to get my divorce as quickly as I possibly can.

Bob   You're shaking and cold. I'm going to give you some whiskey.

Kitty   Go out of this room and don't come back.

Bob (*turning back at the door*)   I'll be damned if I will! You've got to hear *my* side of it. We've got to talk it out.

Kitty I'm going to take the children to mother.

Bob No you're not. Not unless I say you can.

Kitty They're not yours. They're all *mine*. They're mine.

Bob Don't' be a fool, Kitty. The whole business doesn't mean anything more to me than getting drunk. In fact that's just about what it is. It's over. I'm sorry. I wouldn't hurt you for anything in the world.

Kitty You don't even know what you've done to me.

Bob The whole bloomin' trouble is, Kitty, you don't *understand*. You still think and feel and expect just what you did when you were a girl. She's not in love with me. She's all right. She knows her way about.

Kitty Oh –

Bob You still don't know the actual honest to God truth about the man and woman business. If you did understand you'd forgive me. You'd say forget it old man, and let's go on.

Kitty I've made up something that never *was* at all. I believed you were *just* exactly to me – what I was to you. I thought that *being* that way made – the children – more wonderful – made – made everything more – (*Her voice breaks.*) I know I was a fool. I thought it was the most beautiful thing in the world and it never was there at all.

Bob (*deeply moved and a little awed*) It *was* there. It *is*.

Kitty Oh –

Bob Before God it is, Kitty. (*He goes to stand beside the bed.*) And just as much to me as it is to you. You're sacred to me.

Kitty Don't come near me.

Bob Of course I'll come near you. I love you. You're my wife.

Kitty I'm not. I'm not. It's *never* been what I thought it was at all.

Bob It has.

Kitty Don't touch me!

Bob (*dropping on his knees beside the bed*) You wouldn't stop what we are to each other? You wouldn't smash everything? You wouldn't take the children away from me?

Kitty Get *up* – and go away.

Bob I love you.

Kitty You never have. You never did.

Bob I've never stopped loving you – not for a minute.

Kitty Then this couldn't have happened. It couldn't. It *couldn't*.

Bob How can you be jealous of somebody I don't love?

Kitty *Jealous*? Is *that* what you think? You've lied to me.

Bob No –

Kitty Every minute—day and night – while this was going on. Nothing's been true—*nothing* . And I thought everything about you was as true as God.

Bob Kitty!

Kitty If you're like this nothing in the world is what I thought it was. I can't ever believe in anything or anybody – ever—*again*.

Bob (*rising*) It's horrible what you're doing. Killing everything, busting it all up. You're doing a great deal worse thing now than I ever did in my life. I never meant to hurt *you* – never – and you're hurting me as much as you can. You're smashing up the only thin gin the world I care a hang about and the only thing that means a damned thing anyway.

Kitty Go away!

Bob I belong to you, Kitty, and you belong to me.

Kitty No!

Bob Will you forgive me?

Kitty No!

Bob Can't we try again?

Kitty No!

Bob If I go out of this room now I'll never come back. Do you want me to go?

Kitty Yes.

Bob *goes – slamming the door.* **Kitty** *stares at the door – half crying out – then throws herself across the bed as the*

CURTAIN FALLS

Act One

Time: Three years later—an afternoon in August.

Place: A sort of outdoor living room in the country house of **Mrs. Boucicault** *– some place in Westchester.*

The room has an air of great comfort and luxury and smartness—achieved with severe simplicity.

At Curtain: The room is empty – then **Perkins** *comes in from the hall at Left.*

Perkins *is a neat and substantial maid of about thirty, wearing a gray uniform and small apron. Her disposition is somewhat ruffled at the moment, as she brings in a palm leaf fan—a book—a light wool rug—a black silk handbag and a small pillow—all of which she puts in and about the large chair at Right Center.*

Whitman, **Mrs. Boucicault**'s *major-domo of long standing, comes onto the terrace from the Left and into the room with an observant eye as* **Perkins** *is placing the things.* **Whitman** *is gray and venerable, English and imposing – and only enduringly tolerant of other people and their shortcomings.*

Whitman (*with great dignity and deliberation*)   It would be just as well if you did all that at the proper time.

Perkins   I *had* all this stuff in the garden once, when she changed her mind and told me to put it *here*.

Whitman   Certainly, *I* told her it would be cooler here.

Perkins   It would be just as well if you minded your own business. It's bad enough to keep up with *her* notions—hopping all over the place – without you changing her mind for her.

Whitman   I have been changing her mind for her for forty years—and I expect to keep on doing so, without any suggestions from you, Miss.

Williams, *a well set up chauffeur, with a slight Irish brogue comes onto the terrace from the Right and into the room.*

Williams   Hadley just telephoned from the station that nobody got *off* that train.

Whitman (*turning slowly towards* **Williams**)   He was *instructed* to meet the five-fifteen and wait for a train that somebody *did* get off of.

Perkins   God knows who *will* get off – or how *many*. They may be Chinamen or monkeys this time – or the King of the Fiji Islands.

Whitman   Again I suggest that is none of your business, Perkins.

Perkins   I suppose it's *yours*. I suppose you suggested the guest to her also.

Whitman   I have been known to do so. (*Turning again to* **Williams** *who is slightly amused but brings himself to perfect order as* **Whitman**'s *stern eye fixes him.*)

Williams, telephone Hadley, at the station, to wait until someone *peculiar* and *distinctive* arrives. (**Williams** *starts to go – but turns back as* **Whitman** *goes on.*) Someone *likely* to be coming here.

Perkins Something *queer* enough likely to be coming here.

Williams Male or female?

Mrs. Boucicault (*coming out from the hall at Left*) Whitman – her name is Brown – Mrs. Courtland Brown – and I want her put at the end of the north wing.

At the sound of **Mrs. Boucicault***'s voice* **Williams** *has gone quickly onto the terrace and out Right.* **Whitman** *stands still more perfectly and* **Perkins** *again busies herself with the articles she has placed on the small table by the chair – managing to drop one of them much to* **Whitman***'s annoyance.* **Mrs. Boucicault** *is seventy-six – half Victorian – half ultra-modern – an enormous amount of dominating personality radiating from her hardness and her insatiable thirst for life. Her clothes have rather a grand manner of having been well made but not modish—and a good deal of jewelry is mixed up with chains and three kinds of glasses hung about her neck. Her hair—iron gray—is worn rather high in puffs—her voice warm and deep and her sense of humor dry and sharp. She has one slightly stiff knee and walks with a stout stick with a curved handle. She is followed on by* **Struthers**—*a good looking footman in a dark conservative uniform. She moves now in state towards her chair at Right where she sits a little heavily.* **Struthers** *places the foot piece and lifts the foot of the stiff leg carefully, putting it on the stool.*

Whitman (*with controlled insistence as* **Struthers** *moves back*) I have a suite on the south side ready, madam.

Mrs. Boucicault The *north wing* I said.

Whitman (*with tolerance – knowing he is right*) Very good madam. The south side would be better.

Mrs. Boucicault North. Poke that pillow in the right spot, Perkins. (*Indicating the middle of her back.*) Why would it be better? How could it be better?

Whitman That suite hasn't been open at all this summer, madam.

Mrs. Boucicault Open it then. Open it. Why isn't is open?

Whitman You gave orders to close it, madam.

Struthers *goes onto the terrace and off Right.*

Mrs. Boucicault (*knowing she is wrong*) Rubbish! I didn't. Open it – open it.

Whitman (*with resignation*) Very good, Madam.

Mrs. Boucicault No—no—not over my feet. (*As* **Perkins** *starts to put the rug over her feet.*) In this heat? Use your head a little, Perkins. You use yours for her, Whitman. Not that you've *got* any. Watch for the motor and bring Mrs. Brown here as soon as she comes—and get somebody *at those rooms*. Isn't that a motor now? Go on—go on. Be quick.

Whitman (*as he goes off at Left with great deliberation*) I don't think so, Madam. My ears are very sharp.

Mrs. Boucicault How am I, Perkins? If I didn't have to go through this confounded performance of dressing, life would be a much pleasanter business. Did you ever hear of the man who cut his throat because he got tired of the eternal shaving?

Perkins You look very nice indeed, Mrs. Boucicault. Very nice indeed.

Mrs. Boucicault What else could you say – poor thing? Here, undo this. Oh, what a pest! Don't get old, Perkins. The longer you live the more you have to regret.

Perkins (*untangling one pair of glasses*) You aren't old, Mrs. Boucicault.

Mrs. Boucicault Don't be a fool! Thanks. Get away. Oh this heat! This damnable heat! Why *am* I here in August! Why am I fool enough to keep this place open for other people to live in! Go and see if that *is* – Hello, child –

As **Dierdre Lessing** *comes from the hall at Left.* **Dierdre** *is a tall, dark, exotic creature of twenty—just now very startlingly beautiful in a one piece bathing suit of orange and black and a black coat.*

Dierdre Oh darling – I didn't know anybody was out here. I'm going to jump in the pool before tea.

Mrs. Boucicault I thought you were playing golf.

Dierdre I did eighteen holes this morning. Bit fed up. Awfully hot.

Mrs. Boucicault Bored – you mean?

Dierdre Not a bit. Do you mind if I go across this way?

Going onto the terrace and off at Left.

Mrs. Boucicault You'd better come *back* the other way. Tea will be here. Not that *I'll* mind you dripping and more *emphasized* than if you were stark naked. (*She raises her voice a trifle as* **Dierdre** *has gone.*) Oh –

As **Bob Brown** *comes out from the hall – also in his bathing suit.*

Bob Oh—sorry. I didn't know anybody was out here.

Mrs. Boucicault I thought you were playing golf.

Bob I did eighteen holes this morning. Rather hot.

Mrs. Boucicault Sounds like a well trained chorus. Have you been trying to keep cool in the house?

Bob Trying to keep cool – yes.

Mrs. Boucicault Did you succeed?

Bob Um—so-so.

Mrs. Boucicault Bored?

Bob Not more than usual. In fact not quite so much so. Thanks to you for taking me in.

Mrs. Boucicault You'd better hurry unless you want to run into a very pretty woman.

Bob Another one?

Dierdre (*coming back in time to hear this*) Come on, Bob.

Bob You *are* a perfect hostess.

Dierdre Don't excite yourself. You never can tell what grandmother's going to pick up in her travels.

Mrs. Boucicault Wait till you see her. I know something choice in women when I see it, as well as you do.

Bob (*going to* **Dierdre**) I'm sure of that – but you've let me see your granddaughter *first*. Anything after that is bound to be disappointing.

Dierdre (*smiling at* **Bob**) Keep it up.

Bob She's more dark and glowing and mysterious than ever this afternoon.

Mrs. Boucicault (*exasperated and helpless at their bold flirtation*) Go jump in the pool.

Bob But she's still more so in the water. I think I hear a motor now. Perhaps that's your pretty lady. Let's bolt.

Bob and Dierdre go out on terrace and off Left.

Whitman (*coming on from Right of terrace*) Mrs. Brown is here, Madam.

Mrs. Boucicault (*raising her voice*) Is that you, Katherine? Come on—come on.

Kitty (*calling from off Right*) Coming – coming!

Whitman North or South, madam?

Mrs. Boucicault You know what I said!

Whitman Very good madam.

Crossing to hall entrance where he waits. **Struthers** *enters from Right on terrace and stands Left Center. He is carrying* **Kitty**'s *jewel case.*

Kitty (*coming on from the Right and stopping at Center*) Oh, my dear! It's too wonderful to be here! And I've had the sweetest welcome. Your chauffeur looked at me very doubtfully till I asked if he was waiting for me – and then he said, "Oh, oh, I beg pardon, madam – I was looking for something much more *peculiar*." (**Struthers** *looks at* **Whitman**, *who in turn raises his eyebrows and goes out followed by* **Struthers** – *through the hall*.) Will I *do*?

Perkins *enters from terrace, carrying a small hat box.*

Mrs. Boucicault (*putting out her hand to* **Kitty**)   Come here, you goose.

Kitty (*coming down to* **Mrs. Boucicault**)   What a duck you are to send for me! I want to kiss you. (**Mrs. Boucicault** *turns her cheek enduringly.*) But I won't.

Mrs. Boucicault   I'm honestly and gratefully glad to see you. You're just what I need.

Kitty   And what is that? I'm a little suspicious now.

Mrs. Boucicault   Have you got a maid?

Kitty   A what? Oh, my word, no. No such swank. I s'pose I should have *rented* one in New York. What shall I do? Does it embarrass you?

Mrs. Boucicault   Stuff! Perkins will look after you.

Kitty   Thanks so much. I'm clever and awfully neat. I shan't need much, Perkins. Take the hat out right away, please, and put it on a jigger – and here are my keys.

Perkins (*catching the keys as* **Kitty** *tosses them*)   Thank you, Madam.

Perkins *goes out through the hall at Left.*

Kitty   I saw it in a window – dashing through town – the *hat* – and couldn't resist it. The shops are full of the most *ravishing* August things for nothing at all – absolutely nothing *at all* – if one *has* anything at all – which I haven't. (*Pulling off her gloves she goes out onto the terrace – looking off.*) Oh, how sweet! How *sweet!* It's as peaceful as England.

Mrs. Boucicault   And just as dull. Are you looking for peace?

Kitty (*coming back into the room*)   I'm not looking for anything. I know better.

Mrs. Boucicault   Blessed are they who expect nothing for they shall not be disappointed.

Kitty (*going to sit on the sofa at Left*)   Well—I made it. This *is* a hurry call, Bouci. What's it all about? I was on my way to California. Mother hasn't seen the children in three years. I wiped everything off the slate—threw some things into a trunk and *dashed* without thinking – let alone dressing. I'm feeling horribly exposed – I forgot my lip rouge.

Mrs. Boucicault   What have you been doing since I picked you up in Paris? April – May—June—July—August –

Counting them off on her fingers.

Kitty   Different men—for different months. April was the most exasperatingly interesting man I have *ever* known —May was –mm—so-so—and *June*—Well, we'll skip June—You aren't listening anyway, you're dying to talk yourself.

Mrs. Boucicault   I'm not sorry I asked you. You look just as well as I thought you would. At least I suppose you do. Come here und untangle this pesky thing. By the time I've got them loose and on my nose I've forgotten what it was I wanted to look at.

Kitty (*having gone across to* **Mrs. Boucicault** *and extricated the glasses*) You were going to look at me—I believe—but don't—if they're too penetrating. What a love!

Taking up a small parasol and moving away with it.

Mrs. Boucicault I want you to do something for me.

Kitty (*opening the parasol and twirling it*) Yes?

Mrs. Boucicault There's a man here—

Kitty (*turning quickly to* **Mrs. Boucicault**) Ah! –

Mrs. Boucicault Where are the children?

Kitty In town with the nurse till Monday.

Mrs. Boucicault I was afraid to tell you not to bring them for fear I'd seem rude – but thank God you didn't.

Kitty Don't you suppose I know when to display my jewels – and when not to?

Sitting at Center.

Mrs. Boucicault He's bored.

Kitty Who?

Mrs. Boucicault The man.

Kitty Oh! I'll do my best—till Monday.

Mrs. Boucicault How good is your best?

Kitty Depends on the man. One must be inspired—as well as inspiring.

Mrs. Boucicault A girl is after him—hot footed.

Kitty Is he running?

Mrs. Boucicault Not a step—In fact I'm afraid he's *coming on*. That's what worries me.

Kitty Good. Much more stimulating for me. What's he like? What shall I be like—to get him?

Mrs. Boucicault He's one of those stray dogs I get interested in. I don't know much about him—except that he's been divorced – at least once, and seems to be rather *humble* as men go – and to have a fair amount of money. With your alimony it wouldn't be bad at all.

Kitty (*very much amused*) This is very touching – your interest in me. What do you want really? What's biting you?

Mrs. Boucicault The girl.

Kitty Oh.

Mrs. Boucicault She's one of those gorgeous young things that are running around loose now. Lives alone—*is* alone—father one place—mother another—knows everything—everybody—done everything—and only twenty years old.

Kitty I know. I know. Wonderful—isn't it? They get such a good start, now. I've been *made*. They just *are*.

Mrs. Boucicault When are you going to marry again?

Kitty *Never*.

Mrs. Boucicault What are you going to do *then* – if you don't marry – live in what we used to call – sin?

Kitty (*laughing*) My little talent – clothes – is beginning to make money – and when I'm paying my own bills – men may come and men may go.

Mrs. Boucicault Are you implying that up to this point there haven't been any – either coming – or going?

Kitty (*rising and moving away*) Now, Boucicault, that's clumsy. I'm surprised at you.

Mrs. Boucicault That's my way of being subtle. Come here, Kitty. (*Drawing a small chair out in front of her.*) Will you do this for me – take him away from the girl?

Kitty (*going to* **Mrs. Boucicault**) I thought your religion was hands off.

Mrs. Boucicault It is. But it doesn't work when it comes to *my own grandchild*.

Kitty (*sitting in the chair before* **Mrs. Boucicault**) *Oh*, I see.

Mrs. Boucicault I've got to keep her from going to the dogs before the first of October.

Kitty Why the first of October?

Mrs. Boucicault She's going to marry a nice boy the first of October – an awfully nice boy. He's here too. They've got everything in the world in common to make a go of it – when – bing – out of the blue she takes this shameless damnable passion for this man.

Kitty You don't think you can do anything about *that*—do you?

Mrs. Boucicault That's why I sent for you.

Kitty You never seemed like an old woman to me before, Bouci – not a bit. Always as fresh and open minded about life as –

Mrs. Boucicault Shut up. I'm not talking about life, I'm talking about my own granddaughter.

Kitty Oh, well then, of course you can't be expected to use your common sense at all.

Mrs. Boucicault She's in a kind of danger I don't want to recognize – but I'm frightened, Kitty. I want to beat her over the head and make her behave, but I'm pretending I don't see anything. Now the best thing that could possibly happen is for you to take the man.

Kitty I'm tremendously flattered that you think I could get a man away from a stunning young thing like that – but even if I *could*, don't you know the sooner she finds out everything for *herself* – the sooner she loses her romantic illusions – the happier and safer she's going to be?

Mrs. Boucicault I'm not so sure. Women are getting everything they think they want now, but are they happier than when they used to stay at home – with their romantic illusions – and let men fool them?

Kitty At least they're more intelligent. That's one thing I refuse to be – a happy fool.

Mrs. Boucicault Un! I'd like to live another fifty years – without the bother of living – to see this thing through. I've watched a long procession of men, women and morals through three generations. I'm seventy-six, and I don't know anything.

Kitty That's why you're so wise dearest.

Mrs. Boucicault I always knew my husband wasn't faithful to me, but I lived in hell with him for fifty years because divorce wasn't respectable. My only daughter had three divorces – which I was tickled to death to see her get – and here's my grandchild in the middle of this modern moral revolution and I'm helpless – can't do a thing for her. She's grown up before I knew it – dumped herself in my lap and this thing has happened right under my nose.

Kitty Then for Heaven's sake, let it *happen*. Let it alone.

Mrs. Boucicault No – by God – I won't. She's got to walk up that aisle a perfectly decent girl if I have to lock her up till –

Kitty Now see here, Bouci. I don't think I'm clever enough for this job if it's as important as all that.

Mrs. Boucicault You can do it if you *want* to. Didn't I see you take the Russian away from the Italian princess before she even *knew* it?

Kitty I didn't take him away. I just borrowed him for the week-end. Who else is here besides your piece de resistance?

Mrs. Boucicault I can't remember. I never see anyone till tea. From then on to midnight is as much as I can stand of any guest.

Kitty You don't care what they do after midnight – just so they let you alone.

Mrs. Boucicault Not a bit. They'll be coming in in sections now. Oh —here's Townley. (*As* **Townley Town** *strolls in dragging his golf bag.* **Townley** *is forty—tall, plain and charming—not very vivid—not very weak—indestructible in his inscrutable agreeableness. His golf clothes are well worn and his bag is shabby.*) Townley, this is Mrs. Courtland Brown. She's not quite as sweet as she looks, but you'll think she is. Go and impress her.

Townley (*going down to* **Kitty**) I'm nicer than *I* look – *much*.

Kitty (*giving her left hand to him*) How could you be! How do you do. Oh you magnificent long legged Britishers! I've been avoiding you in Paris – but you *are* wonderful – aren't you?

Townley Yes – we are – aren't we?

Kitty (*to* **Mrs. Boucicault** *as* **Townley** *goes to Left to put down his golf bag*) I thought you said he was humble.

Mrs. Boucicault This isn't the one.

Kitty Oh—I'm sorry! I'll have to say it all over again—for that's the way I'm going to begin.

Townley Begin what?

Turning back to **Kitty**.

Kitty (*moving towards* **Townley**) Bouci has a subtly laid plan for me to get a man. Would that get *you*?

Townley I don't remember what you said – but you *have* got me.

Kitty (*stopping at the sofa at Left*) Oh I like this one. Make it this one.

Mrs. Boucicault Practice on him.

Townley She doesn't seem to need practice.

Kitty Let's begin at the beginning. Who are you?

Townley (*putting his hands on the back of the sofa and leaning towards* **Kitty**) Well – I'm a professional visitor. I get an S.O.S. from Bouci – "Man shy" – and I come. I have a suitcase – sport clothes – dinner clothes and a suit to arrive in. I take on any woman in any way desired – and I use my knife and fork in the continental manner.

Kitty And way down deep in under you're a very sweet person.

Townley You've found me out. Do you mind if I stay hot and wet for tea here at your feet? I'm afraid if I go somebody else will come and –

Sitting beside **Kitty** *on the sofa.*

Kitty Don't leave me. You make me so comfortable.

Mrs. Boucicault Here's another one. (*As* **Bruce Keen** *comes in – also in golf clothes and a bag – without a hat. He is young tall and good looking in a fresh straightforward way.*) Are you wet too?

Bruce Not a bit. I changed at the Club. Why? Do I look messy?

Townley (*to* **Kitty**) So did I change. I only said that to show you I was even willing to catch cold for you. I'm just as dry and sweet scented as he is. So don't push me off on that account.

Kitty I'm hanging on to you. Who's that?

Smiling at **Bruce**, *who has disposed of his golf bag and gone to stand beside* **Mrs. Boucicault**.

Townley Nobody you'll care about.

Bruce (*to* **Kitty**)   Yes I am.

Kitty (*puffing her cigarette which* **Townley** *is lighting*)   I'm sure you are. I can tell that at long distance.

Bruce (*to* **Mrs. Boucicault**)   Where's Dierdre?

Mrs. Boucicault (*evading his question*)   That's Mrs. Courtland Brown. Go and tell her who you are and get it over.

Townley (*as* **Bruce** *comes to them*)   I'll save you that embarrassment. This is Bruce Keen – young – handsome and very much in demand both with the upper bums and the best people. But by Monday morning you'll find *me* very much more satisfactory.

Bruce   Do you think that's clever?

Kitty (*giving* **Bruce** *her hand*)   I didn't hear him. I was looking at you. How magnificent you long legged Americans are! I've been avoiding you in Paris – but you –

Townley *and* **Mrs. Boucicault** *laugh.*

Bruce   What's so funny about that?

Townley   It's deep. You have to be on the inside to get it.

Kitty   Oh, I'm having such a good time!

Townley (*getting up*)   You'll have a better one now. Here's tea. And *such* tea!

Mrs. Boucicault   Katherine, if you want to wash your hands and feet before you have it, somebody will take you in.

Kitty   I wouldn't leave for anything. Do you want me to pour it?

Mrs. Boucicault   I certainly do not. Go and get your own, and if you don't get what you want, it's your own fault. Give me mine first, Whitman. That's all I care about *and who is rattling back there?*

As **Struthers**, *the footman, rattles a cup and saucer.*

Whitman (*frowning and shaking his head at* **Struthers**)   Beg pardon, Madam.

Whitman *takes tea and cakes to* **Mrs. Boucicault**, *placing them on the table beside her – and going back onto the terrace.*

Kitty (*rising as* **Bruce** *picks up the little parasol which she has left on the sofa*)   Are you going to hold that over me while I drink tea? It might add a flattering glow.

Bruce   You don't need any extra glow.

Kitty (*to* **Townley** *as* **Bruce** *goes onto the terrace with the parasol*)   It's not as young as it looks.

Struthers *has gone off Left on the terrace and returned with a tray of Scotch – White Rock, ice – etc.*

Townley (*as he and* **Kitty** *move towards the tea table*) Come and look before its equilibrium gets disturbed. It's like a glorified automat.

Kitty I haven't had any luncheon but a Grand Central sandwich – which is still right here.

Putting a finger on her chest.

Townley What will you have? Hearts or crescents?

Kitty Both. Don't ask me to eliminate anything. What are those over there, the dressy little green ones?

Bruce Try one and find out. (*Coming down to* **Mrs. Boucicault** *with his own highball and sandwich.*) Have you got everything?

Mrs. Boucicault Of course. Let me alone now.

Bruce Is Brown with Dierdre?

Mrs. Boucicault (*drinking her tea*) How do I know?

Bruce He is then.

Mrs. Boucicault (*nodding towards* **Kitty**) She'll get him away from her. Don't you think she could?

Bruce (*looking at* **Kitty** *as she and* **Townley** *talk on the terrace*) Who is she really?

Mrs. Boucicault I don't know. I picked her up in Paris because I like her. What do you think?

Bruce She's got a very come hither look in her eye.

Mrs. Boucicault Think so?

Bruce You know she has, you wise old devil.

Mrs. Boucicault I don't know anything about anybody. Go way. (**Madge Livingston** *comes out from the hall.*) Oh—come out, Madge. How delightful you are! It cools me off just to look at you.

Bruce Marvelous – Mrs. Livingston.

Mrs. Livingston *is possibly thirty-eight – looking younger – tall and frail and beautiful in a pale patrician way. She is now wearing something diaphanous and trailing, which adds to her illusiveness. She moves with a slow grace and slight hauteur.*

Mrs. Boucicault I must say it pleases me to see a guest looking as if she'd spent the whole day dressing for me to look at her – instead of running around day and night in a one piece something.

Bruce What are you having?

Madge I'm not having anything No, nothing, thank you, dear. (*As* **Bruce** *comes towards her.*) Oh – will you be sweet enough to move this for me – just a little nearer?

Indicating the sofa.

Bruce All right?

Having gone back of the sofa and moving it about one inch nearer to **Madge**.

Madge Just, thanks. (*As she sits languidly.*) Oh there *is* a little breeze out here. I thought it was too hot to come out. Wallace has been reading aloud to me.

Bruce *goes to* **Kitty** *and* **Townley** *on the terrace.*

Mrs. Boucicault I don't know any greater proof – (*putting her tea down and throwing her napkin after it.*) Take this, Whitman. Take it away. I can't stand anything after I'm through with it. (**Whitman** *comes from the terrace and takes the tea away.*) I don't know any greater proof of a man's slavish devotion to a woman than reading aloud to her in August. I s'pose you've made him think his voice is beautiful.

Madge Not so beautiful as his *mind*. Have you read his latest book?

Mrs. Boucicault I read *everything*.

Madge Isn't it the exquisite revelation of an exquisite spirit?

Mrs. Boucicault It seems to me to be the tired effort of a *very* tired man. A burned out one.

Madge You refuse to see him as he is.

Mrs. Boucicault You refuse to see him as he is because you've helped to burn him out.

Madge How detestable you can be, Boucicault. I thought you *understood* my *tragedy*.

Mrs. Boucicault I don't see much tragedy in a perfectly good husband with a bank-roll—on one side or the fence—and a perfectly good *beau*—on the other.

Madge I've sacrificed my life to Wallace and his work. I've been his inspiration. He *has* written great books.

Mrs. Boucicault Well – at least he's been devoted to one woman for ten years. That's a much more unusual thing for a man to do than to write a great book. Let's give him credit for that.

Wallace Grainger *appears in the hall entrance. He is about forty. A man with a great deal of manner – the perfection of which seems trying to make up for lost enthusiasms. He is wearing flannels and is in most perfect style. He carries a paper novel and paper knife.*

Mrs. Boucicault Come out, Wallace.

Madge It *is* cooler out here, dear, after all.

Wallace (*stopping in front of* **Madge**) I finished it. It has a nice attitude at the end.

Madge   Oh, really? What?

Wallace   Wallace   I won't tell you. I want you to enjoy it yourself.

Madge   But dearest, I'll only enjoy it with you.

Wallace (*going to* **Mrs. Boucicault**)   Try this, Mrs. Boucicault. You'll find it very amusing and the most delightful French I've read in a very long time.

Mrs. Boucicault   There are only two kinds of French for me – the kind I do understand and the kind I don't.

Taking the book.

Wallace   Aren't you having any tea, Madge?

Madge   No—but I will let you bring me a glass of water – no ice. Oh, there's my handkerchief. Please. Thanks. (*As* **Wallace** *picks up the handkerchief.*) And dearest – will you be an angel and bring me my scarf? I left it on a chair by the door, just inside, I think. (**Wallace** *goes back into the house.*) Is that somebody new out there? Boucicault – (*As* **Mrs. Boucicault** *having opened the book, doesn't hear her.*) Is that somebody new out there? When did she come? Rather effective, isn't she?

Looking at **Kitty**, *whose voice is heard as she chats gaily with the men on the terrace.*

Mrs. Boucicault   Kitty Brown. Mrs. Courtland Brown.

Madge   Another Brown? You seem to be going in for Browns.

Mrs. Boucicault   This is the California variety. Come here, Kitty.

Madge   She doesn't hear you. She seems to be rather absorbed in the men. (**Wallace** *comes back with a filmy scarf which he throws over* **Madge** *– standing back of her.*) Thanks so much.

Mrs. Boucicault   Tell Mrs. Brown I want her.

Wallace *goes to the tea table where* **Townley** *introduces him to* **Kitty**.

Madge   Isn't it a trifle unfortunate that Dierdre has gone in for Browns too – so near her wedding day?

Mrs. Boucicault   Stuff! Nonsense! What do you mean?

Madge (*absorbed in draping her scarf about her shoulders as effectively as possible*)   Would you like me to be perfectly frank, dear?

Mrs. Boucicault   I certainly would not. Go on – what is it? Say it. Say it.

Madge   I thought when I saw them together last night the sooner you got rid of him the –

Bob *comes out through the hall entrance. He has changed to afternoon flannels.*

Mrs. Boucicault   It's just as well you came along before we said it.

Madge I was going to say something very charming about you, Mr. Brown.

She smiles and purrs at **Bob**, *who goes to stand back of the sofa.*

Mrs. Boucicault She was asking me to let her be perfectly frank.

Bob That's always ominous. What a lovely frock, Mrs. Livingston.

Madge Oh, do you like it? I'm glad.

Bob At least you make it seem lovely. I think a woman is well dressed when we can't tell where her own charm stops and her clothes begin.

Madge You're so *understanding*. Oh, (*As* **Bob** *starts towards the terrace.*) I wonder if you'd be sweet enough to give me one of those cushions?

Bob (*taking two pillows from the large chair back of him*) Which one will you have? Green or blue?

Madge A green one, I think.

Kitty *is out of sight – having gone to the Left on the terrace with the men. As* **Bob** *lifts the pillows* **Kitty**'s *laugh suddenly rings out.* **Bob**, *hearing it – stops – and stands rigidly waiting – holding the two pillows.*

Madge (*turning to see why* **Bob** *hasn't given her the cushion*) Green – that's blue.

Bob Oh.

He mechanically gives a pillow to **Madge**. **Kitty** *comes across the terrace followed by* **Townley**, **Bruce**, *and* **Wallace**. *Laughing, she goes to* **Mrs. Boucicault** – *stopping above her chair.*

Townley Tell that last one to Mrs. Boucicault, Mrs. Brown. She'll love it.

Mrs. Boucicault You two Browns must know each other. Mr. Bob Brown – this is Mrs. Courtland Brown. (*There is a slight pause.* **Mrs. Boucicault** *turns to look at* **Kitty**.) What's the matter?

Kitty (*after a deep breath – looking at* **Bob**) How wonderful you long legged Americans are! I've been avoiding you in Paris – but it *is* wonderful to see you again.

Bob (*in level tones, looking steadily at* **Kitty**) Do you mean that?

Townley Don't flatter yourself too much, Brown. She thinks we *all* have long legs.

Kitty Has anybody got a cigarette? (*The three men near her offer her one.*) Oh, not three. That's my unlucky number. The third of June was my wedding day, today is the third of August, and three years ago – thanks.

Taking a cigarette from one, and a light from another.

Bob (*not taking his eyes away from* **Kitty**) What were you going to say – Mrs. Brown? Did anything unlucky happen to you three years ago?

Kitty (*as* **Wallace** *lights her cigarette*) I thought so then. I've grown wiser since. Have you ever been in California, Mr. Brown? I keep thinking I've seen you *some* place.

Moving a little towards **Bob**.

Bob   Yes—I have—but I don't seem to remember the *Courtland* Browns.

Kitty   Courtland was my maiden name. I took it back after my divorce of course, and I'm crazy about it. Mrs. Courtland Brown. Not bad, eh?

Townley   No—if one *must* be a Brown—Courtland certainly helps.

Kitty   That's the way I feel about it. Perhaps you don't mind being Brown. I did horribly.

Bob   You seem to have got rid of it pretty successfully.

Kitty   Where's that nice girl you were telling me about, Boucicault?

Mrs. Boucicault   Where is she, Bob?

Bob   I left her in the pool. She wouldn't come out.

Madge (*still on the sofa*)   I'm Madge Liingston, Mrs. Brown. Nobody seems to be introducing us.

Kitty (*going to* **Madge** *with gracious charm and putting out her hand*)   Oh, how do you do.

Madge   I've been admiring you.

Kitty   How nice! I'm grateful.

Mrs. Boucicault   Go get your tea, Bob. (**Bob** *staring at* **Kitty**, *doesn't hear.*) Don't stand around looking indefinite, Bob! Tea!

Bob   What? Oh—yes—thanks. I'll have about the longest drink of Scotch I've ever had in my life –I think.

He goes out to the tea table.

Kitty (*watching him as he goes*)   There's something strangely familiar about that man.

Townley   I dare say all Browns have something in common.

Dierdre (*coming from the house fresh and handsome in sport clothes – seeing* **Kitty** *and going to her*)   I'm awfully glad you got here. Gran's keen about you. Get me some food, will you, Bruce?

Bruce *goes to the tea table.*

Kitty   If I were a man I should fall in love with her *at once*.

Kitty *says this at* **Bob** *as he comes back with his drink and goes down Left. She sits on the small chair near* **Mrs. Boucicault** *at Right Center.*

Townley   That's what we all do.

Townley *is leaning lazily against the piano.*

Dierdre   I haven't noticed any special ardor on your part.

Townley   If I seem cold it's because I'm deep.

Madge   But the one she's going to marry is so beautifully in love with her.

Kitty   Which one is that? Mr. Brown?

Mrs. Boucicault   Stop your monkey tricks, Kitty. (*Hitting* **Kitty***'s chair with her stick quickly.*) I told you it was this boy – this nice boy Bruce.

Dierdre   Thanks, darling. (*As* **Bruce** *comes back to her with a sandwich and a highball.*) *Are* you a nice boy?

Bruce   *I* think I am.

Madge   Aren't they a beautiful pair? (**Bruce** *and* **Dierdre** *standing together, take a foolish pose.*) I hope you're going to be married in this dear quaint little church out here, Dierdre, instead of in town. The lines are so good. Aren't they, Wallace?

Wallace (*coming to sit in the chair at Center*)   The lines? Yes – very good indeed.

Kitty   Well, at least that's *something*. Good lines in a church are a much better reason than most people have for getting married.

Madge   Aren't you going to do that, Dierdre?

Townley   We could work up something very nice. The wedding procession walking over the grass – with garlands in our hands. What? Tum—tum—te—tum—tum—tum.
Singing the wedding march and moving about a little.

Bruce   Personally I'd rather be married by a policeman on the corner – no fuss.
Leaning on one of the pillars under the balcony.

Mrs. Boucicault   How do you like Madge's idea, Dierdre – the wedding here? You can have the whole place for the autumn if you want it.

Dierdre (*a little absently, drinking her highball as she stands back of the sofa at Left*)   Thanks.

Madge   Nothing could be more romantic. The leaves will be turning and the vines on the stone wall will be – Mrs. Brown, did you notice it as you drove in?

Kitty   Oh, yes, I think I did. I was married in a little church too – But it was spring – Everything was just beginning – instead of dying. It was the most perfect June that ever was – of course.

Bob   You must have been a perfect bride, Mrs. Brown.

Kitty   I was. I believed it all. The holy sacrament and everything. There never was such sunshine as it fell across the altar. There never were such flowers – *and* such bridesmaids. They wore large soft hats and green tulle frocks. Darlings – every one of them. They all have their divorces now.

The others laugh a little with the exception of **Bob** *and* **Madge**.

Bob (*keeping his eyes steadily on* **Kitty**)   I hope the bridegroom was fairly satisfactory *at the time.*

Kitty He was the most perfect part of it. And I was more in love than any girl – any place – *ever* was. Wasn't your wedding like that, Mrs. Livingston?

Madge (*shocked – and with excessive dignity*) A wedding is a very beautiful thing – always.

Kitty Are you still sentimental about your wedding – Mr. Livingston?

Wallace (*embarrassed, when he realizes* **Kitty** *is speaking to him*) I've never had a wedding and my name is Grainger.

He rises and goes out onto the terrace.

Kitty Oh – how stupid I am. Sorry.

There is a swift exchange of amused glances between **Dierdre***,* **Bruce** *and* **Townley***.*

Kitty (*to* **Dierdre** *and* **Bruce***, as* **Dierdre** *sits in the chair which* **Wallace** *left – and* **Bruce** *stands near her*) You both look so clever. Why don't you do something entirely new? Why go on doing the same old things you know won't work?

Townley Yes, why not evolve something called marriage which the human animal could have some reasonable hope of making a success of?

Bob For instance? What do you suggest, Mrs. Brown? What new arrangement do you think might make marriage a success? Have you evolved a solution? You seem so cheerful about it you must have thought of something pretty good.

Kitty (*still sitting at Right Center*) I haven't got far – but some graceful arrangement with all the little annoying things like love and fidelity entirely let out. It's absolutely fatal to marry the ones we're in love with. Don't you think so, Mrs. Livingston?

Madge My marriage was a success – a great success – and I can't bear this flippant cynical talk about the most sacred thing in the world. You haven't given me the glass of water, Wallace.

Wallace Oh, I'm so sorry.

Going to tea table to get it.

Kitty (*rising*) I'd love to walk about and see the place.

Townley May I come with you and point out the best features?

Mrs. Boucicault No, you may *not*. I need you, Townley. I'm going to walk a little myself and you're the only one lazy enough to put up with my knee. I think it most appropriate that Mr. Brown should show Mrs. Brown about.

Wallace *brings the glass of water to* **Madge**.

Bob (*going to* **Kitty**) So do I. There's one spot that reminds me of something I used to be awfully keen about. I'd like to show it to you.

Kitty How sweet of you! But Mr. Grainger has already promised to take me about. You said the view is especially lovely from – where did you say – Mr. Grainger?

Wallace (*with a quick glance at* **Madge**) Well – a –are your shoes all right for it?

Kitty My shoes are all right for anything. (*Going towards* **Wallace**.) Bouci, I broke ten engagements today to get here, but it was worth it. I had no idea I was going to run into anything as delightful as this. Life's so much more unexpected than anything we can possibly make up – isn't it, *Mr. Grainger*? I can't help being – a – little excited that you *are* Mr. Grainger instead of Mr. Livingston.

She takes **Wallace** *onto the terrace. They move out of sight.*

Madge (*rising and standing with the glass of water in her hand*) Well – *really*—what sort of a person *is* she, Boucicault?

Mrs. Boucicault (*in her chair at Right*) When a woman talks as much as that you may be sure she doesn't *mean* much. Isn't that so, Bob?

Bob I think it would be rather hard to say – about the lady in question.

He takes the glass from **Madge** *and goes out onto the terrace – putting both glasses on the table – and moves out of sight at Right.*

Madge She's quite obvious – it seems to *me*.

She sweeps out through the hall.

Dierdre Didn't you love it when she called Wallace Mr. Livingston? You needn't tell me she isn't *on*.

Mrs. Boucicault (*rising*) Hold your tongue. Come on, Townley. Give me my stick. Bruce, where's my parasol? (**Townley** *gives her the stick which is leaning against her chair.* **Bruce** *goes onto the terrace to get her parasol which he has left there.*) Somebody go in the house and amuse Madge.

Townley (*following* **Mrs. Boucicault** *as she moves towards the terrace*) You don't expect me to *amuse you* – do you?

Mrs. Boucicault Now don't *talk*, Townley – I'm tired of you all.

She moves off across the terrace like a ship – and out at Left – **Townley** *in her wake.*

Bruce (*coming down Center as* **Dierdre** *sits in Boucicault's chair at Right*) Awfully nice for some tennis now. Want to play?

Dierdre Um—no—I don't believe I do—thanks.

Bruce Why not?

Dierdre Well – I seem to have done enough. I think I'll call it a day.

Bruce It's been a pretty dumb day for me. I haven't seen anything of you at all.

Dierdre Well –don't you think it's rather a good idea not to be together *every* minute?

Bruce No I don't. Every minute I'm not with you is just so much time wasted.

Dierdre Now, Bruce, old thing, you can't keep *that* up.

Bruce You bet I can keep it up – for the rest of my life.

Dierdre You know you get bored with me, *once* in a while.

Bruce (*going a little closer to her*) Listen. If I was ever bored with you for a second – I wouldn't want to marry you.

Dierdre (*trying to evade his seriousness*) Now, darling –

Bruce (*getting stronger as he goes on*) And that's just exactly the way you felt about *me* till exactly three days ago when this Brown guy hove in sight. I'm jealous as a pup and pretty much scared and I think you're making a congenital idiot of yourself.

Dierdre Sweet mood you're in. (**Bob** *comes from the terrace and starts toward the hall.*) Oh, don't go, Bob. We're not going to fight.

Bruce Well what *are* we going to do?

Dierdre Must we do *anything*?

Bob I've got a lot of things to do inside.

Dierdre No, you haven't. You're only –

Kitty (*coming back from the terrace*) These shoes won't do, after all. I'm going to get some others.

Bob Mrs. Brown – I'm awfully anxious to ask you something about California – if you'll be good enough to give me just a minute.

Wallace (*who as followed* **Kitty** *in*) I'll come right back and wait for you here.

Dierdre (*rising*) Is this going to be a *secret* conference? Do you want us to go?

Bruce Yes he does. Come on with me – if you can *bear* it.

Giving **Dierdre** *a push as they go off across the terrace to the Right.*

Bob (*after a pause*) Why did you do this absurd thing? Why didn't you say who we are – at once?

Kitty Why didn't you?

Bob I couldn't speak. It was –

Kitty Neither could I. It was all so quick. If we'd blurted it out at once – but we didn't – and it's infinitely better this way. Much more graceful.

Bob It's ridiculous. I'm going to tell them now.

Kitty Oh no you're not. I refuse to be made – a—conspicuous. It's done now – and much more comfortable this way—for everybody. Why spoil everybody's week end about a thing that is of no importance really? We were bound to run into each other, some time, some place.

Bob I don't like it. There's no reason in the world why we shouldn't tell them.

Kitty There's no reason in the world why we should. What possible difference can it make to anybody in any way? It will only be for such a little while. Any hostess would be grateful to us for keeping still – especially this one.

Bob Do you want me to go in town?

Kitty (*turning back to look at* **Bob**) And leave this nice girl? How absurd!

Bob She's going to marry the boy.

Kitty Oh, surely not.

Bob What?

Kitty That half baked boy? He isn't up to her. She's ready for life. She's gorgeous. I must tell you something. Boucci sent for me to take you away from her. Now you know that's rather good.

She laughs.

Bob You can't be as hard as you seem.

Kitty You didn't expect me to be soft – did you?

Bob You're making them misunderstand you. They think you're a hard boiled woman of the world – to put it mildly. Is that what you want them to think?

Kitty I think it's all a very amusing situation myself. For goodness sake, let's be gay about it.

Bob I refuse to accept the situation. It's uncomfortable and absurd.

Kitty If *this* is uncomfortable what would it be if you told? Curiosity – watching. Why did it happen? – Who began it? What was it? – Feeling *so* sorry for me because I lost you.

Bob Oh—

Kitty Spoiling the girl's fun.

Bob Absurd.

Kitty (*with sudden fire*) I won't have it *all brought back*. It's a *very* trivial thing to ask – it seems to me. I *do* ask it. I—I shall leave at once if you're going to do it.

Bob If you put it that way – I won't.

Kitty Thanks.

Wallace (*coming back from the hall*) I hope I haven't kept you waiting.

Kitty (*after a slight pause – remembering*) Oh—my *shoes*. I won't be a minute. (*She gets her coat from the piano quickly and crosses to the hall entrance.*) Mr. Brown and I have found a distant relation – by marriage – but *very* distant.

She goes off quickly as the

CURTAIN FALLS

Act Two

Scene I

Place: The same as Act One.

Time: Two days later – Sunday evening after dinner.

At curtain: **Madge Livingston** *comes into the room from the hall – very distinguished in a floating evening gown peculiar to herself. She is shaken with nervous excitement.*

Wallace Grainger *follows – trying to quiet her.*

Wallace   But Madge – dearest –

Madge   I can understand the *others* – but for *you* to be acting as if you'd never seen anything like her before in your –

Wallace   She amuses me. She's refreshing. Why not? I'm stale, Madge – stale – stale – stale!

Madge   You mean I don't inspire you any more.

Wallace   Let's go outside. It's hot here.

Madge (*with sudden tragic tears*)   Oh, Wallace – dearest – if what we have isn't *perfect* – if it isn't the most beautiful thing in the world it doesn't *justify* itself.

Wallace   Why are you saying these things now? Nothing's *different*. You –

Mrs. Boucicault *and* **Dierdre** *come in from the hall.* **Mrs. Boucicault** *is important in her characteristic evening gown.* **Dierdre** *is striking and colorful.*

Madge (*wiping her eyes*)   Forgive me for leaving the table, Boucicault. I couldn't listen to another one of her stories.

Mrs. Boucicault (*sitting on the sofa at Left*)   I don't think they even know you've *left* the table, my dear.

Dierdre   Kitty does you bet. Her technique is marvellous. Think I'll go back. I don't want to miss anything.

Mrs. Bourcicault   Stay where you are. Here's the coffee. (*As* **Whitman** *and* **Struthers** *come from Left on the terrace with the coffee, liqueurs, whiskey, soda, etc. which they put on the table outside.*) Keep it outside, Whitman, and put the bridge tables out there.

Whitman (*coming into the room*)   Pardon me, madam. I'm afraid there's too strong a breeze for playing outside.

Boucicault   Outside.

Whitman (*with resignation – going back onto the terrace*)   Very good, madam.

Mrs. Boucicault He's probably right. He always is – damn him. Go back Wallace, and start them out. I want to get at the bridge or it will be midnight before we begin. (**Wallace** *hesitates – glancing at* **Madge** *who has moved to the piano where she carefully repairs her makeup.*) Well – what's the matter with *you?* – Too strong a breeze?

Wallace Why do we hesitate when you give orders?

Mrs. Boucicault Because you like to hear me bellow, I s'pose – so I'll think I'm having my own way. Go on. Do as I tell you.

Wallace *goes out through the hall.*

Dierdre I'm crazy about you, Gran. You're so onto yourself.

Mrs. Boucicault Tell one of them to bring my coffee. I'll have it *here*.

Dierdre (*starting onto the terrace*) Have a real drink – anybody? You, Madge?

Madge No, thanks.

Dierdre You – darling?

Mrs. Boucicault No. – Neither will you.

Dierdre Oh, lay off, Gran. If Bob comes out tell him where I am.

Mrs. Boucicault He seems to be lingering too – just as hypnotized with Kitty as the rest of 'em.

Dierdre You mean you *want* him to be. You're a scream, Gran.

Madge How in the world did you happen to ask her while Dierdre is here?

Dierdre While *I'm* here? Don't you love it? You don't have to put a crimp in your famous hospitality on *my* account – do you, pet?

Mrs. Boucicault Go on outside if you're going.

Dierdre You're awfully cunning. (*She giggles and comes back to her grandmother.*) I give you good on Kitty, old fox – but it isn't working the way you *want* it to a little bit – is it?

Mrs. Boucicault I don't know what you're talking about.

Madge I suppose you think I don't either – but I'm afraid I do. I think Bruce is behaving extremely well.

Dierdre (*with quick resentment*) What's Bruce got to do with it?

Madge Has the man you're going to marry nothing to say about you falling in love with somebody else?

Dierdre Has the man you're married to nothing to say about the one you're in love with?

Mrs. Boucicault Stop that kind of talk, Dierdre.

Dierdre I don't know why you expect me to be so different from anybody else.

Mrs. Boucicault I expect you to go about your business of marrying Bruce – and – let everybody else *alone*.

Dierdre And I expect to be *let* alone, Gran.

Mrs. Boucicault (*pounding the floor with her stick*) *Stop* it! You're forgetting who you are.

Dierdre I know damn well who I am. That's why I'm going to manage my own business.

She goes out onto the terrace and off at Left.

Mrs. Boucicault Old fool! The last thing on earth I expected to do – say anything to her.

Madge (*rising and floating slowly to Center*) Aren't they appalling? Would you have spoken to your grandmother like that?

Mrs. Boucicault No – but it would have been a darned good thing for us both if I *had*. She was the meanest old woman I ever knew.

Madge Dierdre is going headlong right *at* the man. It's the openness – the casualness that shocks me.

Mrs. Boucicault Oh – you're shocked – are you?

Madge Aren't you?

Mrs. Boucicault Yes – but I think I prefer her brazenness to your slyness.

Madge (*going to sit in the large chair at Right*) You hurt me.

Mrs. Boucicault Poppycock! Don't pose with me, Madge. She's the only one of the whole pack I care a hang about. I love her. I've actually been fool enough to let myself love her. I'd begun to have some pride in her. I'd begun to think the good old stock was coming out. Why did this thing have to hit her? *Why?* And no matter what happens I can't blame *her*. I blame myself and my respectable friends and the disrespectable things they are doing.

Madge (*rising*) I won't stand the things you say to me!

Mrs. Boucicault All right. Remind me to speak to Whitman about the soup. I won't stand *it* either. (**Bob** *strolls in from the hall and laughs as he hears this.*) Come here and give me a light, Bob. Are they moving in there at all yet?

Bob Not yet. I thought I'd come out and remind you that you *have* some male guests, Boucicault. I think they've settled down for the evening. I don't think they're coming out at all.

Going to **Mrs. Boucicault** *and opening his cigarette case.*

Madge (*standing near the piano*) Too fascinated with the fascinating Mrs. Brown?

Bob   They seem to be. Which will you have – mine or yours?

Mrs. Boucicault   You try one of mine.

Taking a tiny cigar from her case.

Bob   No, thanks. I'm afraid your little cigars are too strong for me.

Giving **Mrs. Boucicault** *a light.*

Madge (*frowning at the cigar*)   How can you, Boucicault?

Mrs. Boucicault (*with a puff of satisfaction*)   They've saved me from being "among those present" on many an occasion. The second time I met King Edward and he called me by name – right off the trigger – I said, "Ah, your Majesty, it's my cigar you remember." And he said, "Ah, no, madam, your personality is so much stronger than your cigar." He was a great man.

She imitates the king with a slight German accent.

Bob (*going to* **Madge** *to light her cigarette*)   You've known a great collection, haven't you, Boucicault – sitting on thrones and wallowing in the gutter.

Boucicault   They've all been the best of *their* kind. I will say that for 'em.

Bob (*moving back to Center as he lights his own cigarette*)   It's high time you wrote your memoirs – the truth – the whole truth and nothing but the truth about my famous friends.

Mrs. Boucicault   I don't propose to spend the rest of my life in jail.

Dierdre (*coming back into the room with a cup of coffee in one hand and a highball in the other*)   Here you are, Gran.

Mrs. Boucicault (*taking the coffee*)   I thought you'd fallen in it and died.

Dierdre   Bob, Gran thinks Kitty's much more alluring than I am. How about it? Do you?

Bob   You both have your points. Is that for me?

Indicating the highball.

Dierdre   It *is* not.

Bob   I think it would be a good idea if I had one, too.

They turn towards the terrace. Voices are heard, and **Kitty** *comes in from the hall with* **Townley**, **Wallace** *and* **Bruce**. **Madge** *hurries to sit in the large chair Right.*

Kitty   It was this one song which made her the chic of Paris. Not much of a song and she can't sing. She has no voice – no looks – no style – but *Oh*, the things she *has* got.

Kitty *is very chic in a ravishing evening gown, and carries a charming fan.*

Boucicault   Who's that you're talking about?

Kitty (*going to the piano*)   You remember – Fifine. We heard her – her first night in Paris. You said, "Thank heaven for somebody more diverting than my guests."

Mrs. Boucicault   See here – when you quote me – make it agreeable.

Kitty (*standing before the keyboard*)   Nobody would believe you said it, lamb. Will someone be sweet enough to move the piano – just a little nearer?

Kitty *sits and dashes off a brilliant bit of music.* **Madge** *slowly realizes that* **Kitty** *has imitated her and rises with great hauteur and sweeps out onto the terrace.*

Kitty   Am I disturbing anyone?

Townley (*standing close to* **Kitty**)   Yes – very successfully.

Wallace (*leaning over the piano at the upper side of it – not having seen* **Madge** *leave the room*)   Do you know *"Paree"*?

Kitty   Yes.

Playing a little of the song – and then beginning it again as **Wallace** *sings it.*

Bruce (*after the first strain – speaking to* **Mrs. Boucicault** *as he too leans on the piano at the end*)   That's not what he *thinks* he's singing.

Wallace   Certainly it is. It's a good song.

Kitty (*playing again*)   Come along.

Dierdre   Give the song a chance, Wallie.

Kitty *plays – nodding to them all to make them sing,* **Wallace** *goes on with the song – this time* **Townley** *and* **Bruce** *sing with him –* **Kitty** *joining in a little.* **Bob** *whistles without watching the group at the piano,* **Dierdre**, *with her highball glass – dances a little – before* **Bob**.

Kitty (*as they finish the first of the song – playing a softer strain and speaking as she plays*)   A divine boy sang it all the way over on the boat.

Dierdre (*calling across to* **Kitty**)   I love your frock, Kitty.

Kitty (*talking to* **Townley** *who is bending over her as she plays*)   Only twenty.

Dierdre   What – the frock?

Kitty   No – the boy.

Townley   I was divine at twenty.

Kitty (*smiling up at him.*)   You still are.

Wallace   We all are.

Mrs. Boucicault (*on the sofa*)   Keep still. I can't hear what you're saying.

Kitty *keeps on playing.*

Wallace (*raising his voice to* **Mrs. Boucicault**)   I say we *all* are.

Mrs. Boucicault   What?

Bruce (*to* **Mrs. Boucicault**)   He says we *all* are.

Mrs. Boucicault   You all are *what?*

Kitty   Don't you know what we all are?

She dashes into the chorus and they all sing again – with more abandon and embellishment.

Mrs. Boucicault (*as they finish*)   Is that you making that particularly bad noise, Townley?

Townley   No – I'm making the tenor.

Mrs. Boucicault   Well, *stop* it.

Kitty   No – don't. It makes the rest of us seem so good. (**Madge** *comes in from the terrace – stares at* **Wallace** *and sweeps through out into the hall. As* **Kitty** *plays – she smiles at* **Wallace**.) I think you're being paged.

Wallace   What?

He turns and sees **Madge** *and goes out after her.* **Bob** *joins* **Kitty** *and* **Townley** *at the piano. She goes on playing.* **Mrs. Boucicault** *rises and goes onto the terrace.*

Bruce (*going to* **Dierdre**, *and speaking to her in low tones*)   Let's hop in the pool. It's so beastly hot.

Dierdre   Oh, Lord – not yet. We've just had dinner.

Bruce   I mean after while.

Dierdre   Gran wants to play bridge – anyway. You can't buck that.

Bruce   We could sneak out. Moon and everything. It'll be great.

Dierdre   Yes I know – but – I'm not sure I want to.

Bruce   You've been keen enough about going in with *him* every night.

Dierdre *is watching* **Bob** *who is bending over the piano – whistling as* **Kitty** *plays.*

Kitty (*to* **Bob**)   Do you sing?

Bob   I've let it slide. No incentive. I've let a lot of things go – in the last few years.

Kitty   Have you really? I seem to have been rather busy picking things up in the last few years.

Bob   Such as – ?

Townley   Me?

Kitty (*laughing*)   Exactly.

Townley *strolls out onto the terrace.*

Dierdre (*listening to the music*)   What is that, Bob?

Bob *doesn't hear her.*

Bruce   For Heaven's sake – Dierdre – What *is* this? Have you gone off your head about him?

Dierdre   What shall we do about it if I have?

Bruce   Come outside. We're going to talk this thing out right *now*.

Dierdre   What's the use? I know every bloomin' thing you're going to say – and I don't know *what* I want to say yet.

Bruce   You –

Dierdre   That's straight, Bruce. Let me alone for awhile – please – old man. We'd only ball it up now.

Bruce *strides out.* **Townley** *moves down to* **Dierdre** *and they go onto the terrace together and out of sight at Left.*

Bob (*bending over* **Kitty** *and playing a few notes with one hand*)   Do you remember this? (**Kitty** *plays and he sings* "If Love were All." *She stops suddenly after the second strain and stands up.*) Don't go, Kitty – I want to talk to you.

Kitty (*moving away a little*)   What on earth have we to talk about?

Bob   Plenty of things.

Kitty   For instance?

Bob   Ourselves. You. There are lots of things I want to ask you.

Kitty   I can't imagine myself answering any of them.

Bob   I'm afraid you'll have to answer one or two.

Kitty   Which ones?

Bob   I've got to talk to you, Kitty. That's all there is about it. Now when? Where?

Kitty (*moving towards* **Mrs. Boucicault** *as she comes back from the terrace*)   What an interesting old chain Bouci. Chinese, isn't it?

Touching one of the chains about **Mrs. Boucicault**'s *neck.*

Mrs. Boucicault   Is it any good?

Dierdre (*coming from the terrace and going to sit on the sofa*)   Granny never knows whether the objects d'art she collects around her neck are junk or pearls without price.

Kitty   Where did it come from, Bouci?

Mrs. Boucicault   A pawn shop probably. It can't be worth much.

Kitty   Why not?

Mrs. Boucicault   Because I know who gave it to me.

Kitty Who did?

Mrs. Boucicault My late husband. (*Turning away.*) Where *are* Madge and Wallace?

She goes onto the terrace and off at Left.

Townley (*who has come back from the terrace during these lines and now moves to* **Kitty** *as* **Mrs. Boucicault** *goes away*) Are you wearing anything *your* late husband gave you?

Kitty (*touching a small string of pearls*) Oh, yes – these – modest but pure.

Bob Do you wear them to remember him by?

Kitty No – I remember him very well. Quite distinctly in fact. He was one of the most attractive men I've ever known, and as men go – I still think so.

Townley My God – why did you divorce him then? If a woman feels that way about a man, why doesn't she hang on to him?

Kitty He didn't hang on to me.

Townley Oh, come!

Kitty No – really.

Bob That's very interesting. Just what do you mean by not hanging on?

Dierdre *Why* did you divorce him?

Kitty (*after a pause, looking at* **Dierdre**) Because of a girl so much like you, that it's funny – almost.

Glancing swiftly at **Bob**, *who goes towards the terrace quickly.*

Dierdre Lucky nobody has to divorce *you* because of me, Bob. Come on.

She takes **Bob**'s *arm. They stop under the balcony at Left to talk.*

Townley I'm so grateful to Boucicault for you, Kitty. Usually I'm called in to take on a woman with a club foot or something – because she amused Bouci once in – Labrador. When she gets her here, she wants to shoot her and sends for me.

Kitty (*sitting in the large chair at Right*) Have you got a cigarette, Townley?

Townley *goes to sit on the seat below* **Kitty**'s *chair and lights her cigarette. They talk in low tones.*

Mrs. Boucicault *comes from the terrace trying to hear what* **Dierdre** *is saying to* **Bob** *as they stand under the balcony at Left.*

Dierdre Let's hop in the pool after while. It's so beastly hot.

Bob Is it? I don't think so.

Dierdre Oh – you don't *need* the pool to cool off. Why the sudden drop in temperature?

Bob All your imagination.

Dierdre Am I as dark and glowing and mysterious as ever?

Bob You're marvellous.

Dierdre What are you looking at?

As he glances at **Kitty**.

Bob I'm looking at you.

Dierdre (*lifting her face close to his*) And I'm looking at you, darling – and seeing the most wonderful things in the world.

Bob (*touching her highball glass*) Isn't that enough?

Dierdre Don't be so paternal. Come on. You need one yourself.

Dierdre *goes out –* **Bob** *follows her.*

Kitty Townie, are you trying to persuade me you've fallen in love with me or is this just your week-end charm?

Mrs. Boucicault (*coming down to* **Kitty**) Go on, Townley.

Townley (*rising*) Where shall I go?

Mrs. Boucicault Go to hell.

Kitty (*calling to* **Townley** *as he goes*) And if you *return* – bring me some *very* hot coffee.

Townley *goes onto the terrace to the table to get the coffee.*

Mrs. Boucicaut (*suddenly flaring at* **Kitty**) Why don't you do what I want you to do? Get Bob Brown away from Dierdre?

Kitty (*rising quickly*) Really, Bouci, this is rather disgusting. You're putting a ridiculous thing up to me – an impossible thing.

Mrs. Boucicault You're efficient enough with the others. Why are you so mulish about it? This is the first time I've seen you even *speak* to Bob. I've been watching Dierdre. I heard something she said to him just now. Help me, Kitty.

Kitty I've been watching her too. She *is* in love with him. Why on earth don't you let them alone? Isn't your Bob Brown as good as the other one for her to marry – better – since he's the one she really wants?

Mrs. Boucicault He hasn't the slightest intention of marrying her – and she's throwing herself *at* him. Hot headed young daredevil! Anything could happen. I'm *frightened*, Kitty. (**Townley** *comes back with a cup of coffee.*) What *is* it, Townley? Go away. Go away and mind your own business.

Townley This *is* my business. Don't snort at me, angel. I was sent for this.

Mrs. Boucicault (*going towards the terrace*) Well now that you've brought it in, see if you can take it out again. Come on. They're all out here now.

Kitty (*reaching for the coffee*)   Oh, don't take that away from me. I can't bear it.

Townley *turns to* **Kitty** – *giving her the cup. They stand at Right, talking.*

Mrs. Boucicault (*as* **Madge** *and* **Wallace** *come in from the hall*)   Well – where have *you* been? I thought you were on the terrace.

Kitty (*to* **Townley**)   I've never seen her as bad as this.

Townley   Old girl's on the rampage about something.

Mrs. Bouciault   Where *are* you, Townley?

Townley (*hurrying to* **Bouciault** *as she stops with* **Wallace** *and* **Madge** *up under the balcony*)   Right under your feet, dearest.

Madge   Come and get my liqueur, Wallace.

Madge *goes onto the terrace and out of sight at Right.* **Wallace** *starts after her.* **Townley** *and* **Mrs. Boucicault** *go off Left.*

Kitty (*dropping her handkerchief and imitating* **Madge**)   Oh – my handkerchief.

Wallace *goes down to* **Kitty** *He picks up her handkerchief – gives it to her and stands before her – flattered and having lost his head a little.*

Wallace   The last verse has just come to me.

Kitty   Is it as lovely as the others?

Wallace   More so. It's *you*.

Kitty   I'm thrilled pink. That's one thing that's never happened to me – poetry.

Wallace   I haven't done this in years – you know. "Shadows of understanding in her eyes. Shadow of happiness gone – "

Kitty   Oh! Shadows. I s'pose that's all right so long as you don't say *lines* under her eyes. When are you going to read it all to me?

Wallace   When will you let me? Why don't we cut this?

Kitty   I'd love to – but where can we go?

Mrs. Boucicault (*coming into sight with* **Townley** *up Left on the terrace*)   Now look at that ass! Wallace – Madge is waiting for that drink. (**Wallace** *goes to* **Boucicault**.) Haven't you got the sense you were born with?

Wallace   No. Do you know anybody who has?

Mrs. Boucicault   No – I don't. You go slow on those shadows.

Mrs. Boucicault *goes out* – **Wallace** *follows her.*

Townley   Wait.

Kitty   I don't dare.

Townley Tomorrow will be here before we know it – and we'll all be gone. Have dinner with me tomorrow night in town.

Kitty Oh – I don't think I can.

Townley Of course you can. Why can't you? How many days are you going to be in town?

Kitty (*sitting on the upper arm of the large chair – her back to the audience sipping her coffee*) I don't know.

Townley Yes you do.

Kitty Two – three – maybe.

Townley I'll take you to a nice little place up the river – cheap and cool and –

Kitty Nobody there?

Townley Yes.

Kitty I have to think.

Townley What about?

Kitty I don't know.

They laugh. There is a great attraction between them.

Townley I'm not going to lose you.

Kitty Sweet of you.

Townley Give me something more to remember than this. I've got to talk to you. Let's get away.

Bob *has crossed the terrace at back – coming on from the Left – and going to the table where he pours a cup of coffee.*

Kitty How can we?

Townley (*whispering*) You have a balcony.

Kitty Oh – so I have – with steps.

Townley You're a darling. Thanks.

He kisses her hand as **Bob** *comes down to Right of* **Kitty** *with a cup of coffee.*

Bob I was sent with this and told to bring you out – *after* you had finished it.

Kitty (*still sitting on the arm of the chair*) Oh – (*Taking the cup.*) thanks. I need it.

Townley (*To* **Brown** *as* **Kitty** *gives him the other empty cup*) You're not trying to get rid of me – by any chance?

Bob No – by firm intention. (*To* **Kitty**.) Will you take me on at bridge?

Kitty Were you coached to say that – too?

Bob No – that's on my own.

Kitty Are you good?

Bob Very.

Kitty (*sipping her coffee*) It might be unlucky – for the Browns to play together.

Townley It would. You don't want to play anyway. Why don't we rise up and defy the old girl?

Bob Have you ever tried it?

Kitty We must do *something* – and it isn't ten o'clock yet.

Townley But Boucicault's a fiend. She never stops and I always lose my shirt.

Kitty Never mind. I'll give you one of mine.

Bruce (*coming into sight on terrace at Left*) You'd better come quick, Townley – to avoid a blowout.

Bruce goes back again.

Townley (*as he goes up to table with the cup and off Left*) I *am* a worm. Why don't I turn?

Kitty (*rising and taking her fan from the small table below the large chair*) The situation is getting more amusing every minute. Isn't it?

Bob No. I don't think it is. It's getting more ridiculous every minute. We ought to have told them in the first place. Let's tell them now. It would clear the whole atmosphere.

Kitty The atmosphere doesn't need clearing. Surely you aren't embarrassed – are you? *Don't* let my being here make the slightest difference to you in any way.

Bob About Dierdre – you mean?

Kitty About anything.

Bob You don't think I'm in love with her?

Kitty Aren't you? I'm no judge – of *that*.

Bob And you don't think for a minute she's – it's anything serious with *her*?

Kitty Oh – isn't it? I should have said it was something very serious. But perhaps I'm no judge of that either.

Bob You're implying a lot – but you surely don't think I was skunk enough to go after her.

Kitty (*moving away*) And you surely don't think you have to explain anything to me.

Bob I want you to know how it is. I *was* flirting with her – a little – a little too much – perhaps – before you came – but seeing you has made me stop.

Kitty   Oh – sorry. (*Half turning back to him.*) But I'll be gone in the morning – and it will be just as though I'd never been here at all.

Starting again to go.

Bob   Wait – *please.*

Kitty   Yes?

Bob   I'm not going to ask to see the children – though I want to – horribly.

Kitty (*having looked at him quickly with startled wistful eyes – and speaking with difficulty*)   Bob – it *is* better for them to know only one side – even if that side is – *me.*

Bob   Are they well?

Kitty   Very. Robert is getting to be more like you every minute. And Katherine is marvellous.

Bob (*looking at her eagerly and moving a little towards her*)   Like you?

Kitty   Yes – only more so.

Bob   I hope she'll be just exactly like you – *just exactly* – as you *were*, I mean.

Kitty   She won't, I assure you. She'll be much more intelligent – and much more *prepared*. I believe in preparedness.

Bob   You've changed, Kitty.

Kitty   I hope so. Three years of Paris ought to improve any woman.

Bob   You seem to have had a pretty good time.

Kitty   I've been awfully lucky in the people I've known. Gay, delightful people.

Bob   Like these – you mean?

Kitty   Um – all sorts.

Bob   Tell me some more. You might sit down a minute at least. What have you actually been doing – all this time?

She hesitates in a long pause and then sits on the sofa back of her. **Bob** *brings the arm chair and sits before* **Kitty**.

Kitty   *I've* been working hard, too.

Bob   At what?

Kitty   Clothes. I've made a good connection with a firm in Paris, and I'm going to have a shop out home.

Bob   *What?*

Kitty   Yes. It will keep me going back and forth, which I shall adore. I can stand one place because I'll always know I'm going to the other.

Bob Um. There's something in that – *possibly*. Though the further I go the more I see I'd like to stay put – once I get in the right place.

Kitty *Are* there any right places?

Bob There's just *one* – for me. But I'm not *in* it. (**Kitty** *is about to rise. He goes on quickly.*) Well – *and?*

Kitty I think that's about all – except that in a little while I shan't have to have any more alimony – I can take care of the children myself.

Bob You'll do nothing of the kind.

Kitty Certainly I will.

Bob We'll see about that.

Kitty There's something about one's own money – making it and spending it – that has – I know now how a man feels – only – he takes it for granted – and it's a new thrill to me.

Bob And when you're not working?

Kitty Like you I've been amusing myself with anything and everything that came my way. I know how a man feels about that too.

Bob You're very glib but I don't know just what you mean. What – do you – exactly?

Dierdre (*coming on from the terrace with her highball*) What *is* this? *Are* you trying to vamp Bob – Kitty?

Kitty (*still sitting*) You evidently don't think I could.

Dierdre I don't think you *would* – under the circ. I think you *could* get any man you want. Don't you, Bob?

Bob (*putting the chair back and going down Right Center*) There doesn't seem to be any doubt about that.

Kitty (*to* **Dierdre**) What would you do if I did? Would it be a joke or a tragedy to you?

Dierdre (*lifting her face to* **Bob**) Bob knows what it would mean to me. Don't you, Bob?

Kitty Oh – well—if Bob knows what *you* mean – and you know what *he* means – nothing else matters. Does it?

Mrs. Boucicault (*coming in from the terrace*) We have to play in here after all. The wind blows the cards away – confound it!

Kitty Are you going to let me play with you, Bouci?

Standing up and moving out of the way as **Whitman** *comes in with a card table and chairs.*

Mrs. Boucicault   Yes – with Bob – over here.

Struthers *has brought on a card table and chairs which he places at Right.*

Kitty (*to* **Bob**)   You'd much better play over there. If you take *me* on you'll have to be a good loser as well as a good player.

Bob   It depends on what I'm losing – how good I am.

Dierdre   You're going to play with me.

Bob   I don't think I can.

Dierdre *draws* **Bob** *to the table at Right and goes on talking to him a little desperately in low tones.* **Kitty** *has watched this an instant – and then turns to* **Townley** *who is standing at* **Mrs. Boucicault**'s *Right.* **Kitty**, **Townley** *and* **Mrs. Boucicault** *all talk at once – very gaily for a moment. The* **Servants** *go out.* **Madge** *and* **Wallace** *are seen on the terrace.*

Kitty (*heard above the others after a moment*)   You play *against* me, Townley. You're probably worse than I am.

Townley   I'm rather good – but erratic.

Kitty   That's what all rotten players say. Where do you want me – Bouci?

Mrs. Boucicault   Right there. Put that light over my shoulder, Townley.

Townley *gets the lamp – which is up Left.*

Kitty (*as she sits at Right of table*)   I need more than a light over my shoulder when I play with *you*, Bouci. If I didn't love you so much dearest, I'd hate you.

Townley (*coming to sit below the table*)   I *do* hate her – when I play cards with her.

Mrs. Boucicault   How do you suppose I feel about you – when I have to play with you?

Bob (*sitting below the table at Right*)   Be careful, Dierdre! You don't know what you're doing.

Dierdre (*sitting at Right of Right table*)   I know what I'm doing and what I want. Oh, Bob – I'm crazy about you.

Mrs. Boucicault   Bob – come over here.

Kitty (*as* **Bob** *crosses to the Left table*)   Too bad Mr. Brown can't be in two places at once.

Bob (*sitting at Left – opposite* **Kitty**)   This place will do for me.

Bruce *comes on to the terrace from the Right and goes quickly down to* **Dierdre** *– sitting above the table – pleading with her to stop drinking.*

Kitty   What are we playing for?

Bob   Anything you say.

Townley Anything you say – so long as you make it about twenty-five cents a point – for Bouci.

Kitty Oh my soul! Who's going to pay my losses? Are you?

Townley Yes – if you'll take a bad check.

They cut and deal, all talking at once.

Bruce (*heard at the other table*) Put on the brakes, Dierdre. You've had enough.

Dierdre Don't be young.

Bruce For heaven's sake, let up. Why do you do it? What's there *in* it?

Dierdre Not a thing. (*Turning her glass upside down.*) Not a damned thing. Go *put* something in it.

Bruce You can't have any more.

Wallace *has come down from the terrace and stands above* **Kitty** *– watching the game.* **Madge** *tries to draw him away to the other table.*

Dierdre You give me a pain in the ear, beloved. Whitman – bring me a highball. Oh, look who's here! The Lady Madge!

As **Madge** *and* **Wallace** *come to sit at table Right* **Madge** *sits Left of table.* **Wallace** *below it.* **Kitty** *is leaning toward* **Townley**, *talking to him.*

Mrs. Boucicault Kitty! Keep your mind on your game.

Kitty I don't play bridge with my mind.

Townley What do you use?

Kitty Just my hands.

Mrs. Boucicault Stop talking. What do you make it, Bob?

Bob By.

Townley A heart.

Mrs. Boucicault (*glaring at* **Townley**) What?

Townley A heart – dear heart.

Kitty Three spades!

Townley Oh, God.

Kitty Ask him to help *me* too.

Mrs. Boucicault By.

Bob Pass.

Townley By.

Dierdre (*giggling as* **Wallace** *deals*) Is that a club or a spade hopping around, Wallie?

Showing a card to **Wallace**.

Madge   Well really! Are we playing – or are we not?

Dierdre   We're playing, old dear. *And how!*

Wallace   Go on, child – call it a spade.

Dierdre   That's all right by me. Funny looking little things aren't they? Hi – Whitman –

Banging her glass on the table.

Bruce   Let up, Dierdre.

Kitty (*who is playing while* **Bob** *is dummy*)   Don't tell me I took that trick, Mr. Brown. There must be something wrong.

Bob (*rather grimly*)   You either played it very cleverly or very *Innocently* – I'm not sure which.

Kitty   Innocence is not my long suit.

Mrs. Boucicault (*throwing down a card and shouting at* **Townley**)   You should have trumped my ace – idiot.

Townley   What?

Mrs. Boucicault   Certainly. It's the only way in God's name you could make it.

Townley   Are you spoofing me?

Kitty   No, she's *cursing* you. Poor darling! This is one of those purple moments when the most brilliant thing you can do is to do the thing you've been trying all your life *not* to do.

Dierdre (*getting up*)   There – I'm dummy now. I'm going over there.

Pointing to the left table.

Mrs. Boucicault   Sit down, Dierdre.

Dierdre   Kitty, do you know why Gran got you here?

Bruce (*trying to make* **Dierdre** *sit down*)   Dierdre, stop it.

Dierdre   To get Bob away from me. But it can't be done. Can it, Bob?

Boucicault (*in a low tone to* **Bob**)   Can't you *do* something?

Kitty *lowers her head.* **Bruce** *has pulled* **Dierdre** *down into her chair where she fights him.*

Bob (*rising*)   Let's go outside, Dierdre. It's too hot to play – isn't it? Why don't we –

Townley (*rising*)   Yes – Let's get out in the air.

Madge *rises and moves away.*

Dierdre (*getting up again*) Bob wants to shut me up. Look at him.

Bob Not at all. But come and say it to *me*. I don't think anybody else is –

Dierdre (*moving towards* **Kitty** – *very unsteadily*) But I want Kitty to *know*.

Mrs. Boucicault Bruce, take her out of the room.

Dierdre Why should I leave the room? I'm a great deal more decent than anybody *in* it.

Sitting heavily in the chair which **Madge** *left.*

Kitty (*lifting her head quickly and throwing her cards on the table*) I don't think there's any doubt about *that*. Why don't we *all* leave the room – in the order of our sins?

Townley That's a good idea. I'll start the procession.

He goes to Center and up towards the terrace – stopping at upper left as **Kitty** *speaks.*

Kitty I'll come next.

She goes up – stopping as **Dierdre** *calls out.*

Dierdre But *Kitty* – I want you to *know*.

Bruce (*in a low tone to* **Dierdre** – *standing above her*) Dierdre – *please*.

Dierdre I can't help it, Bruce.

Bruce *turns away quickly and goes on to terrace and off at Right.*

Mrs. Boucicault You've disgraced yourself, Dierdre.

Kitty Why do you say that, Bouci? She's only telling the truth. I think it's delightful.

Dierdre Gran thinks I'm tight.

Her head drops a little over the back of the chair.

Kitty (*going to* **Dierdre**) Just chatty – aren't you? I am too – when I've had a drink or two. If this had been me – instead of you – my word – the things I could have told about the first time I fell in love. Couldn't you, Mr. Brown?

Bob (*standing at the Left of the table*) I don't think anybody would be interested.

Kitty Oh, it's always amusing. Why don't we make it an "I confess" game – and cross our hearts to be as honest as Dierdre? How many times has it been the first time with you, Townie?

Townley Well – a – You'll have to give me a few minutes to think.

Kitty While he's thinking – will you, Madge? May I call you Madge? We're all getting so cosy and real now.

Madge   I find this excessively disagreeable, *Mrs. Brown*.

Dierdre   Bob, you tell Kitty how it is with us.

Bob   Don't, Dierdre!

Dierdre   You wouldn't take him away from me, would you, Kitty? You *mustn't now*.

Kitty   No danger of that – is there, Mr. Brown?

Mrs. Boucicault   Dierdre, Leave this room!

Dierdre   No! I want to tell –

Kitty   Come on, dear. Come outside and tell me. I know just how you feel. How could you resist Bob.

Mrs. Boucicault   Katherine! Are you upholding Dierdre?

Kitty   I'll do my best. She's a little tall for me.

Boucicault   Katherine, I'm ashamed of you.

Kitty   That's good, Bouci. I'm ashamed of *you*, too. You've been very naughty with your heavy intrigue. I told you I wasn't clever enough for this job.

Bob   What job?

Kitty   Oh, to get you, and have you and hold you, forever.

Madge   Boucicault, I can't stand this brazenness!

Kitty   Now if it were *Wallie* you wanted me to take away from somebody – there's no telling *what* might have happened.

She smiles at **Wallace** *– much to his excited embarrassment – and turns towards the terrace as the*

CURTAIN FALLS

Act Two

Scene II

Time: About an hour after Scene I.

*Place: The balcony onto which **Kitty**'s room opens. Narrow steps lead down at the left end. Below the line of the balcony the stage is in darkness.*

*Two long French windows with shutters open onto the balcony—one from **Kitty**'s room—one from a room at the Right. The shutters of the room at Right are closed—the room in darkness.*

*The shutters at **Kitty**'s windows are open—a dim light in the room.*

At curtain: the stage is empty.

Perkins (*after a moment, from within*)   Yes, madam. No—I don't think so, madam. (*A pause.*) I beg pardon? (*She comes on to the balcony.*) Oh yes it is—*full*.

Kitty (*inside—not seen*)   Ravishing—isn't it?

Perkins   It's very nice, Madam—if you like it.

Kitty   Can't you do better than that for the moon, Perkins?

Perkins (*folding the red velvet coat she holds*)   I don't care for it myself. It's too spooky.

Kitty (*coming onto the balcony wearing a very charming dressing robe*)   Skip along now. Mrs. Boucicault needs you and I don't. And bring my coffee at eight. Don't wait for me to ring. I'm taking an early train to town.

She stands at the railing looking down.

Perkins   Yes, madam.

Kitty   Good night, Perkins.

Perkins   Good night, madam. Thank you.

Perkins goes in. The glow of a cigarette is seen below in the darkness.

Kitty (*laughing softly as she looks over the railing*)   Not *really*!

Townley   Inevitably.

Kitty   You're too amusing.

Townley   I'm coming up.

Kitty   Oh—I thought you were taking a walk.

Townley (*starting up the steps*)   My God, how they creak!

Kitty   You don't mind, do you?

Townley Not if they don't break down.

Kitty Shake 'em. How do they feel?

Townley (*his head and shoulders seen as he climbs up*) Very frail.

Kitty Oh! The whole thing's coming down!

Townley That'll be all right—after I get up. How pretty you are in that light!

Kitty You look *better* yourself.

Townley Where do we sit?

Kitty We don't.

Townley Oh yes we do.

Drawing **Kitty** *down onto the top step.*

Kitty I don't think it's safe.

Townley Thanks.

Kitty I mean architecturally speaking.

Townley (*looking along the balcony*) Anybody next to you—architecturally speaking?

Kitty I haven't seen anyone. Don't tell me you'd be—embarrassed if you were discovered here?

Townley I'd be terribly flattered. Would you be—ashamed of me?

Kitty Oh—most *proud*. Why shouldn't I be proud of an irresistible man sitting on my door step?

Townley No reason—so long as you don't resist him.

Kitty (*by way of changing the subject*) Sweet out here. I'm sorry I didn't discover this before.

Townley So am I—

Kitty Listen! There's a bird—way off.

Townley Calling to his mate. I didn't come up here to listen to bird notes—you know.

He kisses her arm. She draws it away.

Townley Why That? Don't you like me as well as you thought you were going to—before I came up?

Kitty More—so far.

Townley How is it—*really*—Kitty dear?

Kitty You're a sweet person. I told you that the minute I saw you.

Townley But you've had two more days of me. How is it now?

Kitty I haven't liked anyone so much in—oh, I don't know when.

Townley I haven't liked anyone so much—ever. It's marvellous to like a girl and fall in love with her too. That's how it is with me—Kitty.

Kitty You're perfect.

Townley You're pretending you don't believe me—but you do. You're the most— Damn!

Slapping his ankle.

Kitty Smoke—smoke—hard.

Kitty *leans forward—her elbows on her knees.*

Townley What are you thinking about?

Kitty Nothing.

Townley Meaning me?

Kitty No—that girl—Dierdre Lessing.

Townley You were a peach. Rather messy—wasn't it?

Kitty It happens so often one gets used to it.

Townley But it always makes me slightly ill-somehow—to see a nice girl get drunk. I suppose I'm much too fastidious.

Kitty Much.

Townley It also rather gets my goat to see them go after a man quite as openly as she went after Brown.

Kitty I'm awfully sorry for her.

Townley In the name of heaven why?

Kitty She's in love with him.

Townley She's made a fool of herself.

Kitty Oh, I don't know. He must have encouraged her.

Townley Well—What's a man to *do*? Brown's a bit fed up, I should say. Men *are*. Even I—in all modesty—prefer to do my own pursuing—but they won't let me.

Kitty Poor you! Besieged, I s'pose.

Townley That's why I'm so mad about you—Kitty. You've kept me—a—

Kitty What?

Townley Wondering.

Kitty Is the wondering all over?

Townley Um—when in doubt—detour. You've got the prettiest ears I ever saw. I wanted to kiss the right one all through dinner, especially with the salad.

Kitty Why didn't you?

Townley I'll do it now.

Kitty Oh no. It would be so commonplace now—and it would have been so diverting for everybody then.

Townley You were letting Grainger divert you in the other ear—in French.

Kitty I had no idea he was so brilliant.

Townley See here—ought I to be worried about Grainger?

Kitty You ought not to be worried about *anything*.

Townley At first I was afraid of Brown. When I got on to Boucicault's scheme I thought you'd mow him down just to please the old girl. I thought it would rouse your sporting blood when you saw the layout.

Kitty Ah, but you see—*you* were here.

A light is seen through the shutters in the room at Right.

Townley I've fallen in love with you, Kitty. What are you going to do about it?

Kitty We'll talk about that at dinner tomorrow night. We'll go on from here.

Townley We'll go on *now*.

Kitty (*standing up*) We'll say good night now—and *drop* down this time. Don't risk the steps.

Townley (*stepping onto the balcony beside* **Kitty**) Don't be in such a hurry to get rid of me.

Kitty I'm only giving you a—suggestion.

Townley I don't need it. I know where I'm going.

Kitty Oh, *do* you?

Townley So do you. Don't you?

Kitty You think so?

Townley You're very wise and very *sure*—aren't you? I love you beautifully, Kitty. What are you going to do with me?

Kitty (*moving to her door*) I'm going to say good night to you now.

Townley But I haven't told you how I—

Kitty But go now while I'm still dying to hear it.

Townley (*catching her hand*) Why did you let me come?

Kitty Because I wanted you to, of course. Why not?

Townley Then don't send me away.

Kitty Townie. Keep charming and clever. I want to see you again. Good night.

He kisses her throat. She moves away from him into her doorway.

Townley (*moving beside her*) Kitty, I'm mad about you. I can't go.

Kitty I like you frightfully, Townley—don't spoil it.

Townley Kiss me good night then—

Kitty No—*No!*

Townley But I—

He kisses her. **Bob** *throws open the shutters at Right and comes onto the balcony.* **Kitty** *hears the noise and pushes* **Townley** *out of sight, inside her door.*

Bob Kitty!

Kitty Oh—it's *your* room! Fancy *that!*

Bob Kitty, you don't believe anything that girl said—(**Kitty** *shakes her head at* **Bob**.) What's the matter? No one can hear us. There's no one about. I don't know what she told you, but you've got to know I haven't done anything you could object to.

Kitty (*calling*) Townley—did you find the cigarettes? Come out. (*A pause.* **Townley** *comes out.*) That's Mr. Brown's room. Isn't it amusing? We were wondering. We've been sitting on the steps—smoking—to keep the mosquitoes away. They're awfully bad tonight—aren't they. The vines I s'pose. Mr. Townley was just going. Perhaps you'll stay now. Perhaps you'll bring out some chairs, Mr. Brown? (*The men stare at each other amazed—embarrassed.*) No? Oh—well—I'll see you tomorrow night, Townie. Better ring me up in the afternoon at three—*sharp.* I'll be awfully busy all day. What?

Townley (*after a slight pause*) I'm afraid I don't understand quite.

Kitty You will. I shall have something frightfully amusing to tell you at dinner. Good night.

Townley It seems Boucicault's scheme *did* work then.

Kitty Not at *all.* At least not *her way.* That's what I'll tell you about. It's unbelievably funny.

Townley (*coldly*) I *see.*

Kitty Oh *do* you! You don't in the least. This seems to be rather too staggering for you. Don't be melodramatic I beg. If you want me to dine with you ring me up. If you don't—*don't.* Good night.

Townley At three—sharp. Good night. Good night, Brown.

Bob *doesn't speak.*

Kitty (*putting her hand out impulsively to* **Townley**) You're a darling.

Townley *takes* **Kitty**'s *hand for an instant—and goes down the steps.*

Bob What does it all mean?

Kitty All what? Townley on my balcony? That ought not to need an interpretation—for you.

Bob What?

Kitty Yes. Good night.

She starts to go.

Bob Is it—what it looks like?

Kitty Nothing very novel about it—is there?

Bob What was he doing in your room?

Kitty That's a very naïve question—for *you*. How silly it all is. I'm going to bed. Good night.

Bob Kitty!

Kitty Yes?

Bob It's horrible! I can't *believe* it. It isn't *you*.

Kitty I don't think you know much about what is—or *isn't*—me.

Bob I *do*. You can't have changed like this. It simply *is not possible*.

Kitty Why not?

Bob Are you doing this sort of thing all the time? God—what are you laughing at?

Kitty It's so funny!

Bob No it isn't! I want you to know I've absolutely done nothing wrong towards Dierdre Lessing. I'm horribly sorry and ashamed about the whole thing downstairs—and you've got to tell me exactly what *you* mean by this. In the name of heaven, why did you let that man come up here? Is he—

Bob *stops suddenly as* **Dierdre** *comes onto the balcony from his room. She is wearing the same gown as in Scene I. She stops as she sees* **Kitty** *and* **Bob**—*looking from one to the other with quick suspicion.*

Kitty Hello. Come out. Don't look so suspicious. It's quite all right—I assure you. I've been sitting on the steps with a man—and Mr. Brown was inconsiderate enough to come out at the wrong moment.

Dierdre (*trying to be at ease—but very doubtful*) Oh—

Kitty The man was Townley—if it interests you to know.

Dierdre Oh I say, Bob—It's a wonder you wouldn't stay inside.

Kitty That's what *I'm* going to do. *I'm* going *in* and *stay* in.

Dierdre Don't go on my account.

Kitty Sweet of you—but I've got to pack and I'm awfully sleepy.

Dierdre Wait a minute—please, Kitty. I know everything I said downstairs—and I *meant* it—only I didn't mean to *say* it. You were terribly nice. Thanks a lot. I came in to talk to Bob about it and since I *am* here—there's no use pretending I'm not. So that's that.

Bob You came to say you were sorry.

Dierdre Oh no I didn't.

Bob We understand—but it wasn't a very wise thing for you to do, Dierdre. A—Mrs.—Mrs. Brown will go back with you.

Dierdre What?

Kitty You mean chaperone her back to her room—in case somebody else might be strolling about?

Bob Yes—that's *just exactly* what I mean.

Dierdre Don't' you love it?

Dierdre *and* **Kitty** *laugh*.

Bob Listen, Dierdre. You can't stay here.

Dierdre I want to ask Kitty something. She can help me.

Dierdre *goes closer to* **Kitty**. **Bob** *moves to the right corner of the balcony—his back turned to the others.*

Kitty I'm not so sure of that. I don't know that I'd have chosen myself to come to for help—*just now*.

Dierdre I've thought till I'm woozy—but I don't *get* anywhere. What shall I do? I've promised to marry Bruce but I'm crazy about Bob.

Bob Dierdre—*stop* this.

Dierdre She *knows*. I spilled it all down stairs anyway. What would you do—Kitty—if you were in my place?

Kitty If I were in your place—I'm sure I would marry Bob. (**Bob** *turns to watch* **Kitty**.) I'd believe that he was the one man for me—and that I'd be the *one woman* for him—*always*. I'd believe that *nothing* could ever change him. That's the way I know I'd feel about Bob—but I suppose you're much too intelligent for that.

Bob (*forgetting* **Dierdre** *entirely and going to* **Kitty**) Are you still laughing?

Kitty Do I sound too old fashioned and sentimental to be true?

Bob Not if you mean it.

Dierdre Look at *me*, **Bob**. *I* mean it.

Kitty (*to* **Bob**)   Then why don't you two try it? You must know pretty well what you want by this time.

Bob (*looking steadily at* **Kitty**)   I do know just exactly what I want. I was never so sure as I am this minute.

Kitty   You may be two of the lucky ones who *do* find the most wonderful thing in the world.

Dierdre (*drawing* **Bob** *away from* **Kitty**)   Couldn't we make it that—Bob? I know now—I could.

Bob   Dierdre, you don't know what you're doing. You're only a child.

Dierdre   I'm not. I love you, Bob. I love you.

Bob   I blame myself terribly, Dierdre—but it's better for you to know the truth now. I—I didn't think for a minute it was—like this—with you.

Dierdre   Don't you want to marry me?

Bob   Dierdre—dear girl—it wasn't that way at all.

Dierdre   That's a damned lie. You were just as keen as I was—for *anything*. What's changed you? Oh—What were you and she doing here—alone—together?

Bob   What?

Dierdre (*to* **Kitty**)   Did you take him away from me?

Kitty   Did I *what?*

Bob   For God's sake tell her the truth, Kitty—or I will.

Dierdre   You needn't, I *know*. You *did* what Gran wanted.

Bob   You can't believe any such rot.

Dierdre   Why wouldn't I believe it? Before she came you were crazy about me. Now you're not.

Bob   Dierdre—Kitty and I are—

Kitty (*stopping* **Bob** *with her hand*)   Don't Bob—let it alone—it's better this way. (*To* **Dierdre**.) Since I—since *anything could* take him away from you—aren't you glad to know it now—before you—married him?

Dierdre   Oh—you did—you *did!*

Bob   Kitty—

Kitty   Don't, Bob. (*To* **Dierdre**.) Now you—*know*.

Dierdre   It's vile—it's beastly! Right here in grandmother's house!

Kitty   And what are *you* doing here—right in your grandmother's house? I suppose you thought you were very *brave* to come—to take life in your own hands and look it straight in the face. Well—here we are. If you want to find things out for yourself you'll have to accept things *as they are.* You've found *this before* you married him—instead of afterwards. I think you're rather to be congratulated.

Dierdre (*with a half sob*) Oh—

Bob Dierdre, you can't stay here. Go to bed and get some sleep and tomorrow we'll talk this all out clearly and honestly.

Dierdre I wouldn't believe anything you said to me. I wouldn't believe *anything*—ever again. Everything in the world is horrible—horrible—

She goes out the way she came.

Kitty (*after a pause*) I seem to have heard that before. Well, it turned out beautifully—just exactly as Bouci wanted it.

Bob I don't care what the old woman wants. I'm not going to have her think this rot about you. I'm going to clear it all up the first thing in the morning.

Kitty If you do you'll spoil it. This is the best thing that could possibly happen to Dierdre.

Bob At your expense.

Kitty Well, why not be the goat in a good cause once in a lifetime?

Bob But I'm thinking of *you.*

Kitty And I'm thinking of her. The whole world will never be so completely smashed for her again. It doesn't happen twice. And since you seem to be tired and through, it's an easy way out for you—and I think I've got rather a kick out of it myself. So let's call it a day.

Bob Kitty—how much did you mean of what you said about love?

Kitty Now, really, Bob. I was trying to say the right things to a very young girl, very much in love with you. It was working well, when all of a sudden she believed this pleasant little thing she thought she saw right before her eyes. Very easy for her to believe. A très sophisticated young person she is.

Bob Stop talking about her. Kitty, I'm more in love with you than I ever was in my life.

Kitty Oh—Mr. Brown, this is so sudden.

Bob I adore you.

Kitty It's the moon.

Bob (*taking her by the shoulders and turning her towards him*) Stop this. Look at me. Talk to me like—like—

Kitty Like what?

Bob Like your own honest to God self. You haven't said a real thing to me since you came.

Kitty (*getting away from him*)   I don't know any real things—do you?

Bob   Stop bluffing and hedging. I love you. Doesn't that mean anything to you at all?

Kitty   Yes—that I'm something new to you.

Bob   How much does this Townley thing mean?

Kitty   Nothing in particular. Only that you're not used to seeing other men aware of me.

Bob   I'm not used to seeing other men treating you as though they had a right to—to—

Kitty   To what?

Bob   To come up here.

Kitty   Townley had a perfect right to come up here. I invited him.

Bob   God, Kitty. I can't stand this. What does it mean?

Kitty   It means I like him.

Bob   And what else?

Kitty   I don't know what else—yet.

Bob   How far has it gone?

Kitty   Just as far as—as—

Bob   As—what?

Kitty   As the door.

Bob   Are you in love with him?

Kitty   I always like to think I'm in love with somebody.

Bob   Is there nothing left of what you used to feel for me? Is every bit of it gone?

Kitty   Every little bit.

Bob   Is it?

Kitty   Do you think I'm a fool? I've filled my life with other things.

Bob   What things?

Kitty   Things—*things*—to take the place of the ones I used to think were everything and found were *nothing*.

Bob   What about you—yourself? What's become of that?

Kitty   I find myself a much easier person to live with than I used to be. I don't take myself as seriously as I used to.

Bob   Oh, Kitty, you were the sweetest thing in the world, and you still are.

Kitty   Was I? I don't remember.

Bob I don't believe you've changed. You're the same adorable thing I loved, and you're even more so now. Kitty, I—I—

Kitty No—no—Bob.

Bob (*drawing her close in his arms*) Please—please—darling.

Kitty Oh, no—Bob, not that.

Bob I can't help it, Kitty. Why can't I have you again?

He kisses her.

Kitty It's over—it's finished.

Getting away from him.

Bob (*after a pause in a low, hard tone*) Is there anybody else?

Kitty Yes. Why not?

Bob Is this the way you've been living? Have there been other men? Have you—have you—

Kitty And if I have, what of it?

She stops as a soft whistle is heard from below.

Wallace (*not seen in the darkness*) —Kitty, are you there?

Kitty (*to* **Bob**) Well—we're both having a busy evening—aren't we? It's Wally. Hello, lovely night, isn't it?

Looking over the railing.

Wallace I want to say the poem to you.

Kitty I'm dying to hear it—but you can't now. Somebody else is here.

Wallace Oh.

Kitty Sorry. Ring me up at three o'clock tomorrow—sharp.

Wallace At three sharp.

Kitty Perhaps I'll have dinner with you tomorrow night.

Wallace Thanks.

Kitty Good night.

Wallace (*softly*) Good night.

Kitty (*after a slight pause*) Well—I don't expect anybody else—but perhaps you do—Mr. Brown. Good night.

She goes in as the

CURTAIN FALLS

Act Three

Time: 9 o'clock the following morning.

Place: The same as Act I.

At Curtain: **Dierdre** *comes out quickly from the hall—dressed for going away.*

Bruce (*coming after her*) If you're going in I'm going with you.

Dierdre No you're not. I may not go to town. I'm just waiting to hop in the car and drive till I get ready to stop.

Bruce But you—

Dierdre Don't Bruce—*please.* I want to be alone for awhile.

Bruce Then let me take you some place and you can stay if you want to.

Dierdre *No!* I'm getting away from everybody.

Bruce (*after a pause*) You needn't be so cut up *as all that*—about last night.

Dierdre Because I got plastered and made a fool of myself? Believe me I'm not. I don't give a damn about that.

Bruce Then what *is* it?

Dierdre Oh, let me alone, boy—my nerves are jumpy.

Bruce Sorry.

Dierdre I mean—I want to get off by myself and *think*—before I *do* talk to you. I'm fed up with these people.

Bruce But they're all leaving this morning—every one of 'em—and we'd be alone.

Dierdre I want to get away from *you!* Can't you get that?

Bruce (*after a pause*) Are you going to meet Bob some place?

Dierdre None of your business.

Bruce You *have* made a fool of yourself. For God's sake let him alone—Dierdre. He's *through.*

Dierdre (*with sudden anger and abandon*) And why is he? Because Gran crashed in. Because she got that Kitty woman to come here and vamp him.

Bruce Oh bosh!

Dierdre (*going to sit on the sofa at Left*) Of course she got him. I couldn't compete with *her.*

Bruce He cooled off himself.

Dierdre He *didn't*.

Bruce Why she never even looked at him.

Dierdre Not so anybody could *see* it. It was all on the side—on the sly.

Bruce How do you know?

Dierdre Because I *do*.

Bruce That's a pretty low down thing to say about her.

Dierdre I *found* them—last night—on his balcony—chummy enough. They've been right there together all the time.

Bruce You found them? *How?*

Dierdre I went to Bob's room—to talk to him.

Bruce You didn't. You didn't do a damn fool thing like that.

Dierdre I put it up to her—and she acknowledged it.

Bruce For Heaven's sake why did you go into his room?

Dierdre Because I *wanted* to.

Bruce Then thank God she *was* there. Thank God you know now about Brown. Oh, Dierdre—how *could* you?

Dierdre If he came down here right now and asked me to go away with him—I'd go.

Bruce You wouldn't.

Dierdre I would.

Bruce You're not in love with him. It's just a –an—infatuation.

Dierdre Whatever it is I've *got* it.

Bruce (*touching* **Dierdre**'s *shoulder and sitting on the seat at Left of the sofa*) You'll get over it. I've been that way—lots of times.

Dierdre Of course you have. But I haven't. It *means* something to *me*.

Bruce Not a thing. Not a damn thing. If you threw yourself away on that man you'd want to kill yourself afterwards.

Dierdre Applesauce!

Bruce (*leaning towards her over the back of the sofa*) Dierdre—dearest—I want to see you through this. Believe me there's nothing in it but what you'll be terribly sorry for—and ashamed of afterwards.

Dierdre Awfully wise—aren't you?

Bruce You bet I'm wise. I want to marry you. I love you. I want to make it the—the greatest ever—and we could, too-if you'd—

Dierdre Yes—*why* do you want to marry me? *Why* do you love me? (*Breaking a little.*) I think it's perfectly marvellous that you do, Bruce—but why?—It's because you've lived enough to be sure. Well, I haven't.

Bruce You don't have to go through that.

Dierdre (*softening and putting a hand over his*) Listen, Bruce—I like you better than anybody in the world. Maybe we are the best bet for each other. But I'm not crazy about you the way I am about Bob.

Bruce Take it from me—liking is a better bet than craziness.

Dierdre (*drawing her hand away*) Now, don't talk to me like Santa Claus. I want to know what I'm doing because I know—*myself.* Not because somebody's telling me what I ought to do.

Bruce If you'd use your bean and tell yourself the truth you'd know what to do.

Dierdre I *am* using my bean. That's just it. I'm not swallowing any old stuff.

Bruce Now get this. There's no new slant on this old stuff at all. Either a girl's decent or she isn't. There's no half way business about it—and when a fellow gets down to brass tacks, he wants the girl he's going to marry—the one who is going to be the mother of his kids—to be the straightest, finest, cleanest thing in the world.

Dierdre Pearls you learned at mother's knee. And if a girl wants the darling boy she marries to be the same thing—where the hell is she going to find him?

Bruce It's not the same thing at all for you and me.

Dierdre It is!

Bruce It isn't!

Dierdre It is—exactly the same thing. Why should I marry you and settle down and pretend that's all there is to it when I know damned well it isn't?

Bruce Because you can't do anything that—

Dierdre Why shouldn't I have Bob for a while and marry you, too?

Bruce (*rising and walking away*) *Because you can't.* You simply can't. That's all there is to it.

Dierdre Do you mean to tell me if I'd *had* an affair with Bob—and it helped me to know I wanted to marry you—you wouldn't marry me?

Bruce Oh, Dierdre, I love you. I want to help you. There isn't anything I wouldn't do for you. Can't you see you're—

Mrs. Boucicault *enters from the terrace—followed by* **Perkins**—*who carries the morning mail in a small basket.*

Mrs. Boucicault What are you two doing down here at this ungodly hour? How I loathe Monday mornings—coming down to speed the parting guest. I don't know why I do it. I don't know why I don't just let 'em go—unless it's because it gives me such intense pleasure to actually *see* them go. What's up? Where are *you* going, Dierdre?

Dierdre (*rising and going towards the terrace*)   Away for a few days—by myself.

Mrs. Boucicault (*siting on the sofa at Left*)   Get along, Perkins. (**Perkins** *puts the basket of letters on the table above sofa and goes out through the hall.*) That's a good idea. Go off and come to your senses—and then—

Dierdre (*turning back to* **Mrs. Boucicault**)   It was a rotten low down thing for you to do, Gran.

Mrs. Boucicault   What are you saying?

Dierdre   You were terribly clever, weren't you? It worked all right. I found them last night. I went to Bob's room to talk to him—and there they were. It's lousy—that's what it is—filthy.

Mrs. Boucicault   What are you—

Dierdre   The sneakiness of it!

Bruce (*who has gone to the end of the piano standing with his back to the others*)   Be careful Dierdre! Don't talk so loud.

Mrs. Boucicault   You went to Bob's room last night? You *didn't*. If you did you didn't know what you were doing. I won't *have* it.

Dierdre   Won't you? How about the other lady—what *she's* done? That's all right, I s'pose. You can swallow what's going on in your house—so long as you get what you want.

Bruce   Shut up—Dierdre!

Mrs. Boucicault   How *dare* you say such a thing to *me!*

Dierdre   Oh how dare—*bunk*, Gran! You sent for her, didn't you—to do *just that?*

Mrs. Boucicault   Just what? Just what? Kitty's not that kind of a woman.

Dierdre   You put them off there in that wing—alone—together—so this *would* happen—didn't you?

Mrs. Boucicault   No—no—*no!* I don't know what you're talking about. But whatever *has* happened, has opened your eyes—hasn't it? Aren't you through with Bob Brown now? Aren't you ready to behave yourself and marry Bruce?

Dierdre   Do you think that has anything to do with *me*—and the way I feel toward Bob? Just because you cooked up a nasty thing with that kind of a woman—

Dierdre *stops suddenly as* **Kitty** *comes out from the hall.* **Kitty** *is wearing a summer gown appropriate for going to town—but without hat or coat.*

Kitty (*coming further into the room*)   I suppose I'm the woman.

Mrs. Boucicault I know this is all ridiculous nonsense, Kitty. I don't believe a word of it.

Kitty Why don't you? You wanted it to happen—didn't you? That's why you offered me your hospitality—isn't it?

Mrs. Boucicault Bruce—go away.

Bruce Why should I?

Mrs. Boucicault Because I *tell* you to.

Kitty Is this going to be too bad for his young ears to hear?

Dierdre He knows the whole business.

Bruce I think I have a right to know anything that concerns Dierdre.

Mrs. Boucicault No you haven't. Go away, I tell you.

Bruce Do you want me to, Dierdre?

Dierdre Yes.

Bruce *hesitates and goes out across the terrace and to the Left.*

Mrs. Boucicault Kitty—tell Dierdre that what she thinks—isn't *true*.

Kitty She must tell me what she *does* think—before I can do that.

Dierdre (*fighting back her angry tears*) You took him away from me—didn't you?

Kitty I can't say I tried to.

Dierdre You didn't even *have* to try—I s'pose—with your methods.

Mrs. Boucicault Dierdre—

Kitty And what are my methods supposed to be? Oh, let's be quite frank—please. Just exactly what is it you think I've done?

Dierdre Something too rotten to say.

Mrs. Boucicault The child is *insane* with jealousy, Kitty. Tell her that what she thinks—is—is—is *impossible*.

Kitty Did *you* think it would be so impossible, Bouci? Would you have cared so much *how* I arrived at what you wanted—just so I *did* arrive?

Mrs. Boucicault I'm shocked beyond words, Kitty, that *you* could think that *I* could want—

Dierdre (*going back of the large chair at Right*) Don't take me for a blithering idiot, Gran. I *know*.

Kitty (*with sudden anger—moving a little towards* **Dierdre**) And *what* do you know? There was just a minute last night when I *wanted* you to believe I'd done that rotten thing—because I thought it would save you a *bigger* heartache—later on. More or less the same thing happened to me—once—and I was sorry for you—with all my heart. I intended to hold my tongue—and go through with it. But since *you've* talked—in not quite a good sportsman way—we'll talk a little *more*. You came to the gentleman's—balcony—and found me there first. Surely you can allow me the same comfortable freedom—without question—which I grant you. Besides—I wasn't alone with him—remember. Mr. Townley was there too.

Dierdre You don't think I'm sap enough to believe *that*—do you?

Kitty Here's Townie himself. Ask him.

As **Townley** *comes out of the house—ready to leave.*

Dierdre *Were* you there?

Townley Are you speaking to me?

Kitty (*laughing at* **Townley***'s confusion*) She means were you on my balcony last night—or were you not?

Townley (*trying to keep his equilibrium*) Well—a—a—was I?

Mrs. Boucicault What are you splashing round about—for—Townley? Can't you say a little something?

Kitty I hope you don't mind being compromised a bit for my sake, Townie.

Dierdre (*as* **Wallace** *comes out from the house—dressed for going in town*) Here's another one of your admirers. I suppose you'll tell us *he* was there too.

Kitty (*laughing at* **Wallace**) Almost—not quite.

Wallace I beg pardon?

Kitty We're discussing the balcony scene.

Dierdre We *all* seem to have been there—some time—during the night. I suppose *you* were among the number.

Wallace *looks astounded, tries to speak and flounders.* **Townley** *laughs.*

Mrs. Boucicault What are you laughing at, Townley?

Townley I'm not quite sure.

Kitty Don't *you* think it's funny, Wallie?

Wallace A—I don't seem to know what it's all about.

Mrs. Boucicault No—I dare say.

Kitty What's the matter with *you*, Bouci? You have a *very* peculiar tone in your voice. Don't' tell me you aren't *pleased* with me.

Mrs. Boucicault I'm not sure what I've got to be pleased *about*. I'd like to enjoy the joke if there is one. Just where do these two come in?

Kitty They didn't come in. They came *up*.

Mrs. Bouciault Up *what*?

Kitty My steps. You don't mind a man or two sitting on my steps, do you? Why did you put me there—if you do?

Mrs. Boucicault Are you pulling my leg?

Kitty God Forbid! It was this way—Bouci. After Townley and Mr. Brown—and—*Dierdre*—and I had all—*happened* upon my balcony—and chatted a little—all more or less on the same subject—I was about to say good night—when I heard a soft whistle and there was Wallie at the foot of the steps—in the moonlight—asking if he couldn't come up and recite his poem to me.

Kitty *and* **Townley** *laugh.*

Wallace Well—I was—just passing by and—I—

Mrs. Boucicault Yes—there must be a *little* something in it, Wallace. You look like a sick cat.

Bob (*coming out from the house—also dressed for going to town*) Good morning—What's the joke?

Kitty (*hardening quickly*) The joke's on me—Mr. Brown.

Bob Yes? Why?

Kitty It seems to have been necessary to *check up* the incidents of last night.

Dierdre But she's left *you* out. How about the you and Kitty incident?

Bob We—

Kitty No—

Dierdre Go on. She's so keen about telling *everything*—Go through with it.

Mrs. Boucicault Dierdre—

Bob I won't let them think—

Kitty I don't care what they think. I have your word.

Bob I don't care a hang about my word.

Kitty I won't have my personal affairs aired like this.

Mrs. Boucicault She's quite right. I don't like it either.

Dierdre No, but you've let her make a fool of me. You've let her make a joke of the whole rotten thing.

Kitty And what are *you* trying to make out of it? I know I asked you to believe that inconceivably vile thing—and now I ask you *not* to. That's where the joke comes in. I'm afraid I've tried to be a little *too* clever, Bouci. I'm afraid I've got myself in too deep. There doesn't seem to be anything about me to tell—what I am—(*her voice breaks*) or how things are. That's rather a joke too. I know exactly what *each* and every one of you is thinking about me—each in his own way. (*To* **Dierdre**.) If *you* think I took your Mr. Brown away from you last night—allow me to give him back to you this morning.

Dierdre I don't *believe* you.

Mrs. Boucicault *Dierdre!*

Bob (*stopping* **Kitty** *as she starts to go*) Dierdre—listen—Kitty is my wife—or was. (*There is a murmur of amazement from them all.*) She divorced me three years ago. But she still is my wife—to *me*. There never has been and there never will be anyone to take her place. The greatest thing that could happen to me would be for her to take me back—but that—I know—is a lost hope.

Kitty You always *have* had good manners, Bob. He's only being magnificent, Bouci. This accidental meeting doesn't change anything for *us*. That was settled three years ago. Don't let it change anything for *anybody* else.

She goes out through the hall.

Bob (*after a pause*) Dierdre—I'm sorry I—

Dierdre (*in a low tone*) Don't—please.

She goes out across the terrace and off at Right.

Mrs. Boucicault (*rising, after a pause and going up Center*) Well—I can't think of anything worth saying at the moment, except that you may miss your train, gentlemen. (**Whitman** *enters from the terrace.*) Here's Whitman to remind you of that. He's even better than I am at shuffling people off.

Whitman The motor is—

Mrs. Boucicault Quite so, Whitman. They're coming.

Whitman *goes out.*

Bob Well—good-by, Bouci.

Mrs. Boucicault You're not going.

Bob But I must—

Mrs. Boucicault You've got to wait. I want to talk to you. You can't throw a bomb like this and walk right off. I've got *some* curiosity—you know. Good-by, Townley.

Bob *goes onto the terrace at Left.*

Townley (*shaking hands*) Thanks so much, Bouci—It was—

Mrs. Boucicault I know—I know. Put it all in your letter. (*She waves* **Townley** *aside and puts out her hand to* **Wallace**—*going onto the terrace.*) Come along, Wallace.

Townley (*going to* **Kitty** *as she comes back from the hall, wearing her hat and carrying her coat and gloves*) It's been marvellous to know you. At least I haven't missed that.

Kitty Why so final? What about that dinner tonight?

Townley (*in low tones—his back to the others on the terrace*) Oh—is there any hope?

Kitty Hope? Why not conviction? Everything's just the same as it was when I saw you last. Isn't it?

Townley Will you come?

Kitty You're going to phone me at three.

Townley Oh—am I?

Kitty Don't you want to?

Townley More than anything on earth.

Kitty Then for goodness sake *do* it. Bye-by till three.

Townley Until three.

Townley *goes out on the terrace.*

Mrs. Boucicault (*to **Wallace**, who has been talking to her on the terrace*) Madge is going to stay all week. Run up again if you can.

Wallace Thanks, I'd love to.

Mrs. Boucicault Bob—you've got a car of your own here—haven't you?

Bob Yes—why?

Mrs. Boucicault I'll tell you later.

Wallace (*coming down to **Kitty** who has crossed to look at her hat in the mirror which is on the piano*) You've done something awfully sporting I'm sure—though I don't know just what.

Kitty I haven't done *anything*. Things just *happen* to us. Heaven knows this is the last thing on the calendar I would have brought about.

Wallace Something has happened to *me*—too.

Kitty What?

Wallace *You*. Am I never going to see you again?

Kitty Why so doubtful?

Wallace Because I want it so much.

Kitty At *three*.

He kisses her hand.

Madge (*coming out of the house in a delectable morning outfit in time to see the kiss*) Good morning—everybody.

Wallace *drops **Kitty**'s hand and moves away.*

Kitty (*going to sit on the sofa*)   Good morning.

Madge (*going to* **Wallace**)   You'll have to come back this evening.

Wallace   Eh?

Madge   I have a headache. You'll have to bring my powders to me.

Wallace   Oh, I'm so sorry.

He lets **Madge** *pass him, then holds up three fingers to* **Kitty**. *She smiles and nods and holds up three fingers.* **Wallace** *goes out after* **Madge**.

Mrs. Boucicault (*coming down into the room*)   You're a devil, Kitty. You might have let that poor thing alone.

Bob (*following* **Mrs. Boucicault**)   I have my car here. I'll drive you in.

Mrs. Boucicault   That's *my* idea.

Kitty   Not *mine*.

Mrs. Boucicault   Well, I'd rather hear what you two people have to say to each other now—than anything going. But I'll clear out. Don't be a mule, Kitty. My advice is—take him again. If you don't—you'll be sorry all your life. If you do—you'll be still *more* sorry—so you have my blessing either way.

She goes out through the hall.

Kitty   Well—good-by, Bob. I'm sorry I messed up your week end. I seem to be always spoiling your love affairs.

She goes to him—with her hand out.

Bob (*putting both hands behind him*)   Kitty, I haven't slept a wink. Those men—last night. You've got to tell me the truth in plain English.

Kitty   Are you going to begin that again?

She goes to adjust her hat at the mirror which is on the piano.

Bob   You can't keep the children, Kitty.

Kitty (*turning to* **Bob** *with sudden fear*)   You gave them up. You can't take them away from me.

Bob   I gave them up because you had the things that made it right for them to be with you.

Kitty (*going towards* **Bob**)   The things that bored you stiff.

Bob   The things that are right. Why have you changed like this?

Kitty   Why have I changed? Oh, God—you don't know yet —you don't know *now* what you did to me—what you took away from me.

Bob   And you took just as much away from me.

Kitty Well, then this is what we've done to each other.

Bob Yes, this is what we've done to each other—over something that didn't amount to a hill of beans. Surely you know that now, Kitty.

Kitty It wasn't even a hill of beans to you—but it took away everything from me—everything. See here, Bob—why are we digging this up? It's the last thing on earth I wanted to do. I've spent three years trying to forget it. Let's stop and say good-by as sensibly as possible.

Bob It's not so easy for me as it evidently is for you. Three years haven't made me forget. I've been footloose and home sick and done for. If you'd forgiven me that one time we'd still be together.

Kitty And I'd still be forgiving you.

Bob I'm not so sure of that.

Kitty Do you pretend for a minute that that one crash would have pulled you up forever—changed you entirely for the rest of your life?

Bob I could change now.

Kitty (*sitting in the large chair at Right*) It looks like it. If I hadn't accidentally happened to be here—how far would it have gone with Dierdre?

Bob Just exactly as far as she wanted it to. I told you last night I've amused myself with anything and everything that came my way—since I lost you. How about this Townley? How far would that have gone if I hadn't been there?

Kitty Don't you suppose I knew you were there? Don't you suppose I hoped you would find me with him? Don't you suppose seeing you carrying on with a girl again brought it all back so I couldn't stand it—so I wanted to hurt you as hard as I possibly—

Her voice breaks.

Bob (*drawing a chair close to her and sitting*) Oh—that was it. Then there's nothing in it. There haven't been other men—since you left me?

Kitty (*after a pause—in a low firm tone*) Yes.

Bob *Kitty!*

Kitty What did you expect?

Bob I don't believe it.

Kitty (*rising and going behind the chair*) Then why did you ask me?

Bob How could you! How could you!

Kitty (*with sudden full abandon*) Because I loved you so.

Bob What?

Kitty (*moving up and to Center—letting her feeling carry her away at last*) Heaven and earth and God were all mixed up in *you*. When that was gone *nothing* was left.

Can't you understand that? I suppose you think I ought to have stayed at home with a broken heart, for the rest of my life—hugging my ideals. But I didn't seem to be able to do that. I had to get out and find out what it was all about—to see why *you* did it.

Bob Well, then if you've found out so much—if you've got so wise and experienced—you know now how little that affair meant to me.

Kitty Yes, I know now. I know both sides. I wanted to find out whether I'd been a fool or not—whether I had exaggerated what you did. Well, I hadn't. It was just as horrible as I thought it was. Bob, marriage means just one thing—complete and absolute fidelity or it's the biggest farce on *earth*.

Bob I could make our marriage now what you thought it ought to be then.

Kitty (*sitting on the sofa at Left*) That I should live to hear you say that, Mr. Brown!

Bob (*standing in front of her*) How can you be so hard?

Kitty Because I refuse to be made unhappy again.

Bob (*sitting above her on the sofa*) Kitty, darling—if you'd let me begin again! God—what we've lost! Two people who loved each other as we did!

Kitty Don't harp on *that*.

Bob We had the great chance and muffed it.

Kitty The chance is gone now, Bob. Let's be sane and look this in the face. What if we *did* go back—what of it? What is there *in* it?

Bob Well, not so much if we're only thinking of ourselves. The thing that's been hitting me in the eye in the last three days is that there *is* something a damned sight bigger in it than ourselves—and that's what we ought to grab now—and hang on to.

Kitty The *real* thing, yes. But as it *is*—as we've all *made* it.

Bob Well, it *is* the real thing—to plenty of people.

Kitty To whom, for instance? Anybody you know?

Bob Yes, of course.

Kitty Who are they?

Bob Well—a—a—

Kitty Exactly. Now let's get over this and not be sorry it happened. And the next time we see each other we'll be more game about it.

Bob All right. Then we're going to be friends. Have dinner with me tonight in town.

Kitty I have to eat *two* dinners *now*.

Bob Eat three. I'll make it any time you say.

Kitty Why not all dine together?

Bob Cut out Townley.

Kitty But not Wallie. You don't mind Wallie. He's having the time of his life.

They laugh together. **Bob** *bends over her and kisses her hair.*

Bob Give me a chance to make you love me again. That's fair, isn't it?

Kitty Love isn't enough, Bob.

Bob The children.

Kitty We *had* the children. We had love—but that didn't keep us together. No, Bob, I'm not going to give you a chance to hurt me again. *It's the awfullest hurt in the world* and it would still be there, if I'd let it.

She rises and moves away from him.

Bob (*following her a little*) But I *wouldn't* hurt you again.

Kitty No, Bob—I'm not going back. I'm going *on*. I don't know to just *what*—but *on*. For heaven's sake let's be gay about it.

Bob To see you like this is a worse tragedy than losing you. Aren't you sick of this damned batting around—trying to fool yourself into thinking you're having a good time?

Kitty Maybe you've had enough—you've been at it longer than I have—maybe you're ready for your slippers at the fire—I'm not.

Putting on her coat.

Bob Oh, Kitty, marry me again.

Kitty You're out of your senses.

Bob It's what I want. It's the only thing I do want—you and the children. Can't we make a fresh start?

Kitty It's too late.

Bob Do you hate me?

Kitty (*putting on her gloves*) No.

Bob Then why—

Kitty Oh, it isn't you.

Bob What is it then?

Kitty It's myself. I couldn't. Neither could you, Bob. You're just making a gallant gesture.

Bob No. From the minute I saw you, something pounded in me so hard—an idiotic hope—a something bigger than I ever had—or ever knew there could be. This is tougher than the first time I lost you. Good-by, Kitty.

Putting out his hand.

Kitty (*taking his hand after an instant's hesitation*)   Good-by—and good luck. You'll get over this, Bob, in no time at all.

Bob   Oh—

Kitty   Yes, you will. I know. It doesn't take long.

Bob   Well, how is it going to end? What will you do? Where are you going?

Kitty   I don't know, I'm sure. Life's a very complicated business, isn't it?

Bob   Do you think I could make you love me again? That's the point?

Kitty   That's what I'm afraid of. That's why I'm running now.

Bob (*going to her*)   Kitty—

Kitty   If I left myself go, I could be fascinated by you again in no time at all.

Bob   You're adorable!

Kitty (*holding him off*)   No, Bob, let's not make fools of ourselves. It would be no joke for either one of us to try to settle down again.

Bob   But we—

Kitty   No, I'm afraid, Bob. I'm honestly, *afraid*.

Sitting in the large chair at Right.

Bob   Why? Why, dearest?

Kitty   I don't know. I've been so gay—so—so full of—so *empty*.

Bob (*dropping on his knees in front of her*)   Kitty!

Kitty   So lonely—

Bob   Darling!

Kitty   Oh, Bob, I love you so. (*Putting her arms about his neck.*) Take me back.

THE CURTAIN FALLS

Appendices

Selected Production History

He and She (1911–1920)

** First written in 1911 as *The Herfords*, produced in Albany and Boston in 1911 and 1912, respectively. Crothers later changed the title and took the play on tour before opening on Broadway in 1920.

1. 12 February - March 1920
    The Little Theatre
    Produced by Lee and J.J. Shubert
    Sets by Norman Bel Geddes
    Original Cast:
    Tom Herford . . . . Cyril Keightley
    Ann Herford . . . . Rachel Crothers
    Millicent . . . . Faire Binney
    Daisy Herford . . . Margaret Vivian Johnson
    Dr. Remington . . . Arthur Elliott
    Ruth Creel . . . . . . Ethel Cozzens
    Keith McKenzie . . Fleming Ward
    Ellen . . . . Frances Bryant

1. March 1971
    American Theatre Company
2. 22 May – 15 June 1980
    Brooklyn Academy of Music
    Directed by Emily Mann
3. 9-27 August 1997
    East Lynne Theatre Company, Cape May
4. 4-11 April 2010
    University of Illinois Department of Theatre
    Directed by Deb Alley

A Little Journey (1918)

1. 26 December 1918 – c. 1 September 1919 (252 performances)
    The Little Theatre
    Produced by Lee and J.J. Shubert
    Directed by Rachel Crothers
    Original Cast:
    JULIE RUTHERFORD . . . Estelle Winwood
    JIM WEST . . . Cyril Keightley
    MRS. WELCH . . . Jobyna Howland

            MRS. BAY . . . May Galyer
            LILY . . . Nancy Winston
            LEO STERN . . . Paul Burns
            FRANK . . . Victor LaSalle
            CHARLES . . . Theodore Westerman, Jr.
            SMITH . . . George Mortimer
            ANNIE . . . Gilda Verasi
            ETHEL . . . Vera Fuller-Mellish
            KITTIE VAN DYCK . . . Elma Royton
            THE PORTER . . . Richard Quilter
            1ST CONDUCTOR . . . George Hadden
            2ND CONDUCTOR . . . John Robb
    2. 27 January – August 1919
            Produced by Lee and J.J. Shubert
            Directed by Rachel Crothers
            Julie Rutherford played by Estelle Winwood
    3. 10 June – 10 July 2011
            Mint Theater Company
            Directed by Jackson Gay

Mary the Third (1923)

    1. 5 February – June 1923 (152 performances)
            39th Street Theatre
            Produced by Lee Shubert
            Original Cast:
            Mary The First . . . . . . 1870 . . . . Louise Huff
            William . . . . Ben Lyon

            Mary The Second . . . . . 1897 . . . . Louise Huff
            Robert . . . . Ben Lyon
            Richard . . . . William Hanley

            Mary The Third . . . . . . 1923 . . . . Louise Huff
            Mother . . . . Beatrice Terry
            Granny . . . . May Galyer
            Father . . . . George Howard
            Bobby . . . . Morgan Farley
            Lynn . . . . Ben Lyon
            Hal . . . . William Hanley
            Lettie . . . . Mildred McCleod
            Max . . . . John A. Kirkpatrick
            Nora . . . . Elinor Montell

2. January 1933
    Forest Theatre
    Produced by O.E. Wee and J.J. Leventhal, Inc.
    Directed by Rachel Crothers
3. 14 November – 7 December 2013
    West End Theatre, NYC
    Produced by Women Seeking . . . a Theatre Company
    Directed by Katrin Hilbe

Let Us Be Gay (1929)

1. 19 February – December 1929 (353 performances)
    The Little Theatre
    Produced by John Golden
    Directed by Rachel Crothers
    Original Cast:
    Kitty Brown . . . . .Francine Larrimore
    Bob Brown .Warren William
    Mrs. Bousicault . . . . .Charlotte Granville
    Dierdre Lessing . . . . Rita Vale
    Townley Town . . . . Kenneth Hunter
    Bruce Keen. . . . . Ross Alexander
    Madge Livingston . . . . Adele Klaer
    Wallace Grainger . . . . Gilbert Douglas
    Whitman . . . . .St. Clair Bayfield
    Struthers . . . . George Wright, Jr.
    Williams . . . . James C. Lane
    Perkins . . . . Natalie Potter
2. January 1932
    Palm Beach Playhouse, Inc.
3. 23 – 28 August 1942
    Bucks County Playhouse (Philadelphia)
    Directed by Harold J. Kennedy
    Kitty Brown played by Gloria Swanson

Plays by Rachel Crothers

Criss-Cross (1899)
Nora (1903)
The Rector (1905)
The Three of Us (1906)+
The Coming of Mrs. Patrick (1907)*
Myself-Bettina (1908)*
A Man's World (1910)+
Ourselves (1913)
Young Wisdom (1914)*
The Heart of Paddy Whack (1914)
"Old Lady 31" (1916)+
Mother Carey's Chickens (1917)+
Once Upon a Time (1918)
A Little Journey (1918)+
39 East (1919)+

He and She (1911-1920)
Nice People (1921)+
Everyday (1921)**
Mary the Third (1923)+
Expressing Willie (1924)
Six One-Act Plays (1925)
A Lady's Virtue (1925)*
Venus (1927)*
Let Us Be Gay (1929)+
As Husbands Go (1931)+
Caught Wet (1931)
When Ladies Meet (1932)+
Susan and God (1937)+
We Happy Few (1954)*

* These titles have never been published and reside in either the Illinois State University or New York Public Library archives.
+ Hollywood adapted these titles to the screen, multiple times in some cases.
** Crothers published a revised version of *Everyday* in 1937 under the title *The Valiant One*, The Northwestern Press.

Selected Bibliography

Archives

The Billy Rose Theatre Division at the New York Library for the Performing Arts and the Illinois State University Archives house much of the archival source material on Rachel Crothers. In addition to the Crothers's papers listed below at the NYPL, there are documents pertaining to Crothers that can be found in other collections at the Billy Rose division. The extensive online archive of the author's hometown newspaper, *The Pantagraph* (Bloomington, IL), is also replete with articles about Crothers and her family members.

1. Rachel Crothers's Papers, 1882-1957. Billy Rose Theatre Division. New York Public Library. *T-Mss 2016-002 (3 boxes)
2. Rachel Crothers's Papers, c. 1920-1940, 1964. (arranged into 4 series, organized by material type). OCLC: ocn892913022; includes three volumes of scrapbook used by Irving Abrahamson for his 1956 dissertation (Abrahamson, Irving I. *The Career of Rachel Crothers in the American Theater*. 1956. University of Chicago PhD, dissertation.)
3. *The Pantagraph Archives*. 1838-2013. https://pantagraph.newspapers.com

Andes, Anna. "Feminism, Sentimentality, and Realism in Rachel Crothers's Working-Women Plays." *Working Women in American Literature, 1865-1950*. Ed. by Miriam Gogol. Rowman & Littlefield, 2018. 123–142.

Ashton, Jean. *The New York Times*. 25 May 1980, D3.

Barlow, Judith E. *Plays by American Women, 1900-1930*. Applause Theatre and Cinema, 1985.

Boston Evening Transcript. 14 Feb. 1912, 21.

Gottlieb, Lois C. *Rachel Crothers*. Boston : Twayne Publishers, 1979.

Johnson, Katie N. *Sex for Sale: Six Progressive-Era Brothel Dramas*. University of Iowa Press, 2015.

La Rocco, Claudia. *The New York Times*. 24 Sept. 2013.

Lindroth, Colette, and James Lindroth. *Rachel Crothers: A Research and Production Sourcebook*. Greenwood, 1995.

Orel, Gwen. "Susan and God." *Back Stage East*, vol. 47, no. 26, June 2006, p. 51. *EBSCOhost*, research.ebsco.com/linkprocessor/plink?id=c3575695-a818-38a5-832f-8c3bcb927f67.

Rooney, David. "Go West, Wide-Eyed Easterners: [Review]." *New York Times*, 10 June, 2011. *ProQuest*, https://www.proquest.com/newspapers/go-west-wide-eyed-easterners/docview/871136546/se-2.

Stevens-Garmon, Morgen. "Rachel Crothers, Sign of the Times." Museum of the City of New York Blog: New York Stories. 1 Nov. 2016. https://blog.mcny.org/2016/11/01/rachel-crothers-sign-of-the-times/

Teachout, Terry. "WEEKEND JOURNAL; Theater — View: 'Susan and God': Forgotten but Fresh." *Wall Street Journal*, 30 June, 2006. *ProQuest*, https://www.proquest.com/newspapers/weekend-journal-theater-view-susan-god-forgotten/docview/399025295/se-2.

Teachout, Terry. "Welcome Back, Rachel Crothers." *Wall Street Journal (Online)* Dow Jones & Company Inc, 2011. *ProQuest*, https://www.proquest.com/blogs-podcasts-websites/welcome-back-rachel-crothers/docview/873191945/se-2.

Watt, Stephen, and Gary A. Richardson. *American Drama: Colonial to Contemporary*. Heinle and Heinle Publishers, 1995.

"One of the Wonder Workers of the Town," *The Pantagraph* 18 Dec. 1932.